"In words that whisper intimately, scream helplessly, and reflect honestly the impossible tragedy of a daughter's suicide, Strouse carries the reader into—and somehow through—the heart of grief. Written as a decade-long correspondence to her child, this unique journal rivets the reader with the stark reality of traumatic loss, focusing artfully in text and collage on the felt sense of an anguishing death as it shatters and gradually transmutes the life of survivors. Never has a loss been more tellingly told, and never has the raw immediacy, agonizing recollection, and uneven progress toward once again inhabiting a life of purpose been conveyed with greater clarity. This book is strong medicine, gripping in its imagery and unadorned in its searing prose. I recommend it to every would-be healer who has the courage to walk beside those bereaved by suicide, and who seeks orientation in a wordless catastrophe somehow given voice."

ROBERT A. NEIMEYER, PhD
Professor of Psychology
The University of Memphis, Memphis, Tennessee
Editor of *Techniques of Grief Therapy:
Creative Practices for Counseling the Bereaved*

"There are many ways in which one heals from the suicide loss of a loved one. In *Artful Grief*, Sharon shares the details of her journey: she coped by writing in a diary and creating collages. Her story of healing keeps her daughter Kristin alive in both her struggle and in her mother's memory of the child she loved."

MICHELLE LINN-GUST, PhD
President, American Association of Suicidology
Author, *Conversations with the Water: A Memoir of Cultivating Hope*

"In *Artful Grief* Sharon presents a path through pain that will guide thousands to come and give meaning to their own loss. Thank you, Sharon, for the gift of healing through art. You have poignantly described your own struggles in ways that allow your readers to gain insight and inspiration. You have shined a light into the darkness of suicide loss."

BONNIE CARROLL,
President and Founder,
Tragedy Assistance Program for Survivors

artful grief

artful
grief

A Diary of Healing

Sharon Strouse

BALBOA.
PRESS

A DIVISION OF HAY HOUSE

Balboa Press books may be ordered through booksellers or by contacting:

Balboa Press
A Division of Hay House
1663 Liberty Drive
Bloomington, IN 47403
www.balboapress.com
1-(877) 407-4847

Because of the dynamic nature of the Internet, any web addresses or links contained in this book may have changed since publication and may no longer be valid. The views expressed in this work are solely those of the author and do not necessarily reflect the views of the publisher, and the publisher hereby disclaims any responsibility for them.

The author of this book does not dispense medical advice or prescribe the use of any technique as a form of treatment for physical, emotional, or medical problems without the advice of a physician, either directly or indirectly. The intent of the author is only to offer information of a general nature to help you in your quest for emotional and spiritual well-being. In the event you use any of the information in this book for yourself, which is your constitutional right, the author and the publisher assume no responsibility for your actions.

Certain stock imagery © Thinkstock.
Any people depicted in stock imagery provided by Thinkstock are models, and such images are being used for illustrative purposes only.

Cover Art: Kristin Rita Strouse, "The Yellow Dress," 2001.
Cover Photograph: Renee Fischer
Cover Design: Zack Marsh

Printed in the United States of America

ISBN: 978-1-4525-6802-7 (e)
ISBN: 978-1-4525-6801-0 (sc)
ISBN: 978-1-4525-6803-4 (hc)

Library of Congress Control Number: 2013902309

Balboa Press rev. date: 2/26/2013

This book is dedicated to:

Kristin Rita Strouse

Douglas, Kimberly, Kevin,

and all those whose hearts are broken open.

t a b l e   o f   c o n t e n t s

Part II: Thriving

introduction

Artful Grief is a tour de force in the study of grief and loss. Through her writing and collages, Sharon invites us to join her in an underworld journey that is not for the faint-of-heart. Her words and images are terrifyingly beautiful, unflinchingly direct, and utterly heartbreaking. The hope she describes is unsentimental and even savage, requiring the reader to bear witness to the unbearable: the senseless suicide of one's child.

Sharon writes part one of *Artful Grief* as a letter to her dead child, Kristen, a seventeen-year-old aspiring artist with considerable talent and unrecognized mental illness. Sharon's letters and accompanying collages are riveting, intimate, and instructive, and they make visible the suffering of a survivor: the shame, guilt, regret, and longing. They expose the despair of never being able to hold a loved one again, and the fear of never being able to return to life. Sharon's letters and collages chronicle her descent into an underworld of intense emotion, a rage that threatens to overtake, and a mystery with unexpected moments of stillness and even ecstasy.

Sharon notes that talking to others was of limited benefit because there were no words for her experience, though she searched for something or someone that would mend her brokenness. Her sense of being torn apart is vividly expressed in her collages. Making collages became a way for Sharon to speak the unspeakable. The basement studio that had once been Kristen's now became her mother's refuge, a sacred space for Sharon to be with grief in all of its shapes, colors, textures, and intensity. The basement studio also became Sharon's laboratory, a place of alchemy and transformation.

Through Sharon's letters and collages, we meet figures from her dreams, some which came as harbingers of future healing. In part one, Sharon also speaks about new relationships and ways of being—a process she describes as radical acceptance. Sharon allowed herself to break open, to embrace that which most terrified and disturbed her. She let go of her desire for a neat and orderly world, and she abandoned hope of fixing or changing what could not be changed while simultaneously learning to trust an inner, instinctual wisdom that was emerging. Like characters in Greek myths that were also pulled into the underworld, help came in unexpected ways.

Part two is written retrospectively. Now, Sharon is looking back, gathering jewels strewn along the way that she was unable to see in the darkness, recognizing clues to her eventual transformation that were evident early on in her dream journal entries and collages. Sharon's reflections offer hope that a heart broken by grief can once again give and receive love, and that it is possible to return to relationships with the living without forsaking a connection with the deceased. Sharon is no longer frozen in time at the moment of Kristen's death; she has learned to fall apart, to let go at the deepest levels, and to love again.

Sharon pays homage to others who have made the descent, however uninvited, like Inanna of ancient Sumeria and characters in myths and legends across cultures and time. The poets and mystics have become her companions and guides, as have other bereaved parents and family members whose stories provide inspiration.

Artful Grief is a labor of love, now ready for delivery on the eleventh anniversary of Kristen Rita Strouse's death. May it be of benefit to others who are suffering and offer reminders that the darkness can become the light.

Barbara Thompson, OTD, LCSW, OTR/L
Professor of Occupational Therapy
The Sage Colleges, Troy, New York
Editor, *Grief and the Expressive Arts*

c o l l a g e

www.artfulgrief.com

part I

surviving

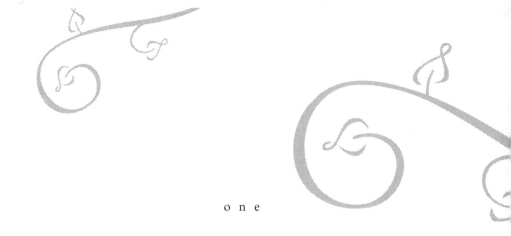

o n e

suicide

October 12, 2001:
Shattered

The phone is ringing, and I reach over Dad to pick it up. It is 2:30 a.m. The man on the other end identifies himself as an officer of the New York City Police Department. He asks if I am Mrs. Strouse. He asks if there is someone with me, and then he says there has been an accident. My heartbeat quickens; time slows. Cold. Still. I anticipate his words. I anticipate my greatest fear. "I am very sorry. Kristin is dead." I repeat the officer's words out loud, "Kristin is dead." Dad begins to scream, I am rendered silent, and his scream becomes my scream. I slide out of myself. I break into a million pieces. I detach from this world and observe it through some other eyes. I am gone. Dad jumps out of bed and continues screaming as he stomps wildly around the room, beating his fist on his thigh and grabbing his head. I look at him and cannot grasp what he is doing. I tell him to be quiet—I cannot hear what the officer is saying. I sit quietly at the edge of the bed and take out a pen from the bottom shelf of the night table. Some part of me writes all the necessary information on the cover of the *TV Guide*, while under the surface the realities of the coming day's events begin to arrange

3

themselves in layers just beneath my skin. I believe that it is the weight of those details—telling Kimberly and Kevin, identifying your body, planning your funeral, and burying you—that keeps some of me in my body. But after that, the details fall away, and I become nothing, bones stripped of flesh suspended in darkness.

I take a shower. I comb my hair. I do my makeup. I see a fool in the mirror trapped in an everyday ritual at 3:30 in the morning. We are on our way to collect your body. I notice that a part of me is missing. I hear my missing part running and screaming throughout the house. I pack a change of clothing and a few necessities in a brown overnight case. Should I wear black to the morgue? I want to tear my clothes off. I want to tear the skin off my bones. I tuck the piece of paper with the scribbled information the officer gave me into my purse. I want to fall down and have a raging fit while I lose my mind.

I make my bed and put the dirty clothes in the laundry room. I write down all the personal numbers I can think of on a small white note card and fold it into my pocket. I will not remember these numbers when the time comes for me to make phone calls. I look at our little poodle, Sienna, sitting in a corner of the kitchen; she is shivering just like me. I must remember to call someone to come and get her in the morning. We walk out the door. We do not talk in the car except to reassure ourselves that it would not be a good idea to drive to New York, especially under the circumstances. Taking the train is a better idea when one is on one's way to claim a body. Dad drives too fast in the darkness. I wonder where the other cars are going. I wonder if we are the only ones in the middle of a nightmare. We park in the lowest level of the train station's underground garage. We buy one-way tickets to Philadelphia. We have decided to tell your older sister and brother in person. Kevin is first.

We arrive at his apartment just a few blocks from campus at six in the morning, ringing the doorbell incessantly until he answers. He can tell by our presence that something bad has happened. I look at his confused face and into his sleepy eyes, and I hear him worriedly asking, "What's wrong?" We sit on the bed with him, with the soft morning light filtering through the shades. He is in his boxers and a University of Pennsylvania tennis shirt. His six-foot frame slumps forward in anticipation.

I say, "We have terrible news about Kristin. She's dead; she took her own life last night." He falls back onto his white rumpled sheets and covers his eyes with his arms as tears begin to stream down his face. He does not move. I look at him, feeling his senior year slipping away. We sit in the folds of his unmade bed for what seems an eternity. We tell him what we know. We pack and make our way to another train that will take us into Manhattan.

We stand at the end of a row of polished wooden pews as Thirtieth Street Station in Philadelphia begins to fill with commuters making their way to unknown places. They move past us, consumed in their own thoughts while we struggle to keep ourselves together. Kevin calls his tennis coach to tell him that he will not be at practice for a few days because his sister has died. His calm voice cracks until he cannot speak. Dad finishes the conversation for him. It all seems out of place amid the flurry of people rushing by as they make their connections. Nothing makes sense. My surroundings feel distorted, as if I am looking through broken glass.

I am suddenly hungry and nauseated at the same time. I take a sip of water and feel it slide down my throat and into my stomach. Liquid moves through me as if I'm a paper straw.

I sit with Kevin. Dad sits in the seat next to me, across the aisle. The train slowly fills around us. Mercifully, no one sits next to Dad. I am sitting on a seat in a train. I am here, but I am not. I am floating in pieces, moving about the space like wisps of delicate white dandelion seeds dispersed in a sudden gust of wind. I look out the window. Everything is moving fast. We decide to wait until a reasonable hour before Dad starts to make some calls, canceling everything "due to a family emergency." We are afraid to tell anyone that we are dealing with your death. We fear the information will get out before we have time to personally tell family, and we have no idea exactly when that will be.

I feel strangely cloaked in the secret of your death. Our secret is contained and controlled for the moment. I rest in this pause because it allows me the opportunity to hope for a miracle, even through deep inside I know it's an illusion. I close my eyes as fragments of multiple conversations get louder inside my head. These voices have no manners and talk over and around each other with no consideration.

Kristin's dead. It's not possible. It'll be straightened out. It's a mistake. Kristin's not dead. She couldn't kill herself. It must be a joke. It's not a joke. Kristin's on a table in a morgue. They did an autopsy; they cut her body open. I didn't give my permission. They can't do that. She's alive. It's not possible. Kristin's dead. It's a mistake. It's not her. They're confused. She's in her room. She's under the covers in her bed. She's alive. The person they found must be Kristin's twin. I just talked to her last night. She can't be dead. She didn't kill herself. She said she would never do something like that. It's not possible. She's not in a morgue. This isn't real.

The conductor brushes by and announces our arrival at Penn Station. The door of the train opens, and I watch my foot meet the platform. I know the foot belongs to me, but I do not feel like myself. We are in New York.

We take a cab to the place where Kimberly works. We stand together on a small landing at the top of narrow stairs. I knock on the door and ask to speak to her. I take an extra moment because the next moment will change her life forever. I search for some kind way to prepare her, some gentle introduction to the unspeakable. I say, "Kimberly, it's about Kristin." I wait so that she can brace herself, and I then say, "She is dead; she took her own life." Before I can move, she rushes past us and down the steps as the sound of "No!" begins to echo off the walls. I turn and run down the steps after her, my right hand moving along the surface of the stairwell to steady myself. A single chip of paint dislodges itself from the wall and falls at my feet. Kimberly throws open the entrance door and collapses onto the sidewalk. The sound that began in the hallway reaches its full potential: she screams uncontrollably, a primal wailing that consumes her as she breaks into her million pieces. I fall to my knees with her. I pull her to me in a clumsy embrace. I hold your sister until there is silence. Just beyond our crumpled bodies, foul water trickles along the gutter, carrying pieces of trash with it. Dad and Kevin crouch beside us, protective but unsure of what to do.

While she is screaming, passersby stop to ask, "Is there anything wrong? Do you need some help?" Smiling, I look up and say, "No, we're fine. She's just upset. Really, we're fine." I feel like laughing. I cannot speak of you. I feel everything in my body. I feel as if I am sliding out of myself into the street. I feel a dissolving of everything I have ever held and loved.

We go back up the stairs and into the loft in which Kimberly works. We sit on sofas, with the morning light streaming through floor-to-ceiling windows; it carries the aliveness of Manhattan and is intrusive as your death creeps in and fills the space completely. Kimberly's boss offers us something to drink and the time to gather ourselves as a family. He seems afraid, and I sense he does not know what to say or do. He leaves and gives us privacy. We share what we know. There is silence. There is crying that deepens to sobbing. There is wide-eyed staring. Kimberly's boss calls Joseph, Kimberly's boyfriend, telling him, "Get over here right away because Kristin killed herself."

Joseph immediately makes his way to us. You were with them at their apartment just twelve hours ago, and now you're dead. His arrival is cause for additional disintegration as we move more deeply into the unreal. He and Kimberly cry in each other's arms. We stand and watch. He embraces each of us in an almost savage attempt to hold together what is so obviously falling apart. His warmth feels reassuring as we join together to face what's next.

Another taxi takes us in the direction of the New York City Morgue. All five of us pile into one cab; we cannot be separated. I ask that the window be open as we drive. I feel faint and dizzy. The breeze blows my hair away from my face. Joe snaps a picture. He does what photographers do: he takes pictures. I don't care. I hope I will not be sick, although there is nothing in my stomach. We get out and have to walk a distance, because the morgue stands behind a series of barricades erected as extra security after September 11. Uniformed police stand guard at the entrance. The air feels unusually heavy and difficult to breathe. I am trembling in the warmth of the noonday sun.

It gets worse as we ascend the morgue's steps and walk through the doors. The stuffy, dank odor of the street gives way to something antiseptic and lifeless. We walk toward the police officer behind the Plexiglas window and introduce ourselves. "We are Doug and Sharon Strouse. We are here to identify our daughter Kristin. She was brought in early this morning."

She looks up and tells us to sit against the wall. "Someone will be with you shortly." I feel like I am at a checkout counter, trying to claim a missing package, something mistakenly discarded, something no one really cares about except the family searching for what is lost.

They usher us into a barren room and seat us at a round metal table. I am aware of the unusually cold temperature of the chair seeping through my clothing. Dad sits to my right and places his hand gently but firmly on my thigh. There is a moment of warmth in his touch. There are a few windows high above us, the panes filled with frosted glass. The room is dull and unyielding. A uniformed woman officer comes in and sits down across from me. I try to steady myself. The officer asks if we are ready to identify you through the picture she is about to show us. I cannot look in her eyes and focus on her lips as she says, "Do not make a sound, and do not move." She places two Polaroids of your shrouded face on the table directly in front of me. My arms reach for you, surrounding the two images of your face, encircling you, protecting you in a kind of embrace beyond which none of us move. I breathe a yes from my body. Joseph stands behind me and snaps a picture. It startles the officer, and she orders him to stop. She is incensed at what he just did. Our focus shifts away from you. We find ourselves reassuring her that it is all right, no harm intended. She is angry and orders him to put his camera away and not to take another picture. She removes your dead face from the table and gets up to leave.

We beg to see your body. She says no; they are too busy. We beg to see your body again, and again she says no. We do not accept her answer and ask again. She finally agrees and allows us to see you. They bring you up from the basement, on an elevator. You are behind a wall of glass. The curtains part, and there you are in front of us on a gurney, wrapped in white sheets, swaddled and gray. We are only allowed to look. I see you in front of me, yet I cannot believe my eyes.

We leave that room. They allow us to sit in the hallway off the busy lobby, as Dad goes through the Yellow Pages and makes a dozen or more phone calls to various funeral homes. In his most official and business-like voice, he pleads for help and explains our situation over and over to each funeral director. Finally someone agrees to help us, to take care of you on short notice so that we can see you late in the afternoon. Funeral homes in New York City are busy these days.

We walk down the street together and stop by a quaint cafe to get something to eat. I wonder how we can be doing such a thing right after seeing you dead; it does not make any sense. The five of us sit at a worn wood table for six and look at a menu. Everyone is hungry, or at least we think we are hungry. When my plate comes, I cannot eat, although I have not eaten since last night at dinner. I move the food around with my fork. I am sickened by the smell and the sight of the food. I force myself to take a bite or two but then push it from me as waves of nausea move through me. No one talks. We watch people walking past, through the open windows next to us. Tears run down my face. I am fixated on the empty chair across from me just beyond my reach. Joseph pulls Kimberly to him. I notice the waitress looking at us; I am sure she senses that we are in the grip of something tragic. She serves us quietly, Dad pays the check, and we leave. I watch him going through the motions of caring for us as always—it's just that nothing is the same.

We walk a short distance to your dorm, where you died. Just a few weeks ago, we walked up these same steps as we moved you in for your first year of college. We are greeted at the door by security and ultimately by the vice president of the university, the dean of students, the dean of academic affairs, and the resident assistant. We are escorted into the offices of the university's psychiatrist on the first floor. We sit on a sectional sofa with the college administrators sitting in chairs opposite us. The room feels way too small. I do not know who looks worse, us or them. I look into their glassy eyes. We are all pale and polite in our fear. The appropriate "We're sorry" is awkwardly extended in an atmosphere that is flooded with emotion. I look at the books lining the bookshelf, all texts devoted to the understanding of the mind and body. I wonder what good they have been under the circumstances. They belong to the university's psychiatrist. You and I saw her together when you arrived in August. We discussed your history; she talked to your psychiatrist in Baltimore. I look at the series of diplomas hanging on the wall, which imply a certain degree of competence. I'd like to rip them off the wall and smash them on the floor, as we ask what happened. They fill us in on the events as they know them. They share the findings of the police investigation. We answer their questions to the best of our ability.

The unspoken floats in the space between us. Why? I want to know why. Why, Kristin? Why?

We ask to be taken to the roof. The elevator doors open. We are on the fifteenth floor. We walk down the hallway past the door to your old room, past the room you moved out of just last week because of roommate problems. We go up a flight of steps and open a heavy metal door. We turn to the left and go up another flight of steps and push open the door to the roof. I close my eyes to the glare of the sun. I close my eyes, afraid of what I am about to see. We asked to be taken to the roof, and the university officials did not hesitate. I wonder what they are thinking as we move from the darkened stairwell and into the light. I want to run to the edge and fall. I want to heave myself over the four-foot high brick ledge. I want to have a screaming fit. I take in 360 degrees of New York in one instant. We take a few steps that move us into the middle space on the roof. Kevin slides down along the surface of a steel vent. I place my left hand on his head, both to reassure him and myself.

The moment shifts as we are escorted to the place on the ledge where you sat. Others move in front of me. I observe their invitation in the gesture of their hands and the movements of their bodies; it's as if they are inviting us to view the magnificence of the skyline, rather than to come to the edge, to the place of your descent. I want to die. What if Dad feels the same way? What if Kimberly or Kevin do something stupid? What if we all just end it right here? I stand in the spot you stood. I place my hands on the spot where they said you sat. The police said, "She sat on the ledge for a long time." The sweat from your jeans and the sweat from the palms of your hands were still visible when they investigated the crime scene. Crime scene—I am standing in your crime scene. I turn to look at Kevin, who remains seated. I turn away and look down, over the edge. It's not possible. You could not have fallen. I imagine this view at night. I imagine the lights. I imagine the stars and the crescent moon. I imagine you falling in the darkness. I want to die.

We ask to be taken to the place where your body was found. We stand just outside the dorm's patio door at the back of the building. We stand in front of a raised three by five foot concrete block where your body was found. The six-inch-deep concrete top is cracked in half as a result of the force of your body's fall. I cannot speak and stand there staring. There are chips of concrete in the crack and on the ground. I pick some up and put them in my purse. I am worried about what will happen to the other chips. There are dark stains scattered here and there. I whisper my wonderings about them to Dad. He does not answer. It's your blood.

Joseph takes a picture with his Leica. The university officials turn and look at him; no one says anything. He's been making pictures all day. We've gotten used to his picture making over the years; his camera is an extension of who he is. It's normal, it's natural. He made pictures of you last night. He has a whole roll of pictures of you and Kimberly, taken just hours before you died. He has pictures of you while you were talking to me on the phone. What did he capture through the lens of his camera? What did his eye see that I could not? I want to see those pictures. I hear the sound of the shutter release. I look up to the roof.

Kimberly lies on her side on the concrete slab, mirroring the position of your body when it was found. She is alive. You are dead. I am trying to imagine the unimaginable. You landed perfectly on this slab of concrete. You landed perfectly on this altar. When you were found, they said it looked as though you were sleeping on your side, until the young man came closer and saw your blood. I look into Kimberly's brown eyes, which are just like yours in color but different in shape. Her light brown hair is wavier than yours. She is smaller in frame and shorter than you. The noses are different. Kimberly's is straight and of perfect proportion; yours was more like mine, a little too large for your face with an obtrusive bump right in the middle. I look for you in her and turn away in my process of comparing and contrasting. I am afraid to stare at the living.

I tell myself not to look up, but I can't help it. I find myself counting each floor until I get to the roof. Tears run along the side of my face and down my neck to the center of my chest. I wipe them with the wad of tissues from my pocket. My tears have made dark stains along the midline of my black shirt. I adjust my black sunglasses; they dim the light just enough to make it bearable to look into the faces of my husband and children.

We leave your dorm and make our way to the funeral home. It is an ordinary building on an ordinary New York street. We would have walked right past it except for the brass plaque on the wall that says, "Funeral Home." We walk in and are escorted down a hallway and into an empty, softly lit viewing room. The wallpaper is old and stained in places. It smells musty.

Rows of simple, well-worn chairs and a few tables with brass lamps line the walls. You are against the far wall like a piece of furniture. You seem out of place. You are laid out on a stretcher, covered with a white sheet. They say that we should not touch you because they have not had time to take care of what needs tending to. I do not ask what they mean. They leave us with boxes of tissues and say they will be right outside if we need them. There is no screaming hysteria. I wonder why. Isn't that the way it is supposed to be? It's strange. Dad slides his arm around me. I quietly wipe the tears from my face. Kimberly begins to emit a sound that is muffled when she buries her head in the sheets covering your body. She wraps her arms around you and moves her hands over your ashen face. Your lips have a bluish cast to them. Your freshly washed hair falls in soft waves around your head. You are cold. You are not you. I place my hand over your heart, just to make sure. I feel the hard reality of your death just beneath my fingertips. I do not believe what I am seeing.

Kimberly and I walk back to your dorm. They have offered to pack your room and ship everything home to Baltimore. I do not want anyone touching your things. The university has graciously booked several rooms for us at the Belvedere Hotel. Dad, Kevin, and Joseph decide to go to the hotel; I feel like they will only get in the way as we pack.

We take the elevator up to your room. The entire floor has been cleared of students. The university has prepared boxes and has them stacked in the hallway. We are alone. Kimberly and I walk into your room. I don't know why, but I expect you to be there. The dean of students waits just outside the closed door, ready to take care of anything we ask for. I sit on your bed, trying to steady myself against the windowsill. I pull your yellow comforter around me; we just bought it in June. You loved the delicate white embroidered flowers along its borders. I pull it to my face so I can smell you, but you are not in that comforter. I wonder if I'll have better luck with the sheets. I pull them off the bed and smell them. They smell like you. I breathe you deep into my belly. I fold the sheets, and Kimberly places them in a box. We make our way around the room, folding all your clothes into boxes. How can I be folding all the things you loved into boxes and bringing them home? We spent the summer collecting all the things you wanted in anticipation of beginning your first year of college. I feel confused and don't understand.

We pack everything from your desk. We look at every note you scribbled, reminders to yourself of things to do in the coming days and weeks. How does someone end her own life when her weekly planner is so full? We put it in a box. We pack your makeup. We pack your bathrobe, the fluffy turquoise one from Laura Ashley that you loved. We pack your shampoo, conditioner, body scrub, and lotions. You were so particular about yourself, loving things with peachy smells. How could you do what you did to yourself? I sit on your stripped bed with your jewelry box on my lap. I open it and touch all the precious pieces you treasured: the Tiffany necklace, your watch, the engraved Irish wedding band, and your pearls. We just gave you the pearls a few months ago for your graduation. You wanted pearls, and we gave them to you. We pack them in a box and set them aside. We do not want them shipped. We decide we will carry them home, along with some other personal things of yours that are too precious to part with.

Within a few hours we are finished. I do not know where the time went. We touch all of your things. We touch you. We name them in a strange kind of cadence between us. "It's her favorite shirt. Her walkman has a CD inside. Here's her pink lace bra, here's the family pictures she brought with her, here's her notes for class." And so it goes until we are finished. You are stacked box upon box on your empty bed. We roll up the pink and blue flowered area rug that we bought the day before we drove up to New York; we found it at Great Finds and Designs, one of your favorite antique stores. I wonder where I will put it. We lean it up against your empty desk. We leave your oil painting of a yellow dress up against the wall. I wish we could find a way to take it with us, but it is too big. We would have a difficult time trying to travel with this treasure, this last oil painting of yours, back to Baltimore. They assure us they will take special care of it. My stomach turns over. It's you that needed special care. We have failed you. I have failed you in every way. You said you would never take your own life. You said you could never do something like that. You said you loved me. How could you have done this?

We close the door, walk a short distance down a cinderblock hallway, and take the elevator down to the lobby. During our descent, I wonder if I am standing in the same space that you stood in when you took the elevator to the top floor and walked up a small flight of stairs to the roof. We just moved you in. I feel the energy of you coming and going. I feel a collision, an explosion inside my brain. I cannot process any more of this day.

One of your roommates and her mother wait all afternoon and evening for us. They are so kind and compassionate. They offer to take us wherever we need to go, not wanting to put us in a taxi after all we have been through. I look into Sara's eyes and wonder about the impact of your death on her. I wonder in what way your suicide will permanently scar every student in the building. They pack us into their car and drive us to the hotel where Dad, Kevin, and Joseph are waiting. It is about ten o'clock; I wonder if you were still alive at this time just last night. We pull away from the curb, and I look at the building, my eyes moving toward the roof as we turn the corner.

I stand in the shower for a long time, just letting the water move over me. I want it to wash the day from me. I hope I will feel something different when I finish. I do not. I get under the covers. Dad sits next to me. Kimberly, Kevin, and Joseph lay at the foot of our bed. We sit together making calls to family. On the other end of the line, I hear hushed exclamations and panic in the form of breathy questions. I feel them entering the nightmare, walking through the door of your death, which we open just a little bit more with each phone call. I ask Aunt Donna and Aunt Elizabeth to take care of Grandma; she should not get a phone call from me telling her that her granddaughter has committed suicide. They will go and tell her in the morning, in person. We agree that at her age, she should have another night's sleep. They assure me they will stay with her and take care of her. Dad calls his two sisters and two brothers. Aunt Gale and Uncle Fred will come immediately, from Louisville; they will move in with us. Aunt Rosalie will take care of telling your other grandma. The phone sits on the bed between us. We are finished calling family. We cannot cope with more. It's almost midnight, and we decide to try and sleep. Kimberly, Kevin, and Joseph reluctantly go to their room across the hall.

We turn off the lights, and I close my eyes. I long for sleep, but the darkness behind my eyes fills with the images of the day. I wish to see your beautiful face as I have known it all these years, but I cannot. I see only your dead face. Unwanted memories of the past eleven months push their way in. Your whole life moves through me. Ultimately I feel consumed by the destructive force of your mental illness, which now turns itself on me. It sucks all life from me, and I am left a victim of my own naivety, ignorance, fear, guilt, and shame. I find myself moving forward in time over the days ahead. I imagine you in a coffin, I imagine your viewing, I imagine your funeral, and I imagine you in the ground. I open my eyes, but my imagining will not stop. I stare at the sliver of light streaming across the ceiling through a crack in the curtains. The city is still moving below us. I am acutely aware that we are high above the ground. I am not supported by this structure and feel myself falling.

October 13, 2001:
Trains

It was the train that brought all of us home from New York. We sat across the aisle from each other, heaped in the seats, intermittently crying and staring. The people around us stared too, acknowledging our apparent suffering with eyes that offered brief moments of compassion. We spoke on the phone with University Officials. I wanted the concrete slab your body rested on. They had already removed it; it was cracked in half. I started crying. I wanted them to get it back. I wanted to see it, to touch it. I wanted to lay on it. I wanted it home so that I could enter that space with you. I wanted to get as close to you in the moment of your death as I could.

They got rid of it as quickly as possible because it was a grim reminder of the night's events. It was a tragic piece of evidence, filled with your blood. Did they break it apart with jack hammers? Did they dump the pieces in the garbage? Did they explain to the workmen that they were removing concrete splattered with the remains of someone's child? Did they caution them to be careful? Did they consider the concrete slab as sacred? I sat and rested my head against the window. I stared into my own reflection, it was unrecognizable. Within three hours, we arrived back in Baltimore. You arrived home later by plane, in a coffin.

I never really paid any attention to trains or train stations; they served a function and carried me back and forth between the places that connected me with those I loved. The consuming energy of your death engulfed this train and this station. I felt inhuman walking up the stairs and coming home to something that had only just begun. The last time I saw you alive, we were in this train station. Hollowed-out sounds bounced off the walls, and I was afraid I would be sick. I wondered what would happen if I fainted. I knew that my feet were moving along the marble floor—I just couldn't feel them.

We said good-bye a few weeks ago. You seemed happy during your brief visit home on September 28. You danced in the kitchen to a tune on the radio just before you left. You talked about the classes you loved. You were excited about a young man you had recently met. You worked through a stressful roommate situation and had a new room and roommate. I could still see you turning toward me and waving as you went down the stairs toward the waiting train. You brushed a piece of hair away from your eyes. You smiled and you were gone. That was the last time I saw you.

We walked out the brass-trimmed glass doors and into sunlight that was too bright. We made our way down the steps to the underground parking. It was dark there. It was dirty and smelled. I was startled by a door that slammed shut. I was cold and shivering as we got into our car.

I felt as if I had entered a dream. I watched myself. When I opened the door to our house, I felt nothing. Family and friends arrived, some quiet and some crying. Grandma sat on the sofa next to me and held my hand. We told the story in the form that it had begun to take after being repeated so many times. I noticed a strange kind of separation between words and experience. We were talking about you, yet I felt detached. The others cried, but we did not. Our dear neighbor David leaned against the cabinets in the kitchen, holding himself as he wept.

And so we began the ritual of letting you go into the earth.

October 14, 2001:
Quiet

The doorbell rang, and I heard familiar voices. Their sound made its way into the darkness of our bedroom. I did not move; I did not want to. More family arrived. I pulled the covers around me and turned on my side. I was becoming increasingly disturbed and undone by the influx of energy that entered the house as people arrived. I listened to them until I could not stand it. I called for Dad. My voice echoed over the balcony and into the space below. "Douglas." I told him I needed to be alone. I needed him to send everyone away. I could not stand it. I could not stand the hushed voices, the intermittent laughter, and the fragments of conversation that entered my space. The sound of my heart beat engulfed my body. The intensity of its vibration made it impossible to tolerate even a whisper. I listened as he tried to explain the unexplainable. I was sorry I could not stand it. I was sorry I needed to be alone. They were only trying to help. You were dead, and I could not stand anything. I needed to be quiet.

October 15, 2001:
Anointing

They ushered me into a small private room at the funeral home where they had already rolled you in. I was alone because I wanted it that way. We had so few hours left before all the formal rituals around your body began. We have become comfortable with burying our dead in a certain way. I had my own way. I lit a candle. I took the little blue bottle filled with lavender oil out of my purse. I opened it as I folded down the white sheet and looked at you. I kissed your face and placed lavender oil on your eyes and forehead. I placed some oil at your temples. I placed some oil along the autopsy sutures that cut across your chest. It was my personal benediction to your body. Your beautiful skin was pinched and pulled together. I hated it; they should have left you alone. You fell, you died. There was nothing more to know. The undertakers had wrapped a portion of your arm in plastic wrap. I wanted to unwrap you. You would have hated this so much. I decided to leave it, afraid of what I might find. I held your hand and tried to wrap my fingers through yours. I left what was private to you as private, respecting you. I touched your leg, your knee. Your ankle was wrapped; I left it. I continued anointing you with lavender oil. I held your feet. You had painted your toenails red. I touched each of your toes as I did when you were born. I kissed your feet and asked for forgiveness.

Kimberly joined me. She had your makeup case from home. There were faint bruises on your face, around your nose and eyes. I suspected there were broken bones beneath the tinted cover-up they used. Together we applied your blush. We took special care to get your lipstick just right. We began to laugh at ourselves. You were still dead. I wondered how long it would take for decay to set in.

Dad and Kevin and Joseph joined us. We cried together and held you. I knew we would savor these memories as the days moved from one to the other. They would anchor us in the fact of your death when we became unsure and wondered if it was all a dream.

October 17, 2001:
I Want

I want my Kristin back. I want to hold my child. I have a broken heart. I cannot stand this one more second. I want to turn back the clock. I want my family whole again. I am numb. I am dismembered. I am bleeding. I am nothing. I want to die. I want to live. I hate all the flowers. I hate all the cards. I cannot do this. I am terrified of tomorrow. I want to start over. I have so many regrets—I did it all wrong. I want to kiss you. I am sorry. I could not save you. I want you to forgive me. I miss you so much. I want you home with me. I want to talk with you. I want to laugh with you. I want to take you shopping. I want to cook little chicken wings for you. I want to see you in your blue jeans. I want you to sleep in your bed. I want to see you married. I want to hold your children. I have a hurting stomach, a hurting heart. I cannot breathe. I want to kill everyone. I want to scream. I want to tear out my hair. I want to dress in black. I want to tell everyone you are gone. I want to cry forever. I want to know why. I want to know how. I want to know what you were thinking. I want to throw up. I was so stupid. I should have seen. I want it to be different. I want ...

October 19, 2001:
Burial

We buried you today, a private ceremony by invitation only. It was a quiet ending after yesterday's viewing and evening mass. Father Ray stood before us at your grave this morning, next to your coffin covered in yellow roses. I reached toward Dad and wiped the tears dripping from his face. We stood together just outside the canopy that covered you, and we released white doves that circled over us, round and round, until they disappeared from our sight. Dad and I saw doves released at a wedding and thought it was beautiful. There will be no wedding celebration for you, Kristin, so instead we marked this moment of your internment with white doves. The last few days have been a blur. I wished I could have slowed time. I wished I could have been more aware and present. I looked into the faces of our family and friends. My legs were shaking. I felt like I couldn't stand up anymore. We got into a black limousine. I said, "That was nice." We drove home; no one said anything.

Our neighbors came and fed us. I thank God for their tenderness. I will never forget their love as they came into our home and made dinner for about a hundred of our family and close friends. They took special care with what they made—nothing bought, all homemade. They set up everything in a way that was warm and inviting, so that when we came in from the cemetery, we were tenderly taken care of. They embraced us and left silently, leaving rose petals on the table. I never did eat.

We filled the dining room table with funeral flowers and laid out your picture albums and scrapbooks. That soft pink and white room was your favorite. You said, "It's perfect; don't ever change it." Your image rested in this space, and when people came to visit, they sat quietly, leafed through the pages of the albums, and cried. I sat and watched in silence. These images of you stood in sharp contrast to the images we were shown at the morgue. I breathed another yes as I sat here, free to speak and free to move. There was nothing inside of me.

A little gray wren sat on a branch right outside the dining room. It kept flying into the glass pane, over and over again. I heard its wings beating against the window, no matter where I was in the house. I tried to shoo it away, but it kept coming back.

Flowers kept coming to the house. They came in the front door and went out the back door and into the garage. I couldn't stand them. I couldn't stand anything. I needed the house to be in perfect order. I could not have anything out of place. I needed everything to be just the way it was before, because nothing was the same. I was barely hanging on and was afraid I would break at any moment. I just wanted the day to be over.

All day, I existed in a primitive place where magical thinking held court. I fantasized that this was all a mistake and that you would suddenly appear at the door. At the end of the day, I stood in your room and opened the brown paper shopping bag that the police had given us. It held your blood-stained clothes. These clothes filled with your coagulated blood were all I had left of your body; the rest of you was in the ground. I wondered where I should put something like that. I tucked you into your armoire on the top right hand shelf and closed the door. I thought, *Oh my God, Kristin!*

As I made my way out of your room, I thought of your mass of resurrection last night. It was celebrated in the auditorium of your high school. We sat in that space just a few months ago and watched you walk down the aisle in your white dress, carrying a dozen red roses for graduation. Last night we sat in the front row as your coffin was wheeled down the aisle and positioned directly in front of us. We covered your coffin with a white cloth as a thousand watched. I could feel them behind us. We played your favorite songs, Bach-Gounod's "Ave Maria," Michael Joncas's "On Eagle's Wings," and Billy Myers's "Kiss the Rain." I listened to people crying, coughing, and blowing their noses.

Father Ray stood before us and said, "In the presence of her body tonight, we can have no more powerful call than to leave here and to transform this world that makes people like Kristin suffer so profoundly."

I watched Dad eloquently deliver your eulogy. I did not know where he got the courage. He said, "We would like you to bear with us as we share with you our deepest feelings and precious memories so we can all hold Kristin in our hearts." At the end he said, "We love you."

In the end, your body was escorted back down the aisle in the candlelight of a thousand single white tapers. We got into waiting limousines and pulled away slowly. I turned and watched as the foyer filled with people who lingered to look at your art work, which had been hastily hung in your honor. It was beautifully tragic.

I lay in bed alone and waited for the others. We had slept together, on and off, for days. Kimberly came into our bed and slept between us that very first night home. Kevin made his way into our bed in the wee hours of that same morning. We were together in the stillness of the night, unable to stand the darkness alone. We found comfort with each other during our intermittent states of wakefulness and sleep. I wondered when everyone would sleep in their own beds. The days and nights ran together. There was no separation of time, there was no rest.

October 20, 2001: Underground

Dad took Aunt Gale and Uncle Fred to the airport. I hated to see them go; we would not have made it through the week without them. They took care of answering the phone, recording who brought what dish, acting as sounding boards, guiding our days, and meeting every one of our needs. When they drove away, the last remnants of anything living left with them. I walked back into my house filled with death.

We decided to go to the cemetery to visit you. I was not dressed yet—I was in your pajamas. I had slept in your things since the night we got home. I felt close to you. Kimberly was wearing your things, too. Dad wanted us to change. I didn't care about anything. We got into the car, and within five minutes we were next to the pile of flowers heaped on your grave. Kimberly and I sat down on the ground next to you while Dad, Kevin, and Joseph stood beside us. Geese fluttered in the pond just across the road. The sound of their trumpeting was at odds with the heaviness that engulfed us. It was an extraordinarily beautiful day, except that you were dead. I could not comprehend the fact that you were in a coffin buried beneath the earth, just below my feet. I sensed myself there with you, underground. *I want to be with you. Let me fall into the earth, let me die, let me go.*

I looked a little to the right at the untouched patch of grass that marked my ultimate resting place. I turned away and focused on the flowers, commenting on how beautiful they were. We pulled out the wilted and dead ones. We tidied up what covered you. I watched it all like a movie being played by actors who had nothing to do with me. Everything seemed pointless.

We drove home. I tried to take a nap, but my insides were moving and spinning, nearly out of control. I closed my eyes anyway; there was nothing more I could do. I could not sleep and so just stayed in bed until dinner time. We were on our own now, and I felt the normal rhythm of responsibility pulling at me. I was relieved that the refrigerator was filled with turkeys, hams, platters, cookies, and casseroles of every variety. I was so nauseated I could barely eat. It was only my mother's chicken soup and the big tray of macaroni and cheese from Sloane that was manageable. I had lost ten pounds since you died, maybe fifteen. I was cold and could not find warmth no matter how many layers of clothing I put on.

I had only slept a few hours each night. I found myself consistently waking at 3 a.m. I wandered about the house, looking out the windows. Sometimes I walked out into the yard, searching for you in the night. I sat alone under the stars on the bench in the garden. Why weren't you there? I was terrified. I was in agony. I was in hell.

October 27, 2001:
Your Eighteenth Birthday

The past seven days had been filled with the routines of everyday living. They felt absurd. There was no logic, no order. I could not think. I was confused and in a timeless dimension with past, present, and future endlessly colliding. Nothing made sense. Today was your birthday, and I was consumed with your death.

I sat on the floor in your yellow bedroom. I sat in your room among the empty boxes. I knew I was sitting in your room, but it did not feel like me—it felt like someone else. Some other person had taken up residence inside of me. I did not know who this person was. She had no skin. She was undefined. She was exposed and vulnerable. She was a bundle of frayed nerve endings. She breathed, but she did not.

I felt you in everything I touched. I was careful to put your things away just the way you had them. I noticed how ridiculous this was, but I could not help myself. I opened the medicine cabinet in your bathroom and put your red nail polish away. I wondered if this was the bottle you used to paint your toenails. I wondered about the insidious mental illness that took hold of you and turned you away from the truth of who you really were. Perhaps it was that brokenness inside that caused your love of creams and potions. I could hear you saying, "Let's go to Rite Aid." You loved that excursion more than anything, so excited with your ChapSticks, lip glosses, and cuticle creams. You took care of your delicate, lovely hands every night just before bed. How could you have done what you did to yourself? Did you have any understanding of what you were doing or the impact that your decision would have on those of us left behind?

I wanted to know why. I thought I would find an answer to my questions in a note you had hidden. If I looked just one more time through your things, through your jean pockets, and under your bed, then surely an answer would be there. There were no notes, no answers. Still I persisted and looked one more time. I felt like sobbing. I heard myself crying somewhere in a distant, far-off place. I couldn't connect with it. A single tear ran from the corner of my eye as I looked at your calendar, which I had left open on your bed. You had circled your birthday and placed stars and exclamation points around it.

In a few days it would be Halloween. It was your favorite holiday. We always celebrated your birthday with Halloween themes and costumes. You were excited over the prospect of being in New York for Halloween this year. You had wild ideas for a costume. You were supposed to come home this weekend to celebrate your eighteenth birthday and attend your cousin Cecily's wedding. I planned to pick you up at the train station. Instead I unpacked the things from your dorm room that arrived from New York. Your things came home without you.

I turned out the lights and closed the door.

October 28, 2001:
Journal

I came across the black journal yesterday when I unpacked your things. I did not open it; I couldn't. I entered your room and opened it today. I sat on the floor. You wrote your name in black across the left inside cover. I looked at the lyrical script I was so familiar with: Kristin Rita Strouse. I ran my fingers across your name, touching you. The entries began December 2000 and ended September 2001, just six weeks before your death. I leafed through the pages. My hands were sweating. I wanted to read what you had written, and I didn't want to read what you had written. Certain words jumped out at me as I turned the pages of your journal.

> Hands that stole. I feel darkness and death. I hate myself. I want to die. I am in so much pain. I feel fat. I feel ugly with my sucking tongue and crumpled chin. My body suffers. I hate my life. Why can't I get along with anybody? I feel manic.

I trembled. I felt sick. I turned to your last entry.

> September 1, 2001: Today I will write, yoga, call about work, see my psychiatrist, talk and be friendly, sit in the park, and read.

My heart pounded as I put your journal down. I collapsed on my side and pulled my knees to my chest. I was destroyed. I lay there with your words. My mind began to search for the other diaries and journals I knew you'd kept. I remembered a little pink one with ballet slippers on the cover. I did not have the strength to search for them. I could not move. They wait for me among your things, in drawers, in closets, in chests. I will find them and I will read them. It will take every ounce of strength. I remembered bits and pieces of them all too well, stealing glances when you were not looking. Your words broke my heart. Their memory took on new meaning. You were hurtling toward death all along. I got up and placed your black journal in your closet on the middle shelf, next to your yellow slippers. I closed the door.

October 31, 2001:
Halloween

Lucy got out of the car in front of the house. She is tall and stately with short gray hair and reassuring brown eyes. Those were the eyes that met mine as I began to cry and turned toward Sheila as she got out of the car.

I walked along the brick entrance and through leaves that had fallen. We did not say anything to each other. Sheila embraced me with all of herself, holding me there in that spot. We did not want to let go, and yet we did. She came in, and we all sat in the dining room together. She had come from her home in Boulder. We talked; she cried. She looked through your albums; they were still on the table along with wilting flowers. We had talked almost every day since you died. She said she would walk the labyrinth of grief with me for as long as I needed. She was not afraid. This delicate-boned woman with green eyes and shiny, straight dark hair had been my teacher and my mentor for years. She was the facilitator of the Temenos Center, a woman's meditation and personal growth community I joined on the eve of Grandpa's death almost seven years ago. Sheila offered experiences that were healing during weekend retreats. I was invited into the moment, invited to be with feelings as they arose, and invited to embrace life as it was. She called a few days after your death and continued to call. I would stop what I was doing and lay on my bed and talk with her. She listened, providing a quiet space for me during these early days of death.

I took Sheila and Lucy to your room. We stood together in the yellow space in which you once lived. Sheila touched your clothing I had put out on your bed. She ran her fingers across your white bedspread and pillow. She and Lucy stayed steady in the face of my grief. It was a relief to be in their presence, a respite in the flurry of so many wanting to relieve us of our pain, to make better what cannot be changed. She will return to Boulder in a few days. She will call me and we will talk. She will listen and allow what is happening to happen. She reminded me that many have returned to tell of their descent.

There were no tricks or treats tonight.

November 3, 2001:
Black Shorts

It has been unseasonally warm through November, and I wore the same pair of black shorts for weeks. I wore them in New York. I wore them on the train home. I unpacked your things in them. I practically lived in these black shorts. I guess I would have worn them to your funeral, except that I could hear you telling me to get a grip and wear the cream-colored silk outfit that I wore to your graduation. You always had such a wonderful sense of style. In any case, I needed to wash them, but I couldn't bring myself to actually do it.

You seemed woven into the fabric of this black cotton. I had this strange notion that washing them would cause some added distance between us that I couldn't bear. The shorts rested on the bench in the bedroom as I continued to contemplate this totally irrational idea. I decided to just let them sit a while longer. I put my hand into the pocket and removed the tissues that were there. They were the ones from your funeral, and I couldn't part with them. They had caught all my tears. I held them in my cupped hands and brought them to my face and kissed them. I couldn't throw them away, and so I put them in a little vase in the bathroom cabinet, where I could see them every morning.

Next to my tissues I put the candles from your mass, your funeral cards, a crucifix from Father Ray, an ivory Buddha, and some pictures of you. They formed a kind of altar and, I caught their reflection in my mirror as I got dressed. I looked at my tissues and thought of the thousands of tissues that were in the Virgin Mary's walled garden in Ephesus, Turkey. We walked along that garden wall together and marveled that people from all over the world would come to place their tissues filled with their sorrows in her garden. I wanted a picture of myself next to that wall of sorrow. I looked happy standing there. I was no longer that person. I had become the stone wall.

In retrospect I was glad that we took you on the Mediterranean cruise you wanted for graduation. You didn't want a party; you wanted to see the treasures and art of Europe. You embraced your artistic ability, nurtured over years of hard work and rewarded in your acceptance at a prestigious institution in New York City. You could not wait to see what you had only seen in books. We began in Venice and ended in Rome. You loved Venice with its canals and bridges. You loved the Coliseum and the Sistine Chapel. I remembered how we stood in Saint Peter's Basilica, in front of Michelangelo's *Pieta*. We held each other for the sheer joy of being in the presence of genius. A mother holds her child in death.

I imagined you sitting on the balcony outside our ship's state room, with your hair blowing in the wind. I took a picture of you to capture that memory. Now when I looked at it, I imagined you falling and your hair blowing in the very same wind. What is it that you say to us, as you smile?

November 15, 2001:
Photos

I took pictures of you when you were alive, and so it seemed quite natural to take pictures of you dead. I was anxious to have them developed and worried about their processing at the same time. It took a lot of courage to walk into the Ritz Photo Shop and discretely and softly ask to speak to the technician. "Could I please talk to you a moment? It's about something very personal." She looked at me above the lenses of her glasses. She appeared to be in her early thirties, rather pretty and with soft brown eyes, like yours. She invited me to come inside the photo processing area and assured me that it would be fine.

I explained, "I have pictures that I took during the viewing of our seventeen-year-old daughter, who just died." I could hear what I was saying, but it was like speaking a foreign language about something that had nothing to do with me. I watched and listened to it all from some other place, far away. I smiled. I did not cry.

She was so compassionate. She pushed some papers away and patted the seat next to her. "Come and sit here," she said, "right next to me, and we will do this together. Many people do what you've done. I won't be shocked or upset by the images." I sat silently beside her and felt my very thin body begin to shake and quiver underneath my heavy black sweater. I brought my breath down deep inside of me so that I would not collapse. I felt like a sacred witness. I felt I was given the opportunity to bless and sit sentinel as the last images of you dropped out of a machine and were cut and packaged.

I brought you home and placed you in the plastic sleeves of the photo album. I put you in the closet, thinking it would not be a good thing to leave pictures of you dead out on the coffee table. I could just imagine some unsuspecting person coming over and opening the album as your dead face stared back from the page.

I often go to the cabinet in the family room and take out this album. I open to the pages that hold these last images of you. I stare at them. I do not believe they are real, but there you are. I stare some more and say, "I do not believe it." Tears roll down my cheeks as I put you away.

November 22, 2001: Thanksgiving

I wanted to ignore the day, but I knew I couldn't. We used to have all the family over, numbering fifty or more aunts, uncles, cousins, and friendly strays, anyone who was alone for the holidays. I could not face that kind of Thanksgiving this year. I did not know what to do. Aunt Donna and Aunt Elizabeth came over with their families; they brought everything we needed. We did not celebrate in the basement, like we did in the past. It needed to be different. We stood in the kitchen and made a big circle. We held hands and offered grace. No one looked at each other for fear of breaking down. It was pain-filled and awkward. It was impossible. Memory fragments of past Thanksgivings moved through my consciousness as easily as the smell of the turkey moved through the house. Orange squash and broccoli casserole were dished out on plates along with stuffing and mashed potatoes. The sound of silverware on china made me shudder. It grated on my nerves, a small detail, yet it was beyond my capacity to endure. I watched Kimberly barely fill her plate. This would have been your first Thanksgiving home from college. It made me think of Kimberly's first Thanksgiving home from college and the card you wrote your sister.

> November 23, 1995: Dear Kimberly, I am very thankful for you to come home this Thanksgiving holiday. I envy you. You have everything a girl could wish for, but still you want more, and you get it. I hate you sometimes because you are perfect. Everyone says so. Sometimes I don't want to love you or even want to be your sweet little sister. You're always going to be pretty. It's so easy for you and hard for me. People don't even know it. Mommy is the only one to say that I am special, and no one else says it to me. I cry when I see you because I love you, and yet I hate you. You have it all. You don't understand me; no one will

ever. I hate my life. I wish I could be you. When you see my face sad, you will perhaps know the pain and depression I am in. My mind is soaked and covered in a thousand thoughts. You said in the bathroom, "I love life, I want to hug it." How do you think that makes me feel? After this card you're going to try to find me or something and hug me. No. I don't want that. Happy Thanksgiving. I still love you in my heart. Don't be too mad.

I remembered the tears. I remembered the hours we spent together talking about your feelings. I remembered how initially shocked I was when I read the words you wrote to Kimberly. I remembered feeling that I understood your struggle as a twelve-year-old in the presence of your eighteen-year-old sister. You let your feelings out, you spoke your truth, and you opened your heart. I felt the capacity to tend to you, to help you through your growing pains. I loved you and felt compassion for you because your struggles were not dissimilar from mine growing up. My two younger sisters were prettier and smarter. Their lives were rich and full of activities and friends, and mine was not. I made it through and knew you would make it through, too.

I was wrong. Your card to your sister was a red flag. I did not see it. You were suffering. The twelve-year-old in pain turned into the seventeen-year-old who no longer could bear life's pain and killed herself.

Tears welled up in my eyes. My stomach tightened, and my shoulders moved inward around my rib cage, around my heart. I brushed my tears away quickly, hoping no one noticed. I was not thankful for anything other than the day coming to an end. I made my way through this ritual, but it was an excruciating charade.

December 7, 2001:
Autopsy Report

Getting the mail was usually no big deal, except for today, when I reached inside the mail box and received the autopsy report from the Office of the Chief Medical Examiner, City of New York. We had been waiting for this letter, as if a piece of paper would change the fact of your death. It said,

Kristin R. Strouse Case #: M01-05."

I: Blunt impact injury of head with: contusions and fractures of
skull and nose.

II: Blunt impact injury of trunk with: abrasions and contusions,
rib and pelvic fractures, lacerations of aorta, liver and right
hemidiaphragm, bilateral hemothorax, hemopericardium with
tamponade and hemoperitoneum.

III: Blunt impact injury of extremities with: abrasions and
contusions, fracture of lower legs and left arm.

The next four pages went into details, none of which I understood except
the parts where they said the heart weighs 200 grams, the right lung weighs
170 grams, the liver weighs 1,100 grams, and so on. That part I understood,
and I became breathless and lightheaded at the thought. The autopsy felt
like another form of violence to your body on top of the violence you already
inflicted on yourself. It was more than any mother should have to bear. No
matter how horrific, I wanted to understand every detail.

Aunt Donna, a former nurse, and Uncle Mike, a physician, agreed to
stop by and go over the autopsy report and answer all of our questions. We
sat together in the family room under the portrait of you and Kevin and
Kimberly, taken when you were thirteen and they were sixteen and nineteen,
respectively. I felt you in your innocence, watching us. In the end Uncle
Mike reassured us that you died instantly, that you were never in pain, and
that nothing could have been done to save you that night. We all sat before
the blazing fire. Dad and I never shed a tear.

Aunt Donna and Uncle Mike drove home in silence. I tucked your
autopsy report into the file next to your birth and death certificates. Dad and
I were quiet for the rest of the evening. I couldn't get you out of my mind and
found myself standing in your room next to your bed. For some odd reason I
opened the little drawer in your night table and took out your cuticle cream.
I touched my own finger into it as if I would find something of you there.
You had taken such care of your body. At seventeen you were gracefully
beautiful. Years of ballet and tennis had made you strong and lean.

I stood in front of your desk and stared into the large high school
graduation portrait hanging on the wall. I looked into your eyes filled with

life and light. I looked at the graceful curve of your neck, accentuated by the V-neck of a bright pink, three-quarter-length sleeved shirt. I looked at your hands, the nails polished bright pink, with your high school ring proudly displayed. I looked at your thick, beautiful, wavy brown hair. You often pulled it up and wrapped it in a scrunchy. I loved seeing you like that, relaxed and casual, wisps cascading down your back.

It seemed that you never realized how graceful and beautiful you were. It's normal for adolescents to be uncomfortable with themselves as they grow and change, isn't it? Standing here in your room, surrounded by your things, I knew that your mental illness won and took you from us before we knew what was happening, before we really understood, before our ignorance and fear gave way to clarity. In some ways you were taken from us right before our eyes, over an eleven-month period. In other ways, the signs were all there and were years in the making. If I had been a little more alert, I might have seen the ending in the beginning, in the moment you were conceived.

We normally think of conception happening as a result of the sexual act between loving partners, but your conception happened long before that act occurred. Your conception happened as I stood in a funeral home, next to Aunt Donna, next to the casket holding her twenty-seven-year-old husband, Rob, who died from complications after heart surgery. Your conception happened when I looked into the grief-stricken eyes of Rob's mother and promised myself that I would never stand as she stood, one son dead, one daughter living. Kimberly was two years old at the time. I reached for my belly and felt Kevin move inside of me; I was four months pregnant. It was that moment when I conceived of you. I would have three children. You were my guarantee against the odds, against the fates, just in case. That was the moment when the die was cast, the moment when my consciousness invited you toward me. Your conception happened in a funeral home next to a coffin.

There is no spare part, no assurance, no way of getting around the horror of losing a child. It is not like having one child balances the pain of losing another, or that having three or four children lessens the pain of losing one. It does not work that way. How stupid of me. How irrational my thinking in the face of a mother's grief.

December 10, 2001:
Out of Place

Dad kissed me on the cheek on his way out the door. He did not tell me
to have a good day. I looked into his eyes. He turned and went out the
kitchen door. He went to work. He went to work a week after you died. It
did not make sense to me. It made sense to him, and so he did it. We did
not discuss it after that. He asked me, "What is one supposed to do?" I
did not have an answer. Life pushed him forward. I did not fit back into
my life.

I did not fit inside my skin. I did not fit in my clothes; they hung on
me. I was uncomfortable in my bedroom. I was uncomfortable in my
kitchen. I was uncomfortable in my own house. I did not fit. The familiar
was unfamiliar. I no longer knew my dark blue coffee mug with gold stars
and crescent moon. It did not feel right in my hand like it used to. I drank
my coffee and did not care. I placed a fork down next to a plate with pink
flowers, and I knew that I was setting the table, but it had no meaning.
The action did not fit with your death.

I went upstairs and got in bed, hoping to sleep for a few more hours.
I closed my eyes. My heart pounded in my ear. My insides moved at
lightning speed while the rest of the world proceeded in slow motion.
I had a sense that I was porous and leaking into the mattress. After an
hour I couldn't stand it, so I swung my legs out from under the covers. I
was aware of the bones in my legs that supported my frame. I knew that
I had a body, but I couldn't feel myself as I walked into the bathroom. I
felt disconnected. I did not fit.

I did not recognize myself when I stood and looked in the bathroom
mirror. I wondered what others saw when they looked at me. My shoulder
blades bent forward and inward. I could not seem to straighten myself, as
if my ribcage collapsed because my heart was missing. I took in a sudden
deep breath. I looked away from my own image. I tried to push thoughts
from my mind for there were no answers. I wanted to scream, "How long
will I feel this way?" No one could tell me when the suffering would ease.
No one could do this for me, this death, this suicide.

December 18, 2001:
The Walled Garden and Ecstasy Dreams

With your death, I entered a state of exquisite dreaming, the kind of dreams that I woke from and simply had to write down. During these visitation dreams, I experienced you as if you were alive; we were together again. You reassured me and told me, "I am fine, I love you." They brought me incredible comfort.

Other dreams were of a different variety and seemed prophetic, as if a window had opened to my future. I felt reassured and held onto these dreams as lanterns placed along my path. Their light offered some guidance in this place of total darkness.

I dreamed I was in a walled garden with someone. I thought it was you, but I wasn't really sure. There were lush green plants and flowers growing everywhere. On further investigation we discovered that the garden was heavily laden with vegetables and fruit. We were amazed and happy. On the other side of the garden, we noticed an area of rich soil and began to dig. As we pushed harder into the soil, we saw that there was a very large alligator sleeping just under the surface. As we continued to look at it, it became translucent. We noticed that there were some blue structures in the area of the heart; they looked like rectangular boxes stacked one on top of another. We were afraid of disturbing the alligator. It began to stir and move in the dark rich mud.

On another night I dreamed I was in our old house. I was in an intense experience of suffering and pain over your loss. I could not endure the reality of your death, and I let go of everything as I fell back onto our sofa in a state of ecstasy. As I fell, my body became frozen in midair. I was in a half-reclined position with my arms outstretched, holding a jar of translucent face powder. My body fell away, and I was engulfed in a rush of energy. I felt transformed and began moving through time and space. I realized that I had entered another dimension—I had broken through the veil to the other side. I called for my father, and I called for you, Kristin. Although I found myself on the other side, I had a sense it might be too soon.

I woke from these dreams and felt I was given a gift.

December 26, 2001:
Christmas in Mexico

I thought if we could get away and be in the sun, perhaps it would help. It was awful. The airport was crowded with families and young people; they were in high spirits and filled with anticipation for their upcoming vacations. I was shocked by the obvious. I imagined you among the others waiting in line, waiting with your suitcase, happy and excited. I imagined you standing there with your black backpack, your shoulders hunched under the weight you carried. I saw you and did not see you. You were everywhere we went.

We were a family of stoic, dark figures in a field of vibrant color. I wanted to hide. I wanted to return home, and we had just arrived in Mexico. We were warmly welcomed on an open portico with music playing. There were beautiful fuchsia flowers and palm trees everywhere. I detected the sound of the ocean off in the distance. I stood with a mimosa in my hand and wondered what the hell I was doing. I wanted to gather all the smiling people around me and tell them, "Don't smile, don't look into my face. My daughter just died, and I don't know what I am doing here." We slept with the patio door open, hoping the sound of the waves would help us sleep. It did not.

The color of the water did not lift my mood. The spa treatments were wonderful, but an hour later the dreaded feelings that I wanted to get away from returned. My inner chaos was intensified by the very fact that there was nothing familiar.

On Christmas Eve, we sat on the balcony overlooking the pool and gardens. We exchanged gifts in the full moon's light. We tried to proceed as one would normally do on a holiday, but we failed. Dad gave me a gift that I would have cherished at any other time: a journal that he kept during the past year. Who would have guessed that he would capture the last year of your life in those pages? He wrote, "May this bring you peace and happiness as you reflect on the positive aspects of this precious year; my love to you." I opened it to October 11, 2001, and read, "Please no, no. Tell us this is a dream. Our baby girl died today at approximately 11:30 p.m." I wanted to tear the diary up and throw the pages off the balcony. I wanted the written record of what we had been through stricken from my sight. But it was a gift of love, and I prayed that one day I would be able to open it and read what he had unknowingly recorded. As my heart broke, I smiled and hugged Dad with tears running down his face.

Joseph gave us the words, "You are alive." He saw them painted on the wall of an abandoned building in New York. He took their picture, cut them out, and mounted them on the reverse side of three small mirrors. We broke down as something so simple tumbled into our heart with its multiple meanings.

Dad spent last night vomiting. He blamed it on Montezuma's Revenge. I believe he succumbed to the trauma of your death. He unconsciously threw you up. He got rid of feelings he could no longer contain in his body. He was a shell of a person. I could not help him and he could not help me. He spent the day in bed; I spent the day sitting and looking out over the water. The book I brought with me rested in my lap. I couldn't read. I couldn't concentrate. I couldn't process anything. I needed to be alone. I needed to be quiet.

December 28, 2001:
Chichen Itza

On our last day, we visited the ancient ruins of Chichen Itza, a large, pre-Columbian archeological site that had been built by the Mayan civilization. It turned out to be our best day yet. We loved the ruins, and perhaps that says it all. We loved the history and the fact that it had survived so many years. Something about ruins and survival gave us peace, happiness, and relief.

We were impressed by the large step pyramid, El Castillo. I loved the fact that on the spring and autumn equinox, at the rising and setting of the sun, the corners of the pyramid cast a shadow in the shape of a plumed serpent, which moved along the staircase. We climbed to the top and looked out over the jungle. Its height and steepness had an unsettling effect on us, and thoughts of you falling to your death overtook each of us. We did not stay at the top because our experience shifted toward you and then became all about you. It was a subtle intrusion at first and then mounted in intensity until it consumed us. I felt you falling and felt myself falling with you, noticing the urge to fling myself down the steep set of steps. We climbed down and felt safe as we sensed the earth under our feet. For a few precious moments, we were normal tourists, enjoying a piece of history on a beautiful day in Mexico; the next moment we were cast again into the abyss of your death.

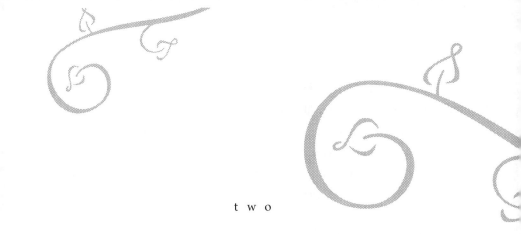

two

image
making

New Year

We returned home. I wanted it to be different, but nothing had changed. Father Ray and Grandma came for New Year's Eve. We sat around the table eating lasagna and talking. Father Ray reminded us that we were each responsible for our behavior, including you. We went to see the movie *A Perfect Mind*. It was a poignant commentary on mental illness and love. My love was not strong enough to see you through. I did not realize the extent of your suffering. I did not understand the dangerous dimensions of your mental illness and the stranglehold it had on you. I failed you. The movie tore my heart out. I cried. We were home before midnight, sat in the garden together under the big maple, and lit candles in the moonlight.

Feeling our movement into a new year was not celebratory. Time officially moved forward, placing distance between our living memories of you. I felt adrift. We had each come through your death in our own ways. I was beginning to realize that we were on very solitary journeys; we shared it as a family, but our paths were separate.

I sat alone at my desk today and made notations in my new calendar, moving over the pages of 2001, transferring birth dates and anniversaries. I felt flat and unmoved as I remembered the past year. I wrote, "First Anniversary of Kristin's death" on October 11, 2002. I tossed the loosened end of my black Pashmina around my right shoulder. The phone rang and I jumped. Its sound as well as other sudden noises were disturbing reminders of life's fragility. I wanted to cover my ears and mute the sound. The ringing was like a gunshot to the chest; it pulled the trigger back to panic and the phone call that destroyed my life. I saw it was Grandma and let it ring. I couldn't talk. Everyone else was asleep.

January 8, 2002:
Defended

In the beginning the suffering was relentless and marginally bearable, because of the defense mechanisms that took over and ensured my survival. They protected me and allowed me to move through each day without falling apart. They were merciful, and I was thankful to have allies. I was familiar with the literature on defense mechanisms; I'd read about them during my training as an art therapist. I talked about them in reference to my own clients. I noted some of myself in the pages of the *Diagnostic and Statistical Manual of Mental Disorders*: (DSM-IV) dissociation, derealization, repression, denial.

> Dissociation: A disruption in the usually integrated functions of consciousness, memory, identity, or perception of the environment. The disturbance may be sudden or gradual, transient or chronic.

> Derealization: An alteration in the perception or experience of the external world so that it seems strange or unreal.

> Repression: Defensive functioning ... that keeps the potentially threatening ideas, feelings, memories, wishes, or fears out of awareness.

> Denial: Characterized by keeping unpleasant or unacceptable stressors, impulses, ideas, affects, or responsibilities out of awareness.

I was further defined by "the apprehensive anticipation of future danger or misfortune accompanied by feelings of ... tension." The experience of your suicide crystallized those words. They no longer were one-dimensional clinical notations resting on a page—I embodied them. I was a living, breathing case study of trauma.

When you died, my grief split me apart. I was like a skeleton tree in the backyard, caught in a hurricane. The part of me standing was naked and vulnerable. My center was impenetrable, protected by layers of hardened bark. The vibrant colorful and feeling part of myself fell away and scattered like so many leaves across a landscape. A tree in shock will lose its leaves to conserve energy and to survive. I was defoliated. In this pause I was both alive and dead.

I knew I would make it through; the sap would rise, and life would continue. When my feelings returned, they were like sharp green buds that pierced my skin and took my breath away. I longed to remain dormant. These defenses offered me a temporary rest. I needed to find my way. In the end I turned to what I was comfortable with: I turned to traditional institutions and traditional therapy in the months following your death.

January 9, 2002:
Endless Talking

Dad and I signed up for a grief and bereavement course offered at one of the local hospitals. Each week we covered one of the five stages of grief: denial, anger, bargaining, depression, and acceptance. The stages were taken from Elizabeth Kübler-Ross's teachings, formulated during her research with dying persons and grieving survivors. I had read her 1969 book, *On Death and Dying*, years ago; it seemed straightforward and neat. I found it irrelevant in the face of my current chaos. I was not surprised when, at the end of the five weeks, the bereaved parent who led the group took us aside and invited us to sign up for another round of the course. It seemed to him that we were in need of more. Somehow we had not gotten whatever it was that he was trying so hard for us to get. His presentation on "Letting Go and Moving On" did not seem possible from where we stood. We smiled and thanked him. Dad said he was not going back as he slammed the car door. The facilitator characterized Dad as angry, constricted, cut off, and analytical. Dad did not want to hear it. I found the group somewhat helpful, in spite of the fact we were the only ones who had lost a child. It was an eclectic group of newly bereaved; it was not Dad's cup of tea. The conversation ended there. Our world was already upside down, and I did not see any need to push things. It gave us some information and exposed us to some others grieving, and we were able to ask questions. I let go of the idea that a group would work for us. Not everything works for everyone.

I thought that individual couple's therapy might work. I wanted a place where Dad and I might find healing together. I wanted a therapeutic container that could support our diverse universes that I feared might spin out of control. I was told that a high percentage of parents divorce after the death of a child. I was determined that we would not fall into that statistical category. We began meeting with a psychologist and committed ourselves to our grief work.

We just got home from our weekly, eleven o'clock session. Dad went back to work. The fifty minutes we had spent together had not changed the way I felt in my body. To a certain extent, it was endless talking. It felt pointless. I struggled to find meaning.

January 23, 2002: Snake Dream

In my dream, I was in the house I grew up in. The basement was unfinished and filled with snakes. I crawled over hundreds of huge snakes and called for everyone to come and see. I was at the foot of the stairs and had on two robes; the outer one was black and the inner one was white. I took off the outer robe. I could see undulation and movement beneath my clothing. I lifted my inner robe, and snakes covered my body. I reached around to my left shoulder. One snake had bitten me there and was attached to my body. I was aware that I had swallowed a snake; it ran the length of my spine. Our mouths were one and the same. I was not afraid—I was calm.

Snakes are symbols of death and rebirth. They are symbols of transmutation. I was covered with them. I shed two layers of clothing to reveal their presence. Snakes shed their skin. This dream awakened in me the notion that I was an initiate in a healing process that was multilayered and involved letting go. The snake also offered me something as it attached itself to my left shoulder, injecting its venom into my body. I felt it was medicine rather than poison.

Tomorrow will mark fifteen weeks since your death. In spite of the dream's assurances, I wanted to go to sleep and never wake up.

January 31, 2002:
Janet

I remember meeting Janet when Aunt Donna called in early December and said, "I'm taking you to have a reading." I don't know why I said yes, but I did. I went with an open mind, not knowing what to expect. I had a vague notion about mediums. Supposedly they had the ability to connect with the dead and pass on pertinent information to family and loved ones. This information subsequently served as evidence to the living that the soul continued its journey after the physical form of the body died.

We drove into the city and turned onto a tree-lined street filled with rows of old homes. I was surprised when Janet opened the door. I did not expect a stately woman with gray hair holding a white poodle, but rather someone in flowing robes holding a crystal ball. Aunt Donna kissed me good-bye and said she would be back in an hour. Janet gave me a hug and showed me the way to her sitting room, complete with desk, comfortable wing-backed chair, and lots of windows that let in light. The solarium allowed in a view of bare trees and tangled branches. In a charming British accent, she explained some of her philosophical beliefs. "Life is eternal. It is without beginning or end. We are essentially energy that is neither created nor destroyed; it only changes form. When someone dies they move out of the form of their body into formlessness, as energy, as consciousness, as spirit, as essence, as love." I believed that. I believed in heaven and imagined you there. At least, most of me believed and hoped it were true. A very small part of me was skeptical and wondered if it was all just wishful thinking. What if there was nothing beyond this world? What if we turned to dust, and that was it?

She began the reading by talking about several dead relatives, all accurate information in terms of physical description and references to personality …

but not the dead relative I wanted to hear about. I was impatient and on the verge of saying something when Janet got very quiet and very serious. She said, "these family members bring forward a shy young woman, a child really, who has recently crossed over. This would be your daughter." I began to cry. She described you as taller than me, with light brown wavy hair. She sensed your death, using the words "falling, flying, quite sudden, and unexpected. She crossed herself over." Janet spoke of you as an artist. She spoke of your struggle with food in the months before your death, and she shared details from the week you died. She described your moods. She was accurate about almost everything.

This experience comforted me in a way I had not expected. I felt reassured and close to you. There was something exceptionally powerful about sitting with a total stranger and receiving direct and personal information. Her apparent connection with you made me consider my own internal conversations with you as more than the ravings of a desperate mother gone mad. I thanked her.

As Janet walked me to the door, she said, "I have a weekly spiritual development circle on Thursdays. Would you like to sit with us beginning in January?" I again found myself saying yes. I had no idea what I had said yes to, but it felt like the thing to do.

On January 3, 2002, I went to my first circle. We met in Janet's basement. I made my way down the narrow steps and felt enveloped by dampness mixed with burning incense. The house was over sixty years old, and the small, pine-paneled room was just big enough for a circle of wooden chairs. I knew I would leave if it felt too weird, but as I looked around, there was nothing weird about the surroundings. There was a black lacquered screen with flowers in one corner and two very large silk wall hangings of an Asian couple adjacent to where we sat. A picture of the Virgin Mary, a few Buddhas, the Hindu Goddess Kali, and a row of carved elephants sat on a shelf above our circle. Small white lights, left over from some distant Christmas, wrapped the steps' banister. There were several cats roaming about. Binki, Janet's old white poodle, sat on her lap. Janet sat in the soft chair against the wall, underneath the shelf of eclectic religious icons. I sat next to her on her right, and I felt safe.

Once the five of us were seated, she began. She started with a guided meditation, designed and structured to raise our consciousness and open our awareness. She said, "This first part is a time of preparation and a time to attune to a higher vibration." She then guided us into the second part, which was like entering a day dream. My mind was relaxed and spacious at the same time that it was alert and alive. My experience evolved from Janet's intuitive prompt, which was like being offered a single note onto which I imagined a whole symphony. After sitting in the fullness of my experience for a few minutes, each circle member then shared what came to them. We closed with a prayer of thanksgiving.

When I got home, I recorded my experience in my red leather book, where I recorded the dreams I have at night. I wrote, "I had the impression that Grandpa was with me. He gave me a gift, a stethoscope. He said, 'Listen to your heart; you are on the right path. Keep learning and studying.'" The following week Grandpa appeared again in his white lab coat and instructed me to "Be in a place of humility, be in the silence and in the quiet of what is being revealed." The experience included images of stars falling from the heavens, coming down, adorning me, covering my nakedness, and making me new to the world.

These gatherings have steadied me more than anything else. I looked forward to the hour and a half in the meditative, altered state of consciousness that provides me a time out from the endless turmoil of your death. My weary body and mind take a break, and I find some peace. I experience healing on a cellular level.

February 6, 2002:
The Wedding Vase

I tried to explain my circle experiences to Dad over the weekend. I took in his wry smile as he said, "Do what makes you happy." I thought he rolled his eyes as he left the kitchen table. I couldn't expect him to understand, because I didn't completely understand what was happening myself. All I knew was that I felt better for a few hours each week. Where did my experiences come from? Did they come to me from the spirit world? Did they come to me from my own subconscious mind? I didn't really care where. As strange as it sounded, it was calming to my nervous system, which was on high alert most of the time due to the trauma of your death. I was suffering. I also didn't care what anyone else thought about what I was doing. I would have sat in a circle with pumpkins and painted myself purple, if it gave me relief.

I'd had conversations with you inside my head since the day you died, long before sitting with Janet. Sitting in this circle allowed me to continue those conversations with you, in a space where I was not judged. Not only did I continue to have conversations with you, but I had experiences that felt nourishing and healing. I was bathed in water and filled with light. I rested in a field of fragrant flowers. I would have gone to Janet's every day if she would have had me. In fact, I went to her Tuesday circle last night, knowing that I couldn't make the circle on Thursday.

Janet's prompts varied, based on what intuitively came to her. She would say something like, "You find yourself in a garden; someone joins you," or, "You climb a set of stairs and enter a room; notice who's there and what's happening." Last night Janet said, "You have been invited to a wedding."

In my experience, Dad and I were on a cliff overlooking water. We were seated on a bench. We realized you were standing before us. You reminded us of the vase you broke on Mother's Day 2001 in a fit of rage. That vase had been a wedding gift, and I loved it. You tried to comfort us and tell us we would be all right, and that a new marriage would be born out of this broken vessel. The idea of a new marriage being born out of what was broken gave me pause as I considered the status of our marriage: the ups and downs, the flaws in the relationship. I sensed more to your words than my thinking mind could grasp. You said, "We are all willing participants."

The energy of this sitting stayed with me. As I drove home, I heard your voice inside my head telling me, "Go to our favorite antique store, and you will find a Lenox vase there. It's not quite like the one I broke, but close enough. You'll know I love you." I was filled with fear and doubt. Was this real or just my imagination? Should I take the chance and follow your direction? If there was no vase, then what?

I struggled with myself all morning until finally I gathered my courage and got in the car. My heart was pounding when I pulled back the heavy door to Great Finds and Designs. The glass and china was located in one section of the consignment store. I had never seen Lenox of any kind displayed there, and I had shopped there for years. I rounded the corner, and there on the third shelf, just as you had shown me, was a beautiful Lenox vase not exactly like the one you broke, but larger and perhaps even more beautiful. I could not believe it. I took it off the shelf and turned it over to see when it had been brought in. The tag read "1/11/02." You died on the eleventh, and I seemed to see elevens wherever I went.

I was glad I listened. I came home and placed my new vase on the counter in the kitchen, in the same spot as the one you broke. The broken pieces of my cherished wedding gift were no longer on the kitchen floor. I decided to keep this experience to myself. Perhaps I would share it with Dad on another day, perhaps on our Anniversary in March. This was an exceptionally happy day.

February 19, 2002:
Tennis

We were a tennis loving family, smitten with the sport because of Dad's passion. He had started playing soon after graduation, when his days on the University of Maryland baseball team ended. We became more serious about tennis in 1987, a year after we moved into our new home. We gave Kimberly and Kevin lessons. You started lessons when you were just a little girl. You would run onto the court with Kimberly and Kevin, screaming, "I want to play, too." The tennis racket was bigger than you. I looked at what you wrote in your journal.

> November 20, 1995: Yes, off school for the whole week. My backhand sucks but my forehand is good. I love tennis. When I grow up I want to be a pro like Steffi Graf. She is the best player in the whole wide world.

> September 7, 1999: I decided to play varsity tennis. I'm #1!

Tennis was a big part of your life. I cherished all the time spent sitting and watching your lessons. I cherished our time at local, regional, and national tournaments. I could still see you in your blue and white plaid NDP tennis skirt; you were fit and tan. I imagined you rushing out the door with your water bottle and tennis bag. I saw your ponytail bobbing and swishing behind you. I felt your kiss as you left me with a, "Bye, Mom." I wished I could go back. Time was precious, and I wondered how I would look back at this moment.

Today was about playing tennis again. My friends called and encouraged me to come back. They said it was time. They gave me the autumn; they were not willing to give me the winter.

The Greenspring Racquet Club was filled with your memory. When I walked through their doors so soon after you died, the walls shifted from their ninety–degree, upright positions as the ground beneath me gave way. I couldn't move or breathe. I wanted to run from the place as I pulled the curtain aside and walked onto the court. There were Debi, Bonnie, and Sharon, waiting for me with open arms and smiles. They hugged me and pulled me back into life.

They made me play. They forced me to put one foot in front of the other even though I couldn't feel myself. They made me move my body and encircled me with their love week after week, even though I could hardly hit a ball. I didn't feel bad about my playing; I showed up and that was good enough. They were a lifeline, and their kindness sustained me in the face of so much change. On Tuesday mornings, from 9:00 until 10:30, I could count on something normal.

February 28, 2002:
Kay Redfield Jamison

We walked down the glass breezeway of Johns Hopkins Hospital toward the Tower Restaurant, just off the main lobby, to meet Dr. Kay Redfield Jamison. We sat at a table by the window and waited for her. She did not know us, and we did not know her beyond her reputation as a professor of psychiatry at the Johns Hopkins University School of Medicine. She was also co-director of the Johns Hopkins Mood Disorders Center and a renowned author of numerous books.

She called personally after receiving the fax I sent, which read in part, "On October 11, 2001, our seventeen-year-old daughter Kristin took her own life. She was a college freshman in New York City. We are in uncharted territory as we attempt to bring greater awareness to the issues of suicide. We feel the need for some expert advice and would like to meet with you for an hour." A few days later, the phone rang. Dr. Jamison introduced herself. She said she was very sorry for our loss and would be willing to meet with us on February 28. I couldn't believe it.

I recognized her from her picture on the covers of *Touched with Fire, An Unquiet Mind*, and *Night Falls Fast*. We stood up as she approached the table. She was taller than I expected with blonde hair. Her white lab coat had her name on the pocket. She was professional in demeanor, quiet and reserved. She was kind and compassionate. She listened and answered questions. She was direct with Dad and me. It was Kimberly who caught her attention, however. Kimberly passionately shared her vision of creating a healing environment called Rita Project, in which those who had lost someone to suicide, and those who had attempted, could come together and let out their grief and anger in a positive way, through the arts. Dr. Jamison encouraged your sister and told her to go after her dream. I wished Kevin was here for this special meeting, but he was at college finishing his last semester.

I left our meeting encouraged to bring awareness to the issues of suicide, depression, and related affective disorders. We planned to focus our attention on quality programs that addressed the serious mental health issues facing adolescents in high school and in college. In addition, Rita Project felt acknowledged and worthy of our efforts.

I admired Dr. Jamison for her brilliance and clear writings about the ravages of bipolar illness. She wrote from personal experience, coming forward herself as an example to others who remain hidden behind the closed doors of mental illness. I wished I had read her books before. I was strengthened by her example and was encouraged to remain open concerning your mental illness and death. I was aware that some try to cover over the facts. We could have tried, but it would have been a lie. Your casket was intentionally open. Your body and bruised hand were there for all to see.

April 16, 2002:
Rain

I felt it before I opened my eyes: it was not going to be a good day. My morning shower did not release my grief. I had tennis in an hour. I finished dressing and drove to the indoor court. I didn't know what caused one day to be different than the next, one more horrible, one less horrible, mixed in with the uneventfully numb days with no labels. I got in the habit of just going with what I woke up to, knowing that tomorrow would bring something different.

My tennis friends were waiting, anxious to get started. We warmed up at the net with volleys. Some part of me watched myself and couldn't believe that I had the audacity to be playing a game. *Kristin is dead. She killed herself, and I am playing tennis.* I moved for a shot. I extended my arm and felt you extending your arm, too. It was just another in a series of strange body experiences, where the story of you and the horror of your death made itself known in the matter of my flesh. I felt terribly fragile and did not know how I was going to make it through the next hour and a half. I fought back tears. We moved back to the baseline and began to practice forehands and backhands. I wanted to excuse myself and go home. The game began even though I did not want to play. I threw the ball high and hit a serve that moved over the net and came down squarely in the appropriate box. I did not feel myself. The experience was supercharged with memories of you that rushed through me like electricity; these sensations came and went throughout the match. I played and no one knew. I was two people, not one, and I struggled every moment until it was over.

I put on my jacket, got in my car, and drove straight home. This had happened before, and it would happen again. I wondered about my life. Your death created a before and an after. Before, I thought I knew who I was and what I was doing. Now I didn't know anything.

I came in from tennis and placed my racket on the shelf in the mud room, right above your tennis gear, which I could not bring myself to move. I plopped myself down in the kitchen, not taking the time to remove my black North Face jacket, which was yours anyway. I noticed the lone dragonfly stenciled by the light switch; you had painted it on the wall. I sat sideways in the arms of the oversized chair and let my legs dangle over the padded curved arm. I rested my head against the cushion and looked at the clock. I sat and listened to the rain falling and imagined it moving through my body, washing me clean.

It was 11:11 a.m. I closed my eyes as I pulled the Irish afghan over myself.

May 11, 2002:
The Price of Rejection

I was up early. I could not sleep. I looked monstrous with a puffy face and swollen eyes from crying so much. I'd never looked so terrible and barely recognized myself. I felt like I was going to fall to my knees. I was dizzy and sick to my stomach. I practiced some yoga poses, ones I remembered from a distant class. I listened to sacred Buddhist mantras being chanted. I went outside and lay on the ground to help stabilize myself. I felt upside down and dark.

In the afternoon, I met your best friend, Kelly, at your grave. We sat and cried together. She said you came to her in her dreams. She brought your favorite potato chips from Rite Aid and scattered them over you on the grass. She missed you so much. She sat for hours with you at your grave. It seemed like only yesterday that Kelly sat with you on the kitchen floor, playing with Sienna, who was just a puppy.

I wondered about your other friends and how they were doing as they completed their first year of college. I remembered what you wrote.

> September 6, 1997: Death. Today is even worse, knowing that I was not included in the sleepover. I thought she was my friend. I need to talk to Kelly. She is my friend. I'm so sad I can't even cry. The mixer was so bad; I never want to go to another one again. I know I will have to because if I don't, I will be such a dork, but I already am one. I knew it would be like this. I want to die and I hate myself. I wish I was a baby again, three years old, lucky number.

I wondered how they felt when they thought of you, especially when memories of your times together filtered through their hearts. I was sure they remembered the good times. I prayed that they remembered the times when they set themselves apart and left you out for one reason or another. Young girls can be incredibly cruel to one another. I remembered a time when you came home from middle school, and in tears you told me, "I sat down at the lunch table filled with girls I thought were my friends. They looked up at me and then got up and moved to another table." I remembered the times when you cried because you were not invited to a dance or a party; you suffered as if someone had lacerated your heart. I wondered about all the hurts you carried inside. You were so sensitive. You had a kind and loving heart. I wondered at the price of rejection: your suicide.

May 12, 2002: Kevin's Graduation

Today was Mother's Day and Kevin's graduation from the University of Pennsylvania. We were all trying so hard to be happy. He deserved a day in celebration of his academic accomplishments, majoring in economics, graduating Cum Laude, and fulfilling his dream of playing Division I tennis. Yet there was a pervasive sense of loss that moved like an underground current of sludge, permeating and fouling everything above it.

I looked at your brother in his cap and gown, so proud and confident, perched on the edge of all that was before him. I saw him in this moment, and yet I was aware of another Kevin, the one collapsed on the floor of the roof of your dorm as we examined the place of your descent. I remembered when I turned toward him that day, I felt as though I was seeing him through the long lens of a looking glass. He seemed transported out of time and place into another dimension. He seemed small and fragile. He sat away from us. He held his head in his hands. He was withdrawn and pale. He did not stand with us by the edge. He did not place his hands on the place where you sat, because he could not.

You should have been here with him today, Kristin, sitting in the stadium, taking pictures, and walking the grounds of the university. I did not understand and was exhausted as I tried to keep it all together.

Both grandmas were with us, and I could hardly stand it. I wanted to run from their presence. I was filled with shame and consumed by my own failure as a mother that was only highlighted when I looked into their eyes. I felt no sense of pride or accomplishment as a mother—your suicide destroyed that and replaced it with self-abasement. None of your grandmothers' children died. I wondered if they were able to sense what I was trying so hard to conceal.

I was comforted by the fact that Grandpa never lived to see all of this. It would have killed him to see you in a coffin. In my daydreams I played with the notion that he was there with you at the moment of your death. I imagined him reaching up to catch you, long before you hit the ground.

I found a certain measure of peace as I considered the two of you in heaven, and in knowing that your bodies rested side by side in your graves. Grandma lovingly gave you her spot beside Grandpa in the cemetery. She said, "Don't worry about me; I'll be happy. Just cremate me and spread my ashes between the two of them." I never asked her to give away her final resting place, but she offered. That's what mothers do.

I welcomed the evening with open arms. It brought this day to an end. I felt a sense of relief. During our drive home, I gazed through the windshield into the night sky and felt quieted in the darkness that was everywhere.

May 17, 2002:
Twin Dream

I dreamt of you last night. I have had many dreams of you. Most fade in the morning light; others seem special and stay with me, like this one. In this dream you were young, crystal clear, and full bodied. I drank in your face. We held each other as I realized I had the opportunity to be with you. You said, "I am happy." Your body began to fade, leaving golden light behind. I called after you, and an exact replica of you returned. There were two of you—you were a twin. I understood you could be in two places at once. I visited with you again, and we embraced. You told me, "I rest my head against you, I lay down with you at night, and I am beside you always." You tried to comfort me and faded into golden light again. There was no fear or shame or darkness around you; you were love and light. I was given two fresh water pearls. I woke and I was filled with the joy of having held you.

June 4, 2002:
Tennis with Kathy

Kathy called in January and asked me to be her partner during the women's tennis interclub season. We met this past summer on the court while taking some tennis lessons. I was completely overcome by her invitation. I got off the phone and cried at the thought that someone I barely knew was willing to be with me. I felt like a leper, contaminated by your suicide.

Kathy included me, and in that inclusion she reminded me that I was more than a mother whose daughter had killed herself. I appreciated her kindness, which came at a time when I felt so flawed. It had been a winning season in spite of the fact that we lost our final match. Those weeks of tennis had nothing to do with the scores we posted. For a few hours a week, I was a part of ordinary life. The fact of your death moved to the outer reaches of my consciousness while I focused on a yellow tennis ball.

July 5, 2002:
Fireworks

Fourth of July came and went. I listened quietly at night to the fireworks and noticed the sky light up here and there. The sounds ignited the interior of my heart. Others were celebrating with their families. We were by ourselves. One expects children to grow and move into their own adult lives. We never anticipated your death and the sudden aloneness that came with it. Kimberly and Kevin did not like coming home. This place was filled with memories and the energy of death. They suggested that we sell the house, let it go, and begin again. It felt too early to know what was right. All I knew was that I missed them terribly.

I was cold in the heat of last night as I remembered watching the fireworks with you last year. You urged us to go and see the fireworks, and so we drove around the corner to the little church that sits high on the hill. We stood in the cemetery among the gravestones and watched the sky light up. Past and present converged. I wondered if there would ever be a time when a day could just be a day without your death being woven through each minute.

July 15, 2002:
Kitchen Drawer

I couldn't stop thinking about you. If I could have turned off my thoughts, I would have. I wondered what you were doing. I wondered if you were sad over what you had done. My stomach hurt. Why was it that one day I felt a sense of peace, and the next day I was flung into the depths of despair again? I had no answer as I stood in the mud room and looked at your tennis rackets sitting with your tennis shoes on the shelf. I still couldn't move them. They seemed to be waiting for you, although I knew you were never coming home.

I sat and opened a drawer by my desk, and I thought of cleaning it. I hadn't cleaned anything in the kitchen since before you left for college. My drawer was filled with fragments of you: a ballet sticker, an old schedule, some pens and pencils. Underneath my papers were the drawings you etched into the wood when you were four or five. I saw you sitting on the chair and looking up at me, saying, "Look what I just made for you." I could not even wipe them. I could not touch them with my cloth, for fear of removing some part of you from my existence. I was paralyzed. I closed the drawer of my desk and walked away. I couldn't do anything. I went and sat outside and remembered.

I remembered Kimberly and Kevin sitting at the kitchen table doing their homework. You sat on the floor with paper and crayons, and your little hand moved over the paper. I looked at the shapes you created, the lines you used, and I already saw the beginnings of an artist, someone special with the ability to capture essence. That cannot be taught; you were just born with it.

I remembered when you were six years old. I held your hand as we made our way up the steps to the art studio. You had been taking drawing lessons for some time. The teacher said she would give you a try. She had her doubts, never having someone as young as you in her classes. You sat right next to her. You looked so little on that chair, in a room filled with art materials and students who were older. I sat in the waiting room just outside the studio, but I was able to glance at you above the pages of my book. You thrived and grew. You created one pastel masterpiece after another. You could copy anything, and we framed your finished pieces and hung them.

You were happy when you were drawing or painting. Your kindergarten teacher had to limit your time in front of the easel in order to force you to take advantage of other learning experiences in the classroom. That love and passion continued through elementary school. By middle school you had years of art lessons under your belt. You were a passionate collector of pencils and pens. Everywhere we went, you seemed to find something special you had to have. You had a drawer filled with treasures: a pencil with ballet shoes on it, one with sparkles, one with a troll on top; pens of every variety, some that glowed, and some that came in small packages complete with little pads of paper, more for an elf than for a person. When I walked by your room, I usually saw you lying on the floor on your belly with your materials spread before you, working, creating, and playing, happy in your own little world.

August 2, 2002:
Kimberly's Twenty-Fifth Birthday

I picked Kimberly up at the train station. She appeared weary, although she said she was fine. There were deer at the crest of the hill. We stopped and looked at them before driving down the driveway. She did not seem happy to be home, but she managed a smile. We sat outside around the table and enjoyed crabs. I made her an apple pie. At twenty-five she had lived a full life—a fuller life than I would have wanted for her. At twenty-five she seemed old. I wished I could sweep all the pain and suffering away and make it better for her, but I couldn't.

We were pleased she came home to celebrate. She seemed to be doing as well as could be expected. There was no light in her eyes other than when she spoke of Rita Project. There was no light in any of our eyes. She blew out the single yellow candle I put at the center of the apple pie.

She went off to New York University, Tisch School of the Arts, filled with passion and on her way to fulfilling her dreams on stage or in film, as an actress. She was young and beautiful; her petite frame was alluring. She had brown eyes that flashed with intensity. People were drawn to her. She liked being at the center. You were always jealous of that.

Kimberly's life turned upside down when you died. She quit her job as a coordinating producer and came home. She stayed with us until the first of the year and then returned to New York. Her vision for Rita Project took over her life. Kimberly wanted a creative place to heal from the suffering of your death. Kimberly wanted something more than she was receiving from traditional talk therapy. Kimberly founded what she desired for herself.

Rita, which is Sanskrit for "truth," was a global movement to stop suicide and to celebrate life, an "organization devoted to using the arts to help survivors of suicide connect with the power of creation and in doing so, foster transformation." There was a spark of life in her when we talked about Rita Project Studio, New York, in memory of you, Kristin Rita.

August 27, 2002:
My Birthday

It was my birthday. I woke up early—too early—walked into the kitchen, and made myself a cup of coffee. I sat at the round glass-top table and stared out into the garden. I felt guilty and ashamed that I was alive at fifty-two, and you were dead at seventeen. I looked over at the birthday cards from Kimberly and Kevin, displayed on my desk. I appreciated that they had at least managed to send the cards before my birthday arrived.

They were not coming home to celebrate with me. They were busy, another in a line of excuses that kept them from coming home. I did not blame them, but at the same time I was filled with resentment as I sat here alone on this day. I had no plans; I wanted it like that. I did not want to be caught in a situation where I was trying to be nice for someone else's sake.

I opened the book that someone had given me as a gift: it was about suicide and healing. People gave me books to read throughout the year. When I opened them, the words sat on the pages and made no sense at all. I could not concentrate. I had no strength to wade through stories of loss and grief. Yet as the months moved from one to another, I had questions. I found myself leafing through this book. I searched for the meaning of "it's really difficult" and "it gets better with time." I wanted details, really specific details. I wanted hard facts. I wanted someone to please tell me exactly what "difficult" meant. I needed complete descriptions so that I could compare my experiences and determine whether or not I was going insane. I wanted someone to please let me know what "better" meant, so I could hold on to something hopeful. It was beyond my conception that I would ever feel really better—you're dead, and that fact would never change. I wanted someone to please tell me exactly how much time "better" took. I wanted to know where the finish line was. I sensed no endpoint, and that was terrifying. I often woke up afraid that this was the condition of my life forever. I would have appreciated a map, one with great directions, so that I would have an idea of where I was going; then I might not feel so lost. I needed to know the lay of the land, to understand the territory of my descent.

Talking with other survivors only helped a little. They shared and answered my questions. I heard what they said, yet their words did not impact my life in a way that altered my grief. There was a limit to what I could talk about. A fine line defined the territory of my imaginary world, filled with bones, blood, and screams. I dared not go there. I was ten months into your death, and I had no idea who I was. I felt disconnected from myself and the story of my life. Time continued to implode on itself.

I was the oldest of three daughters, born to loving but strict parents. We never missed church on Sunday, even the Easter I came down with chicken-pox. We had a comfortable life as the family of a physician. Manners were of utmost importance. We spent much of our leisure time with colleagues and their families. I remember sitting at the dining room table and listening to the adult conversations on politics and philosophy, but I was too shy and unsure to participate. I was a fair student but a disappointment to both parents, who feared for my life based on grades. I was good enough to get into a small Eastern shore college named after our first president.

I came into my own when I left home and was out from under my parents' watchful eye and judgment. I majored in psychology and minored in art. My father was not particularly supportive of my choice, letting me know that "People who enter the field of psychology do so in order to figure themselves out." He was not impressed with what he saw as "a specialty riddled with wounded healers." I respected his opinions; he was a brilliant man, philosophically grounded in Jesuit teachings that he embraced during his years at Providence College and Georgetown Medical School. I loved what I loved and made room for our differences. I did not argue with him; that would have been a losing battle. I quietly moved in the direction I was drawn to and gave myself permission to entertain the fact that he might be wrong. I believed his attitudes were born of ignorance and armored by his own unwillingness to look at himself. He was the second youngest of seven children in a hard-working yet impoverished Irish family. His father was an alcoholic. Grandpa extracted himself from a less than ideal life through education. He was a kind and gentle man, and I loved and admired him. The cornerstones of his life were integrity and hard work. He had high standards and expected nothing less from those around him. I tried to pass those ideals on to you.

I let my hair grow long and bought my first pair of blue jeans during my years at Washington College. I loved my psychology classes, I loved my studio art classes and art history classes, and I loved my sorority. I met your dad at the end of my junior year. He was a business major at the University of Maryland and was an outfielder on the varsity baseball team. He was handsome, we fell in love, and we married in March 1974, between semesters, as he continued work on his master's degree and I began a master's degree in rehabilitation counseling. Rehabilitation counseling did not capture my imagination, and I let it go when we moved from College Park to Catonsville. We bought a brand-new, split-level house right around the corner from Grandma and Grandpa in 1976, and we started having babies: Kimberly in 1977, Kevin in 1980, and you in 1983.

My life was uneventful, normal, and typical for the times. I nursed my babies, and I basked in the enjoyment of watching you ride your bikes, play in our sandbox, and swing on the swings. I baked my own cookies, participated in play groups, and read to you at night. I was a young mother and a college graduate. In those early years, I discovered I needed something of my own outside the demands of raising a family. My interest in continuing my education resurfaced, and I applied to a master's degree program in art education. I enjoyed my studio courses and found a balance to my life during those years. I completed eighteen credits of that program and made an abrupt change when Dad showed me an article in the newspaper on a new master's degree program in art therapy, opening in the fall. Without knowing much about the field beyond what the article stated, I knew I had found what my heart had been searching for: a means of combining my two passions, psychology and art. It was very demanding and challenged me in every way. I grew, I loved it, and I was happy. I proved something to myself when I graduated from Goucher College with a degree in art therapy. You were just a baby, and I held you in my cap and gown. That day I noticed the smile in my father's eyes.

Where did it go off track? At what moment did I make a wrong turn without knowing it? I was responsible. You died. I felt guilty. I was ashamed of myself as a mother. Those feelings churned endlessly in me. Everything goes back to the mother, doesn't it? I looked inside and outside for answers. I looked at my mother. I remembered my own beginning. I was born in Fall River, Massachusetts. I was born in a place whose name defined the single most important moment in my life: your fall. It was there in plain sight, right on my birth certificate. Surely it was her fault for birthing me in such a place. And so on my birthday, amid the memories, I fell with you into a river of tears and found myself swirling and carried away to some distant place, into the unknown.

September 9, 2002:
Books and Therapy

I searched for something, anything, that would mend my brokenness. I was devastated by the condition I was in. We were approaching the one-year mark. I felt like one of the tall reeds in our backyard during a windstorm, being blown this way and that way. There was nothing steady, nothing secure, and nothing dependable, except for Janet's circle. I felt connected to you there, and that felt right amid everything else that felt so wrong. In spite of that oasis, I was robbed of whatever emotional strength I had begun to gather over the summer. I felt totally dismembered and stripped bare to the bone again. I couldn't do a thing. I was so pissed off and upset that I had so easily succumbed. The initial physical and emotional suffering passed by late winter. A watered down version persisted, and symptoms came and went. I wondered if my life was as good as it would get.

I experienced Dad from a faraway place. In many ways we were ships in the night, passing each other as we moved about the house in our separate spaces. He buried himself in his work and in exercise. The pain of your death crushed him. He did not like to talk about it. We tried as best we could. Dad brought me flowers and left little notes for me. I ran the house as usual, cleaning, doing laundry, grocery shopping, and cooking. We had sex. Someone told us to have sex as soon as we thought we could stand it. We did, but it was not the same. It was more like bodies taking care of bodies, and nothing more than that. I was hollowed out and had nothing to give, and I sensed that Dad had nothing more to give, either. There was emptiness and suffering, death behind the eyes that did not change. Dad and I continued therapy, although I felt we were just going through the motions. Perhaps we needed more therapy; perhaps we needed therapy every day. Perhaps it took longer than I envisioned.

In spite of my current mood, I had gradually found some answers, some clarity, and some comfort over the past months. I moved hauntingly between written words and spoken words. However, in my deep soul I acknowledged there were few words that made things "better." I knew that words served their purpose. Therapy did what it did. Books did what they did. In the end it felt like endless storytelling. We went round and round, covering the same territory over and over again. What could be spoken of was spoken, but it was the unspeakable that needed a place to be heard, and that was not happening. Perhaps I should have tried harder, given it more time. I felt like nothing much had really changed in spite of my intention to heal. I was on the lookout for a sustaining process. I noticed my best days were spent outside gardening, sitting quietly, or sitting with Janet. I felt supported by this stillness, and so I released my longing to heal into its vastness and waited.

I did not know what I was waiting for. I just knew there was something more.

September 11, 2002:
New York City

It arrived, this first anniversary of 9/11. I did not expect it to affect me the way it did. It closed in on me slowly, with each passing day of the month, because I was in New York the morning of September 11, 2001. I had spent over a week with you trying to help you adjust to college. You were struggling and considered dropping out and coming home. In the end you decided to stay. I wondered now, if we brought you home, would we have lost you anyway? You were being treated for depression since January of your senior year. I wondered if you were misdiagnosed. I wondered if you suffered from a bipolar illness. It's too late, and we'll never have all the answers.

I sat on the train that morning. It pulled out slowly along the tracks that marked the way just underneath the city, but it stopped moments later. I wondered why and relaxed into the seat, feeling a sense of completion and confidence. I had done all I could do over the past nine days with you. You seemed back on track, and we had moved through the crisis. You were on your way. The train was not moving. People's cell phones began ringing, and hushed voices turned to urgent conversation. People moved toward the windows where there was a view of the New York skyline. There was smoke coming from the Twin Towers. People were crying. Someone collapsed into the arms of the person sitting next to them. My heart began to beat fast. A plane—no, two planes had flown into the Twin Towers. I panicked as I realized that my daughters were in that city. I wanted to get off the train and find my way back to you. It was too late, and the train continued. I felt like crying. We were let off in Philadelphia and told to run from the station. "Run anywhere; just get out of the terminal." The Pentagon had been attacked and we were left to fend for ourselves. The Towers had fallen.

The streets were clogged with bumper-to-bumper traffic that was going nowhere. I ran with a young woman who was no older than you. I tried to help her and offer her what I could, hoping my kindness would somehow come to you or to anyone in need that day. I stayed with her until she figured out what she wanted to do. I left her in a coffee shop after she had gotten in touch with her family. I would never see her again.

I ran with my bag onto the campus of the University of Pennsylvania. I was afraid and did not know what was happening. I was determined to find Kevin as I watched kids playing Frisbee, walking to class, laughing and talking in total oblivion as to what was going on. The day was too pretty. I felt unglued and shaky until I found Kevin at Levy Pavilion, the university's tennis complex. We watched the towers fall over and over again as we sat in the coach's office. I watched in horror as bodies fell from the towers. I could not grasp what I was witnessing. Did they jump to get away from the inferno? Did they choose? I watched until I could not watch anymore. I closed my eyes to those jumping, to those falling, to those flying. I turned away from all the terror, but the sound of bodies hitting the pavement rang incessantly in my head. That stayed with me more than the images of the planes hitting the towers and more than the towers falling. People falling, and the sound of death, entered me.

I got a call through to Kimberly and discovered that you and Kimberly were together in Kim's apartment on West Fourth Street. You heard the sirens and saw smoke rising above the roofs of tall buildings. You were dismissed from your classes. Thankfully you decided to go to your sister's apartment, where you watched the events on TV. Joseph grabbed his camera and ran toward the Twin Towers. Neither you nor Kimberly could reach Joseph on his cell phone. You did not know where he was and whether he was safe. You did not know that he was almost consumed in the plume of debris and smoke from the falling towers. You were safe, you and Kimberly were together. I asked you to call me later, if you could. I hung up telling you each how much I loved you.

When the trains began service again, I got back on and finally arrived in Baltimore some eleven hours later. The officials offered to issue us another ticket for another time. I waited in line with a few others. Date of issue: September 11, 2001. Dad picked me up, and I tried to explain my day. He had been in meetings and did not seem to understand what I was saying. We got home and turned on the TV. He began to see. He was shocked and called to me, saying, "This is unbelievable—people are jumping out of buildings because the fire is burning off their skin." I felt intimately interwoven into 9/11 and could not separate myself from the day.

Your dorm was close enough to the Twin Towers that it stood within the boundaries of the part of the city that was shut down. I asked you if you wanted to come home, but you said no. You did not have a TV; you did not watch the towers fall over and over again, as I did. Classes were cancelled for a week, and you slept in. You caught up on your reading. After talking with you, Dad said, "Kristin seems to be doing well. I'm so glad she has settled down. She is moving forward with her life, finally. We did it." Exactly one month after September 11, you committed suicide.

The memories were violent, and I felt attacked. The images of the towers were everywhere. I felt for the country and for the families who were coming to grips with the trauma they suffered. I stayed quiet today and only took care of the bare minimum. I sat outside and noticed my heart beating. I rested, because there was nowhere else to go and nothing to do. October was a few weeks away.

October 1, 2002: Almost One Year

Over time the defenses that protected me loosened their grip. Emotions crept in that were not dulled—they were still sharp and debilitating. I feared my feelings as much as I would a thief in the night, for they stole my sanity. My emotions were excruciating, but they were real. Amid it all, I hungered for relief and constancy.

Over this year, I noticed there was nothing I could do when I heard one of your favorite songs on the radio. There was nothing I could do when I walked past the potato chips that you loved. There was nothing I could do when I saw a girl with long brown hair who reminded me of you. There was nothing I could do when you were everywhere. I watched, I felt, I gave in to the crushing pain in my chest. I gave in to the burning tears in my eyes. All these thoughts and emotions were exhausting. At times I felt like I was dying. In those moments I did not care that I was alive—which was very different from wanting to kill myself. I was not invested in the living. My life force had gone underground. I was buried alive. It had been a year, so now what?

My grief was heightened with dread of every holiday and special occasion. I made my way through an entire year of firsts without you. They served as endless markers of time. Your one-year anniversary was here, and I wondered what it would be like. I assumed it would be much like all the other firsts, but worse in its own particular way. I was not prepared for the extended trail of tears leading up to it, however. I noticed a marked shift in myself as the light changed in late August, so subtle yet so completely disturbing, especially around my birthday. I had always loved the light of late summer because it heralded the approaching autumn. Now it warned of October, which was filled with your birth and death days. I waited for the eventual lifting of grief, but as the days moved from one to the other, there was no lifting. August was a descent, followed by an even deeper descent into September.

 October 7, 2002:
KRSF and the Yellow Dress Golf Classic

We established the Kristin Rita Strouse Foundation for Mental Health Awareness, Education, and Suicide Prevention (KRSF) after your death. Some of our shame dissolved in our openness. There was nowhere to hide and nothing to hide as a result. We publically moved toward something positive. This was the place where Dad and I came together in our grief. We channeled what energy we had toward something purposeful, in spite of the fact that we struggled with the senselessness of your suicide. There were no easy answers to the contradictory aspects of your life and death. We found a way to carry on because we had unwavering support from our family and friends. They helped to shape the foundation and guided us along this new path.

For the anniversary of your death, KRSF presented its inaugural fundraising event. We chose your last oil painting of a yellow dress as our logo, and we named our golf tournament the Yellow Dress Golf Classic. We had a full slate of golfers and 250 dinner guests. Dad and I welcomed everyone, and we shared our story. We shared you in the video we put together. The pictures of your life stood in sharp contrast to the tragedy of your death. We invited everyone to "Be the One" and to make a difference. Thankfully there were boxes of tissues on every table.

We raised $48,000 for Mental Health Awareness, Education, and Suicide Prevention. I was astonished at what we accomplished, especially since Dad was not a golfer and we had never been involved in fundraising. I knew that the only way I got through this day and all the emotions was by God's grace. I prayed I would make it through the next few days.

October 11, 2002:
First Anniversary

Everyone said it was wise to have some kind of plan for the day. We chose to
be in New York. We chose to make sacred the site of your death and create a
garden for the students of your dormitory. A huge planter was placed on top
of the cement block where your body was found; we filled the planter with
a small tree, plants, and flowers. It was a peace offering to the horror that
had taken place there. Father Ray, the celebrant at your funeral, officiated
in the rain as we marked this day along with university officials. We stood
under large black umbrellas as it poured, and we stared at your name on the
little marker they placed by the flowers: "Kristin Rita Strouse, October 27,
1983–October 11, 2001." I wondered what would happen if I grabbed the
plants, uprooted them, and flung them on the ground. I might have been
happier. Instead I looked into Dad's face, which was as set as the concrete
we stood in front of. His once good looks had faded with your death. Deep
lines ran horizontally beside his nose and around his mouth. His cheeks
were hollowed out. His shoulders slumped like those of an old and broken
man. I watched the rain drip from the umbrella I was holding. I felt I was in
a time warp and could not wait for it to be over.

We supported the university in offering students and faculty an
opportunity to learn about mental health. An afternoon program was created
in which written information was distributed along with a stage production
on mental health issues. We placed our attention on life. By nightfall we were
back in Baltimore because we also wanted time to be home and be quiet.

I turned the lights on in your room and played your favorite song, *Kiss
the Rain* by Billie Myers. I wanted a few moments alone before I went outside
and sat by candlelight with everyone. Under the stars, I was in sync with
the rhythm of the night. I noticed the sound of frogs and crickets beating
in the background and I noticed my own heart. I watched the minutes pass
until it was over. I sat under the maple tree for a while longer than the
rest of the family. I looked up at the moon as I made my way across the
lawn and wondered if you walked beside me. Dad and I were grateful that
Kimberly and Kevin made the effort to be home. It was important that we
were together, especially on this first anniversary.

October 23, 2002:
The Garden

It was unseasonably warm again this year, so I lived in the garden. I couldn't say that I ever loved yard work, but your death seemed to have changed that. I found it grounding as I quietly moved through the beds on my knees, digging and weeding. The bramble of wisteria at the edge of the tennis court was a comforting place to work. I liked clipping, clearing, and hauling away debris. Even picking up sticks seemed to offer me a kind of stillness that shifted the disturbing energy that crawled over the surface of my skin.

I felt ultra sensitive and oddly in communion with the world around me. The earth was dying and decaying. The natural process of autumn served as a grim reminder of all I'd lost. It was a painfully beautiful time of year as reds, oranges, and yellows mixed with periwinkle blue skies. I asked for strength and courage with each passing day. "God, please, is there any way to let this be over?" Perhaps it was the same prayer you murmured to yourself, sitting on the ledge.

October 27, 2002:
Your Nineteenth Birthday

I decided to make one of your favorite dinners: barbecued chicken wings, baked potatoes, and broccoli with apple pie. Dad and I sat alone at the kitchen table by candle light. There was so much to say and no way to say it. I let it all be and kept breathing. Then I cleaned up dinner and went to bed. I gave in to the softness of my pillow and blankets, in to the same place I slept and was awakened by the phone ringing to learn of your death. I longed for sleep, but instead I was haunted with memories of your birth.

You were born in the darkness of the early morning. You came into this world cold, and so they put you in an incubator. Perhaps your little body sensed the life that awaited you. As I think about this now, I wonder about the impact of this initial separation. My mind endlessly reviewed every possible reason or contributing factor to your choice to die rather than live. I remembered when Kimberly and Kevin came to my hospital room to see you. They looked at you through the glass of the incubator and did not understand what was happening. I said you were in a little oven to keep you warm. They couldn't wait to have you home. I loved you. You were my third. You were my spare part, my guarantee. I thumbed my nose at fate, confident and in control of my own life. I would not be the mother of one dead child and one living child, like Rob's mother had been. How idiotic. In the end, I lost you. I became the mother of one dead child and two living children. I had not escaped fate.

The memory of seeing you as a newborn through the glass walls of the incubator stirred the memory of seeing you dead for the very first time. The police at the morgue allowed us to see your body through a glass wall, after they showed us your picture. We had to beg them. We were told that your body was being brought up on an elevator. Someone said, "Don't make a sound when you see her, or we will take her away and you will have to leave." That was the second time we were told to be quiet. We were asked if we were ready as a pair of white curtains parted to reveal you stretched out on a gurney with a sheet covering your body. We were told not to touch the glass. We stood silently. My very last hope for a miracle was destroyed in that moment. I couldn't believe what was before my eyes. We begged them to open the doors so we could be with you and touch you for just a moment. They denied our requests.

How strange that a pane of glass would separate us, in both your birth and death.

October 31, 2002:
Halloween

We had costume parties for your birthday because Halloween was so close. Memories flooded through me. I could see you as a little girl running from house to house all dressed up as a bride, a princess, or a ballerina. You carved pumpkins on the back patio with Kimberly. You counted your candy on the floor in our bedroom with Kevin. We always had a celebration, and I could see you as the years went on, with your teenage friends all dressed in costumes, having pizza in the basement.

I made sure I did not drive past Warren Elementary School today, afraid that I might run into the Halloween Parade of students and teachers making their way around the school grounds. It was a sad commentary on the condition of my life as I took pains to reroute myself, afraid of what I might drive past. The truth was that there was no easy way home. All roads held the memory of our travels together. The simple act of getting into my car, driving down Pot Spring Road, and taking care of what I needed to take care of was filled with pain.

It was Halloween, and our outside lights were turned off. The house was dark; I had no candy.

December 19, 2002:
Holiday Shopping

I avoided shopping as much as I could. It was too painful, especially the stores we used to frequent. I used to love going with you, trying on clothes, picking out beautiful things, and having a soft pretzel or frozen yogurt afterward. You were gone, and I would never do those things with you again. I was all alone—no lights, no music, no tree. It was Christmas, though, and I wanted to get a few gifts. I talked myself into a quick morning visit and made it through one store successfully. As I was leaving, I bumped into girls from your high school, in their navy blue uniforms with white Peter Pan collars. They did not know me and I did not know them, but suddenly there you were in front of my eyes, and I wanted to throw up. They were smiling, laughing, and having fun like teenage girls do. I felt the tears welling up in my eyes, and my breathing accelerated as my heart squeezed shut. I went numb and looked away. I couldn't go on. If I could have run, I would have; instead I reached for my sunglasses and tried to get out as fast as I could. Tears streamed down my face, and I made no attempt to hide them. People passed me. No one looked at me or said anything. I went home and placed my packages on the counter. It was 11:33 a.m., and I was done for the day.

December 28, 2002:
My Image

It was our second Christmas without you. We ran away to Mexico the first year, and it was a pain-filled attempt at escape. There was no getting away from anything; it followed you wherever you went. You would think we would have learned, but no, we tried running away to the Greenbrier in

Virginia and wound up leaving on Christmas Day. We had to go home because Dad was in too much pain, flat on his back with a herniated disk. Last year Dad was throwing up; this year his body was immobilized and broken.

We arrived back home in the late evening to a cold and empty house. My grief felt darker than the darkness we returned to. No tree, no lights, not anything Christmas. We had left this space for another, only to be forced back into what we had so desperately wanted to leave behind. The rest of the holiday loomed before me with nowhere to go and nothing to do. Frankly, I was not capable of being with anyone, because I could barely be with myself. I got into bed and uncharacteristically left unpacked suitcases on the bedroom floor; they were there for me in the morning.

The next few days were heavy and slow moving, filled with the tasks of unpacking, laundry, grocery shopping, making dinner, and cleaning it up. The fact that it was a beautiful day today did not change things for me. Dad was in bed, and Kimberly and Kevin scattered behind the closed doors of their rooms. In the evening I turned out all the lights in the kitchen, except the two spotlights over the sink. In a moment of despair, I leaned over the countertop on the island and rested my head in my hands. I pleaded for God's mercy as I stood in the darkened kitchen for more than a few moments before raising my head. When I opened my eyes, I noticed a pile of magazines on the ottoman to my left. I heard an inner voice that said, *Why don't you make a collage?* Perhaps it was my inner art therapist speaking, reminding me that art heals and that it was time to create and give myself what I had been trained to give others. Talking about your death had not diminished my intense feeling states. I thought, *I might as well go and play with paper.* I turned on all the lights and began.

I pulled the drawer open by my desk and found an old pair of scissors and a very tacky glue stick. Then I went into the basement, rummaged through your materials, and found a sturdy piece of black construction paper. I ran back upstairs and stood as I leafed through the pages of the magazines, tearing out one page after another, oddly excited by the words and images I found. Within a short period of time, the countertop was filled with paper. Some of the pages had dropped to the floor. I took my time noticing what was before me. I was giddy with excitement as I began to arrange the pieces I'd torn out. I had no idea what I was doing; it seemed to be doing itself. I was having fun. The images moved me, and there was a sense of recognition inside. *"Yes, there it is, this is my story. These are my thoughts and feelings; this is what is just as it is."*

"Here begin the terrors, here begin the miracles."
—Parsifal's *The Grail Legends*

December 29, 2002:
Into the Deep

Collage #1: "Caution"

Making a collage was the farthest thing from my mind. As an art therapist, it was absurd that it took me so long to embrace a creative process for my own healing, but life was absurd. It was the highlight of the holidays; it was a gift. I grabbed a handful of the million or more fragments of myself and threw them onto an eleven-by-fourteen-inch piece of black construction paper. Making the collage about your death brought me a measure of serenity. I gave little thought to the images I selected. I deferred to what my body responded to as guidance. For a few hours everything stopped; all the confusion and chaos and all the chatter inside my head. I was quiet and there was relief. I felt like I could breathe more deeply. I felt some space around your death as I stood in my kitchen and looked at my creation. I slept more soundly.

In the morning I came back to my artwork, which was leaning against a kitchen cabinet. I liked looking at it. I was transfixed by the images and couldn't take my eyes off them. I sat in contemplation as one thought connected to another thought. I was receptive to my feelings.

In my collage, you are perched atop a building, spreading your wings and wanting to fly away. What are you thinking? Do you know what you are doing? What are you feeling? You sit there on the ledge for a long time, and that is all we know. Do you know you are falling? I long for answers, but there are none, and so I fall with you into the darkness, I tumble with you into the deep.

I placed death's angel sounding her trumpet into the field of my story; she arrived with her black horse. I looked at that horse and remembered a family vacation when you were only eight years old. Dad and I stood at the split rail fence and enjoyed every moment of watching you during your beginner's horseback riding lesson. You, Kimberly, and Kevin were the only three making your way around the corral. The ranch hand began to dismount each of you when suddenly your horse took off running at full gallop. We all started screaming as we helplessly watched you hanging on the side of the horse. We yelled for you to hold on tight. I do not know how you held on, but you did. The ranch hands subdued your horse, reached for you, and brought you back to us. I began to shake as I enfolded you in my arms. You were safe. You held on despite your terror.

I liked the words I glued over your eyes. "Caution, do not leave unattended!" There were caution signs all along the way. You were on a collision course with death between December and October. My eyes were blinded by ignorance, confusion, denial, and fear. I was ashamed for leaving you. There were no hands in New York City to subdue the beast whose back you rode. You hung on until you couldn't hang on any longer. I was not there to see the terror in your eyes. I was deceived. I trusted you and that you would not let go, but you did. You let go and fell fifteen stories to your death. I fell with you.

I am black and blue, pierced, an open wound. My blood tints the flowers' petals red. I am awash in guilt.

I supported you. You were so determined to realize your dreams, and yet you hid. You were not the angel I thought you were. You wore angel wings but had secrets. You wore those wings to your graduation white dance; we found them at a costume store. You placed a crown of golden beads on your head. You and your best friend, Kelly, drove to the dance together. You were so happy that night. Joseph snapped a picture of you posing just before you got into the car.

Five months later you are dead. Angel wings, butterfly wings, wings of transformation. None of us are the same.

I cut out a diamond moon and glued it over myself, dripping and oozing. In the midst of your ungluing, you said, "I just want to rest in the arms of the crescent moon." What did you mean? Were you warning me that spring? Did you want to leave this world? I thought you were just being poetic. You said, "I feel like jumping," during our conversation on the phone the night you died. I could not hear what you really meant. I did not translate those words into a thought that you wanted to actually die. It was such a casual, common and unnoticed part of our everyday language. People flippantly say, "I'll kill myself." We condone such inappropriate exclamations and in so doing conspire with those who are deadly serious. Did you fix your eyes on the diamond moon that night as you X'ed yourself out amid the stars?

I found a hand that was black and blue. I pasted that bruised left hand over your body. I remembered that the undertaker wanted to cover and put makeup on it. I wouldn't let them. Covering your hand would not make it better or undo the fact that you were dead. There was nothing to hide. I loved your slender fingers. I loved watching the movement of your hands because they were so expressive and beautiful. Kimberly loved your hands, too. She wanted to have a portrait of our hands taken. We never got around to it. Your hands were folded over your stilled body. We placed a small bouquet of flowers in them, along with your favorite pencil and paintbrush. Your hands would never fashion your dreams of being a designer in New York. What a waste, what a tragedy.

I placed a dragonfly over your heart and asked for forgiveness. I had found a way for the unspeakable to speak.

three

terrors and
miracles

January 4, 2003:
Entering the Space

I decided to enter your studio space in the basement. I spread out my materials on the tables that you used for your paintings. I felt like an intruder, but at the same time I felt like I had come home. Kimberly and Kevin joined me in this unexpected collage exploration. We sat together around one long table, under the watchful eyes of the nude women in one of your paintings. We were all quiet and working on individual creations. It felt peaceful. I found words and images that spoke to me in every magazine. They were all fashion magazines. How ironic. You will never fulfill your dreams of creating beauty in the fashion world, and I find myself in the pages of *Vogue* and *W*, in the magazines that you loved.

"Madness" only took a few days to create. It was all madness, every bit of it. The images I was drawn to arranged themselves in a certain way. They did not conform to a standard rectangular shape because grief does not conform to any standard shape. Your death did not come in the neat little packages that I read about: denial, anger, bargaining, depression, and acceptance. It had not been that simple, not that straightforward. My grief demanded its own shape. It took on the shape of a cross.

Touching the Ashes

Collage #2: "Madness"

I cut out an image of a woman running with her arms outstretched. I was in the center of it all, in the space where horizontal met vertical. Image stirred memory, and I ran toward the light where you were sitting outside your dorm.

You saw me coming down the street. You wore a white embroidered skirt with small yellow flowers and a yellow tank top. You ran toward me with open arms. Your hair was loose and full and flowed about you as you ran. I listened to the sound of your flip flops hitting the cement. You reached for me and we encircled each other, holding each other tight, a moment too long. Something deep inside told me to pay attention. Something inside told me to drink in the experience and savor every morsel of it, for it would not last. I was aware of the full length of your body pressed against mine. You were a little taller than I was, but I could feel our hearts beating. It was a moment of fulfillment and contentment.

It was our first visit since dropping you off in August. We linked arms and turned in the direction of the Lower East Side. You said you needed a pair of comfortable walking shoes; you knew just what you were looking for. They had a size six and a half, but you needed a seven. The store was crowded. You sat on a worn leather bench, and I sat next to you. You smiled with excitement as you bent over, removed your flip flops, and pushed them to the side. You took the bright green shoes out of the box and slipped them on without socks. Your smiled receded and your eyes narrowed as you said they were a little tight. You seemed suddenly anxious and were not smiling. You wanted them anyway, you insisted. You seemed annoyed and a little irrational, wanting shoes that didn't quite fit. I bought them, trying to avoid an incident. We had lunch. I bought you a pink lace skirt, and we walked arm in arm back to your dorm. You told me you were thinking about cutting your long hair; you wanted to donate your locks to an organization for cancer survivors. I looked straight ahead and said, "Really?" I knew the less I said the better. You were on the brink of your own adventure, and I needed to let go of you.

You showed me your books. I looked at the view from your dorm room. The afternoon sun cast long shadows across the buildings in the distance. I allowed our visit to wash over me as I sat against the window on the train back to Baltimore. Was it in my imagination? It was subtle, almost imperceptible. I did not connect your moodiness in any way to the problems you had throughout the winter and spring. We had a wonderful day.

I closed my eyes to this memory and continued creating. I pasted a blood-filled tear on myself, just at the corner of my eye. I then pasted a monkey.

A monkey opens its mouth, reveals its teeth, and screams. It stretches out its arms as if they will absorb the impact of the fall. I sit and look at its face, my face. I am upside down and falling. We are falling from the fifteenth story. The primitive part of me wants to scream. It's buried inside, waiting. There is terror in "touching the ashes" of what is left of me. I turn to glass. I run the other way and am swept away.

January 27, 2003:
Other Mothers

I was honored this year to meet other mothers who had lost children. We shared our experiences, and there was a certain degree of comfort in that. We usually ate in the kitchen, a more intimate setting than any restaurant. I wanted the privacy and comfort of home, a safe place in which to share our stories. I took note of the moments in which other mothers found out about the deaths of their children or found their children's bodies. Most screamed. I listened as they described the primal cutting open of their entire beings, the falling to the ground, the weaving back and forth, and the uncontrolled wailing until there was nothing left. My scream was inside. I imagined it would be a relief to let it all out. I engaged my scream in the images I placed before me. I was aware that this was something that I was not in control of. What an illusion to think I was in control of anything at all.

January 28, 2003:
In the Mirror

In the midst of my winter madness, I stood in my bathroom before my makeup mirror and looked into eyes that were not there. I looked into Dad's lifeless eyes, too. They say the eyes are windows to the soul. I looked and there was nothing there.

I saw those same eyes in the faces of the officers at the New York City Morgue. I sensed in their blankness an overwhelming brokenness that could not endure any more loved ones as they arrived to identify a body or a part. I sensed how they had been brought to their knees by September 11. They were rendered silent and insisted we be silent, too. Although I was still stunned by their request, there was at the same time an understanding of the ravages of trauma and how we do what we do in order to survive.

I applied shadow, blue liner, and mascara. Nothing helped; my makeup did not cover my anguish. I appeared a much older and tired version of my former self. The mundane ministering to my own body was fraught with pain-filled associations of every variety. I felt your brokenness within my own body. You were everywhere I turned. You obliterated my reflection.

February 3, 2003:
Groceries

Grocery shopping was one of those relentless obligations I could have done without. The Giant on Ridgely Road was filled with your memory. I felt myself getting anxious as I drove into the parking lot. I quickly went over what I needed so that I could move through the aisles as fast as possible. You would often come with me as I picked up something for dinner. I always knew you had your own agenda, which included Jolly Ranchers, Breyers mint chocolate chip ice cream, and Dr. Pepper. The double doors opened as I pushed my shopping cart in front of me. I felt that cold gust of wind at my back, reminding me that I had entered another space that was filled with you. It felt unreal. I wanted to run away but couldn't.

It was my job to feed you. When you were little, I fed you with my milk. Nursing is one of the most wonderful and intimate experiences a mother can have. I felt the imprint of that in my body, in my breasts. I walked up and down the aisles and cried. I used to worry about what other people might think was wrong with me; I tried to hide the fact that I was crying. Now I just let the tears fall and wipe them away. There wasn't a meal I made that I did not think of you. My grief poured out like an additional ingredient into every dish, rendering them tasteless. I ate quickly and did not linger at the table. I would never feed you again.

I saw the mother of one of your friends. I turned around and made my way toward another part of the store. I did not want to see her and put myself in the position of asking how her daughter was doing in college. I was the mother of a daughter who killed herself. I wondered if she was afraid of me, afraid of getting too close, as if what happened to me was contagious. I got in line to check out. I noticed those around me and wondered how many times I walked past someone with a broken heart. I brought the groceries in and left them on the counter. I opened the door to the basement and walked down the steps to what felt like sanctuary

February 5, 2003:
Branded

Collage #3: "Once Upon A Time"

I felt like I needed to work bigger; I needed more room. I found additional art supplies of yours and worked on a twenty-by-thirty-inch piece of red foam board. I did not have any particular plan or theme in mind when I began my first and second collages. I took my time with this third piece, noticing what I was drawn to and what I had strewn across the floor for consideration. I narrowed the focus of my attention and turned within. This collage was about me. They said the second year was often worse than the first, because the defenses broke down and one really felt the pain. I wished it was a fairy tale with a happy ending, but it wasn't.

I spent hours each day for over a month in the red. Red was for Valentine's Day; red was for blood, your blood and mine. I gave myself permission to see where my blood had gone. It felt reassuring to note my hemorrhage. My life force seeped out of me just like your blood flowed over concrete. I was in pieces and scattered about. This was a snapshot of me and my day-to-day experience. This was my story.

I would like to brand the word "suicide" on my forehead, like a scarlet letter. This would separate me out and mark me as I truly am. I am a shame filled mother who lost her daughter. I am an outstanding "person of the year." My head explodes, and I place a crown of thorns on top in hopes of keeping it together. I drip like water over another part of myself that clutches at my own throat. I emerge out of my own eye. One self rests inside another self like Russian dolls stacked one inside another. Invisible parts scream a scream that is heard and not head. I am cut off at the knees. I am torn in two. Crucifixes are everywhere. I pause. Yes. I cut myself out and paste myself down.

I now created most days and long into the evenings. I was peaceful and content. I easily gave into my need for sleep.

February 8, 2003:
Cup of Tea

I woke up this morning and did not think of you. Your death was not my first thought, and that was a miracle. I sat with a cup of tea and moved one image here and another there. An hour later I moved it all back the way it was again. I could manipulate the pieces, the fragments, and I felt in control. The hours passed by, and when I was finished for the day, I felt calmer. I felt a kinship with the pieces. A yes arose within me, and I felt softer inside. Dad asked what I was doing. I was hard pressed to give any kind of explanation. I said, "I am moving torn pieces of paper around. I am cutting out words, words that I keep inside of myself. I am gluing myself down so that I do not blow away. I can see for a moment what is happening." He said that was nice. He did not want to look at what I had done and went upstairs. He was doing his own thing. We couldn't help each other; we could only make the space for each of us to find our own way. Somehow we both came upon this basic understanding, and that was a good thing, a saving grace for our marriage.

The first collage took me a few hours, the second a few days, and the third a few weeks. On most days there was nothing else I wanted to do. Nothing else really mattered, because the outer world made no sense. I had come inside myself and discovered a refuge, a tangible source of comfort. I worked in the basement, underground.

February 16, 2003:
Snow Storm

The landscape was covered in white, every branch laden with snow crystals that glimmered in the sunlight. Large pine trees edged our property. My eyes were drawn to each needle, separate and distinct. I was alone in all of this.

I looked out the window and remembered all three of you sledding down the hill. I saw you spinning round and round on red plastic saucers. I heard you screaming with delight and let this memory fill me as my heart broke. Beauty and pain mixed together. I retreated inside myself, separate from the world I once knew. I found myself in a space that was completely foreign and terrifying. Nothing was the same. My fingers wrapped tightly around my mug of hot chocolate. I used to open these very same French doors and give you hot chocolate in the midst of sledding and snow angels. As I looked out, I saw my own reflection. I felt that I was discovering my new world as I allowed myself to touch and release the fragments of my old world. I was finding my way through the images I created.

February 18, 2003:
Fatal Plunge

Collage #4: "Suffering"

I did not plan to touch this violent place. It happened as I came across a young girl's image with butterflies in her hair. I looked at it and saw you splattered on the concrete. I could not get away from blood; I imagined it pooling from your mouth. I could easily have turned the page, but instead I tore it out and glued it down. I looked at it and imagined red everywhere; it formed the field in which you were held.

I glue you down in a way that allows the rupture to be seen. I like the torn edges and leave them. There is some kind of physical release in the experience of tearing. I tear and align myself with the truth of the exposed, ragged, and uncontrolled edges of your death.

Cutting with scissors produced a different experience: there was more control; it was clean and neat. There was nothing clean or neat about your death, and so I tore. I touched it, I let go of you falling, turning, and rotating head over heels.

Driving past a tall building triggers my imagination; otherwise there is no rhyme or reason why I feel you falling. I place another image of your descent into my space. My attention rests in the wound of your death, in "The Fatal Plunge."

The feeling part of me gives way to the creative part of me. I cut out the letters to spell "DEAD" and search for the perfect place to glue them. I try them in various places until they find a resting place along the right side of your body. The yellow letters bring balance to the yellow in the sign "Alternate Route."

I wondered if your eyes were opened or closed when they found you dead. Did someone close them? In this collage I allowed Sienna to close them. Your beloved toy poodle closed your eyes. She brought you so much comfort and happiness. She slept with you, and now she sleeps with me. She looked into your eyes, and now she looks into mine. I often sensed you coming to me through the love she offered. She sat on the back of your legs at night when you were doing your homework on the floor; now she sat on my chest. I could feel her heart beating next to mine. She reminded me that I was alive and brought a measure of warmth to what was cold inside of me. I thought of what you wrote about her.

> December 22, 2000: My dog, my little red poodle, she is the only one that sees me the same and will only see me one way. That is comforting. My dog, I love her so much. Am I withering away? Sienna holds me. Her energy is my cradle. I feel so close to her. She encompasses the mother energy.

> December 23, 2000: I need to talk to someone right now, just like I need my dog, Sienna. Sienna, she is cradling me; she is holding

me in her arms. I pray for myself. I pray for God to forgive me. God forgive me, bless me, bless me. I have done such damage to myself. I have ruined everything. I don't know how to act.

I placed an actual photograph of you into this collage. You were in your white graduation dress. You were outside the kitchen door as you let go in a campy moment of happiness. This was the Kristin I held in my heart along with the one who rested in her own blood.

February 27, 2003:
Movies and TV

I was overwhelmed by movies and TV shows that incorporated "falling to your death" as an element of exciting entertainment. I couldn't close my eyes fast enough—the damage was done before I was able to shield myself from it. The simple pleasures found at the movies and watching TV were stripped away. I was living in my own horror show and had no capacity to witness violence of any kind. Grandma saw a lot of movies and so was watchful for those I should not see. She'd call and say, "You can cross that one off your list." There was not much left to watch; even commercials were suspect. I refused to put myself in danger and turned it all off.

If we were not undone by people falling off buildings or jumping off cliffs, we were undone by the continual assault of language we heard on radio and TV. There was a time when I never heard the word suicide; now I heard it every day: suicide attack, suicide bomber, suicide.

Suicide was everywhere.

March 3, 2003:
Laid Out

Collage #5: "I'd Rather Die"

It was seventeen months since your death, and I often did not care I was alive. I played with this notion as well as other notions when I played with images in my studio. This was a place where I gave myself permission to rest in the reality of your death without filtering it. It was a relief to give form to my internal conversations.

I cut you out and laid you out repeatedly, looking at you from various angles and wishing it was not true. "I'd rather die." You fell again. You were upside down and falling not once but three times, as if that would help make it real. I placed a single long-stemmed rose in your bruised left hand. It grazed my face. My charcoaled eyes stared from beneath the fishnet that covered me.

I'd rather die, but it is you in the coffin, not me. The flowers that we place in your hair will not bring you back. Your suicide is not softened by yellow and pink rose petals. I know that over time I will remember you in a different way, but for now I see you gray, cold, and broken. I pretend that you are sleeping. You are forever young, until the other visions of your face and body come into my consciousness. I want to stare at you, and so I do. I stare at the images before me.

I am glad that I took hours of private time to be with you, to look at you, to hold you, to kiss and touch what I would never see again.

I would rather have died than discuss this with anyone. Your image haunted me; the story of you was endless. For weeks I continued to imagine you as you lay on the gurney in the basement of the funeral home. The memories arose and the paper held the experience of your body for me. It was sacred. I was grateful for that holding.

March 12, 2003: Dark Secrets

Most of the other mothers I talked to would rather die, too, at least part of the time. We whispered about this in private. It was a deep, dark secret only to be shared with those who knew.

One mother threw up every day for over a year and lost thirty pounds; another mother hardly left her house for nine months; another one was not able to function without tranquilizers and sedatives. I had lost close to fifteen pounds. I got up, got dressed, put my makeup on, played tennis, cleaned up the house, did the wash, went grocery shopping, made dinner, worked in the yard, spent time with Dad, and saw friends and family ... but in the end, I'd rather die.

Permanence

Collage #6: "Grand Illusions"

As soon as I finished one collage, I started another. My creative process fit nicely into the flow of my life, which altered after your death. I wasn't interested in the life I once had. I wasn't sure who I was anymore. I took care of necessities and made my way to the basement.

I had black-and-white images mixed in with colorful images. I played along the subtle edges that separated us; you were alive in the warm skin tones, and you were dead in the blacks and whites.

You are here and you are not here. You are form and formless. You are physical and non-physical. You are body and soul. We all come to death sooner or later. What is it? What is this impermanence? What is real? Is this all just a grand illusion? Where are you? I feel you now, in this moment, and that is real.

I placed the thirty-by-twenty-inch black board I had selected for this collage on the table and began the process of arranging what I had selected. I had a lot of images and words with which to work. It was a process of elimination, and it had nothing to do with my thinking mind. I felt my way through it. It had an energy all its own; I just stepped aside and let it be. It was a reflection of what was currently inside me.

One afternoon I cut out two rabbits, one black and one white, one innocent and one not so innocent. I positioned them under the red cross that marked the danger on the roof. You were the little girl dressed in a white rabbit costume. You loved bunny rabbits your whole life and used to call them "bobbies." I looked into the sweetness that was you. I placed an actual image of you taken when you were seven onto the page. Who would guess that just ten years later, you would end your own life?

I thought I knew you. I thought if I loved you with all of my heart, that would be enough. It wasn't.

You turn and look at me through your windswept hair. You turn your back on life and fly away. One last look, and you are gone.

March 30, 2003:
Little Girl Dream

In my dream, you came to me as a little girl. We both knew that you had died. I was crying because I was afraid that you didn't have the things that you loved and that brought you comfort. You reassured me that you were fine and enveloped me in your energy. I was able to hold you and scratch your back. I was able to touch you and feel my fingers on your soft skin, even though we both knew you were dead. We were mother and daughter again on this date, marked with a series of your favorite number, three.

I remembered you in my arms as a newborn, wrapped in that pastel pink, blue, and yellow plaid blanket. I remembered you sleeping with it pulled up over your little blond head as you sucked your middle fingers. You named your blanket *bunkaleena*. You cried because we had to wash it. When you got older, you put it on the top shelf of your closet. I noticed you had torn off a small piece, which I could not find. We laughed and teased that you would carry *bunkaleena* down the aisle on your wedding day. I wrapped *bunkaleena* around you in your coffin and pulled it up over your head like you used to do in your sleep.

April 1, 2003:
Saving Your Voice

There were three messages from you on our phone. We saved them. I used to listen to you often, in the early days when the numbness made it possible. Now it was too painful to listen to you, and yet I continued to save your voice. I continued until today. We found a company that would record your voice and make us a CD. We had that CD, so there was no reason to continue to record your voice each month. It was a relief to let go of what I was compelled to do. It was a relief not to count the days, not to mark the time, not to sit and sweat, knowing that one wrong move and your voice would be gone. In a few hours your voice disappeared. It was another letting go. It was another death.

> *October 2001: So, I'm fine and wanting to see what you were doing, and um, bye.*

October 2001: Hi. Um, what are you doing? Mom, I miss you. I'm going to the bathroom right now.

October 2001: Hi, Mom, I just woke up and made myself bacon and cereal. I don't know what I am going to do today, probably just read and take a nap. What are you doing, you little bop bop a little. You better come soon. Bring the dog. Bye.

April 10, 2003:
Analyze This

Collage #7: "Field of Screams"

The images were dark and horrible. I could not fit them all on the paper. I tried to arrange them on two separate pieces of paper, but they demanded to be together for the sudden impact of it all. I taped the black paper together and formed a twenty-five by twenty-eight-inch space. I tried to place words with the images, but they would not go where I wanted them. The collage had a mind of its own. I listened carefully, and it told me what it wanted to be. I got out of my own way.

There was an intensity about this "peace" that was beyond words. Perhaps that's the reason words were not necessary, because pure sound emanated off the page—it screamed. At one point I removed the face of a beautiful girl, leaving only her hair. I placed a tall building within that emptiness.

I breathe. I imagine you falling, your hair blowing in the wind. I paste a photograph of you in the center of it all: you are white-faced and dressed as a ghost during a high school event. You hold a headstone with "RIP" painted on it. I continue filling the space with images of death. A baby falls.

I worked on this collage longer than any other collage. On the surface of it, one might have envisioned agony in the creative process. My experience was one of tenderness as I continued to touch your life and death. I noticed I came back to your hand over and over again. I came back to your black and blue left hand as a way to assuage the pain filled memory. Your entire body should have been black and blue, yet it was not. Why was it that only your left hand was bruised as a visible reminder of your complete internal destruction?

I remembered the photo of you taken when you were three years old. Your left hand caught my attention.

You stand in the basement of our old house. You stand by your easel, brush in hand. You pause and look at your left hand; it is covered in blue paint.

Your left hand traveled through time from that moment to the moment of your death. I had forgotten about that picture. You discovered it when you were working on your college applications. You fell in love with it and had me make a copy for you. You framed it and placed it on your desk. I looked at this picture when I entered your room.

Your painted blue hand reminds me of you as artist and the years at the Maryland Institute College of Art. You began when you were twelve. Two of the professors there took you under their wing, and you painted with them every Sunday for years. You knew just where you were going. We did not worry about you during those formative years, like we worried about Kimberly and Kevin; their career paths did not seem as easy and as clear cut as yours.

You were determined to make a mark, to make a difference. The world was yours for the taking, and we had no doubt that you would be successful. Now you were dead, and there would never be anything from your hand to this world. I grieved all that was unseen, I grieved all that you took with you to your grave, and I wanted to scream.

I looked at all the horrible images I'd created over the weeks and wondered when I began to worry about you, when my worry moved from normal worry to extraordinary worry, when my worry over you far exceeded any worry I ever had over Kimberly or Kevin. Perhaps if I had defined my experience in October as worry, if I had noticed it more, I might have observed the beginning pages of the final chapter unfolding before me.

I remember you were working on a collage piece for your college portfolio. You seemed anxious and were having trouble finishing the collage. You had spent a week over something you would normally have completed in a day or two. You had images all over the floor. The hallway, dining room, and kitchen were covered with torn pieces of paper. It was not like you—you were all over the place. I thought it very uncharacteristic but chalked it up to senior jitters, which are quite normal. Now I wonder if something more was stirring inside. You finished the piece, and we placed your application in the mail. You seemed fine after that and were a normal senior enjoying your senior year. I watched you play in the number one spot on your tennis team. I made cupcakes for your birthday and served them to the team at one of your tennis matches. You went out with your friends. It was a wonderful fall, our favorite time of the year.

Your hands, one that created and one that destroyed, both entered my consciousness as I remembered the events of December 18, 2000. It shook our foundation and shattered something inside each of us. That was the night I consciously began to worry, the night when store security called and said you had been arrested for shoplifting.

April 11, 2003: Corpse Pose

I couldn't sleep last night. I was not sure what time I woke up but made a point to not look at the clock when I got back into bed. I tossed and turned to the sounds of crows outside my bedroom window. My body ached from lying on my left side, so I rolled over on my right side. I turned over once again as my body found rest, lying on my back. My mind geared up for another assault, sensing impenetrable walls around your death; it moved further back in memory and attached itself to December 18, 2000. It would not let go of this rupture that marked the beginning of the end. My defenses were not fast enough to construct the necessary boundary. I could not control it once it began.

On that December evening, I was by myself; Dad was away. At six o'clock I was sitting at my desk in the kitchen, listening to the news and finishing my dinner. The phone rang. The person asked if I was Mrs. Strouse and told me you had been arrested for shoplifting. I said there must be some mistake—you would never do something like that. The voice said there was no mistake. I threw on my coat and felt sick. I got in the car and drove carefully to the store.

I was sure there had been some mistake as I went to customer service. They escorted me upstairs to the security office and opened the door, and I saw you sitting in the corner hunched over. You did not look at me; you had pulled your hands inside the sleeves of your black sweater. I said your name, and you looked up. There was fear and shame in your eyes. Your eyes were red because you had been crying. You wrapped your arms around yourself and did not get up when I tried to hug you. I told you I loved you and that it was going to be all right as the police officers began to read me your charges. There was nothing to say, nothing to explain. I was shown a stack of clothing you did not pay for. I was read the riot act as if I was the one who stole the clothes. I felt victimized, traumatized, ashamed. I was confused and on the verge of tears. I wanted to get you out of there. Security detained you for almost two hours before they called me. I couldn't imagine what you'd been through. I couldn't imagine you a shoplifter and didn't understand what was happening.

We left the store together. We got into my car, and I drove you through the deserted parking garage to your car. You wanted to drive yourself home. I worried about your capacity and asked if you felt together enough to drive safely. I told you to follow right behind me. I worried about my judgment, letting you drive, and I kept looking at you in my rearview mirror. Your face looked very white in the darkness. I wondered if you would do anything stupid. Suicide crossed my mind for a split second, one irrational set of behaviors leading to another set of irrational behaviors. Not you, not my Kristin.

When we got into the house, before I took off my coat, I collapsed over the kitchen counter, my head and arms flung from my body in fear and anguish. You stood frozen before me. I gathered myself and then gathered you in my arms. You needed your mother, you needed love and reassurance, and we entered that place together. You couldn't explain yourself and said you couldn't help it. You didn't understand why you stole. You had access to money; we never denied you anything. I did not understand what was happening, either. I knew you needed help, we needed help. I questioned my trust in you. You had stolen. I wondered if you would hurt yourself in the night. I made you sleep with me, although we hardly slept. I held you close and told you I loved you still. You missed the Christmas Liturgy, held in your school auditorium, the next day. You were in no shape to attend that holiday ritual in candlelight. We moved through the day, intermittently talking about it while we baked cookies. I wanted to scream but knew I needed to stay calm. Now I read the words you wrote about that event.

December 22, 2000: My hands are the hands that stole. I have a story to tell, true story: a shoplifter. Last night I prayed for God's forgiveness. I don't know how to act. I'm analyzing my every thought and move. I suffered. I have suffered so much already. I don't feel like crying; the pain is too hard to deal with. I need to heal from this. I hate this so much. There are good and other parts of this that aren't good. I have lost my mother's trust that I took for granted. Why is it that beautiful things and people are important to me? How am I feeling right now? Fear that I will steal again. I want to but I don't. I want to because it satisfies me. Stealing the purse I didn't even need gave me satisfaction even though I will never be satisfied from my stealing. I am so broken. I am shattered pieces or is that an illusion. Am I completely whole?

December 22, 2000: I feel such darkness and death now. I am black. Where is the light? Come, light; nurture your rays upon me. I am not falling apart. I am keeping it all together. This is a separation into a new self. At the end of this, if there is an "end," will I ever fully heal? Will I ever find myself? I was burning at the stake of my heart. It was a catalyst. I've grown quickly from this. I have lost my child within. I am still that little three-year-old girl; she never left me. Ahh, life is so hard, you never expect such things to happen. If someone had told me on my sixteenth birthday that on December 18 I would be arrested for shoplifting, I would never have believed it, but it did happen. This is my truth.

December 23, 2000: Every day is so torturous. I want to die. I
feel like my life is over. I should die. I have caused too much
pain for my mother. I lied to her point blank, to her face. How
much more lying am I going to do? I hate myself. I hate that I
have allowed myself to get caught, caught completely. Now I
have nothing, nothing. I am so empty.

We got through Christmas. You insisted on keeping the incident from
your sister and brother; we agreed for the time being. We were in a fog and
played out the charade. We found a therapist immediately. You entered
treatment. You would be all right. We would figure this out. The December
eruption was contained. I did not anticipate an eruption surfacing in January.
You couldn't sleep at night. You came and got me early in the morning, and I
got in bed with you. I held you, sang, and chanted mantras to you until you
calmed down and slept.

You lost weight, and I suspected you were purging. You never did that
before. You never had any issues with food or eating. You denied it. I smelled
it in your bathroom. You denied it. I watched your every move. You missed
classes. You told me your heart was beating too fast. You could not concentrate.
Your therapist assured us she was handling everything. I was not so sure.

The eruption subsided until February rolled around, and then the
symptoms returned, intensified and with verbal aggression added to the
mix. We had been close. We never fought. I didn't know what the fighting
was about. You seemed very angry and screamed at me. You never did that
before. I watched you drive too fast out of the driveway. I couldn't stop you.
Suicide crossed my mind. I wondered if you would hurt yourself in the state
you were in. I was afraid.

We changed therapists; you were now being seen by a psychiatrist.
We had hope. During a week when you were calm, we walked arm in arm
from your bedroom around the balcony on our way toward the stairs to the
kitchen. You told me you loved me. You said, "Thank you, Mom, for all your
help. I could not have done this without you."

I didn't know why, but I asked, "Have you ever thought of hurting
yourself?"

You said, "Yes."

I was not surprised. Everyone imagined killing themselves at one time or another. These are common thoughts, passing thoughts. I asked, "If you had a plan, how you would do it?"

You said, "I would jump off a bridge." We laughed. It was a light conversation on a bright morning, musings that had no bearing on us.

I said, "That's terrible. It's too scary."

You said, "No, it would be like flying." We walked into the kitchen together, and I asked if you would like some blueberry pancakes.

The eruption subsided for a while and surfaced again in March. Each month you got worse and worse. The eruptions were more severe. In one of your screaming fits, you said you were going to rip my eyes out. You told me how much you hated me and that I was a terrible mother. You threatened to kill me. I was afraid of you and of what you might do. You got right in my face, without touching me, and screamed. You smacked your car keys so hard on the counter that you chipped the Formica in the kitchen. I stood in front of the drawer with the knives, shaking. At night, Dad and I locked our bedroom door and braced it with a chair. You were worse.

I mentioned to the therapist that there seemed to be a pattern to your eruptions: one week out of each month, you went crazy. It was a week that happened to coincide with your period. Your psychiatrist told you to stop acting out and giving in to impulsive, self-destructive behaviors before your therapy appointments. I listened, because she should know, but a voice inside me said she was wrong. A voice inside me said to pay attention to the patterns. I let those voices inside me drift away and listened to the psychiatrist.

On April 1 you received a card from Kimberly, with a tiny red ladybug on the front. She said, "Kristin, I loved seeing you today. I really look forward to palling around with you here in New York City, going to yoga, movies, the beach, walking, whatever. I think you are going to flourish here, change, grow, inspire, and love it. I know you are scared now, and that's okay. I was scared, too, but you are dealing with it and being in it, so it won't paralyze you later on. I'm here. I'm with you. I love you."

The eruptions subsided for a while and surfaced again for a week in April. They continued to escalate. You continued to scream at me and were more verbally aggressive. We took away your car keys and hid them. You wanted to go, to get out of the house. You found the keys. I couldn't stop you. I watched you as you drove too fast out of the driveway. You went to Kelly's house. I followed you there, and we talked in their front yard. I called your psychiatrist. When you returned home, we discussed the possibility of you being admitted to the hospital for a few days. You began screaming and thrashing around on the floor like you were a two-year-old having a temper tantrum. I called Dad and told him he must come home—I was afraid to be here alone with you. You were out of control. We admitted you to the hospital for a few days. They put you on more medicine and observed you. They released you. You were despondent. You came home on Good Friday.

We planned to have family over for Easter brunch. You wanted to go through with it and wanted to see everyone. You wanted to be with your cousins. You wanted to be normal. We made a coconut bunny cake together. It was the last time most of your cousins saw you alive. We took a picture of you all standing around the kitchen table together. We took a picture of you and your cousin Erin hugging each other by the sofa. My family did not know all the details. I had shared some, but I had kept some a secret. I gave into your request to be private because I wanted to protect you. I failed you. I conspired with you and your secrets. If I had shared everything, perhaps my sisters would have seen things differently. Perhaps they would have sensed that something was not right. Perhaps they would have challenged us to consider other opinions. Perhaps they would have encouraged me to have confidence in my own inner knowing, rather than pushing my intuition from my consciousness.

That Sunday, the you I always knew was back again, and yet I was ravaged by the months of upheavals. I was fractured and broken, thrown back and forth between your intense states. One week of insanity followed by three weeks of damage control. I was in shreds. The fact that spring had arrived gave me a measure of hope. It was Easter, a time of resurrection. It was the beginning of a new week.

These memories of you ran through me like a river. I threw off the covers and realized from the Yoga classes I'd taken that I had been laying in corpse pose. The memories of your arrest on December 18, 2000, opened the door to more memories of you through the winter and spring. I moved myself out of the torrent of suffering as I got out of bed. It was daybreak. I looked out the bathroom window into the backyard. Everything looked gray, in the morning mist. Today was an anniversary of sorts, marking thirty months since your death, seventy-six weeks, or five hundred forty-seven days. I got in the shower and stood there, letting clean water remove the residue of those memories.

April 19, 2003:
Cousin's Wedding

We traveled to Memphis for your cousin's wedding. We'd had to attend other weddings over this past year and a half. I could never predict what the experience of the celebration would be like for us. Kimberly and Kevin were flying in, and I was worried about how this would be. I did well for a while, until the actual day of the wedding, and then I noticed a familiar process taking place, one that I was powerless to stop once it had begun. My skin dissolved, and the self inside began to move outside, giving way to the trauma of the moment. I had no solid boundary and no protection. I was not a body, only energy.

I felt your absence deeply as I watched the processional and heard the wedding march. I wanted to cry. Kimberly reached her hand toward mine. I looked up at Kevin, but he turned his head to look at Dad. I wondered when your sister and brother would get married. Grief had halted their emotional development and sent them on a backward spiral. They had regressed. Hope carried one into the future. I had no sense of future. I was crushed in the face of other people's hopes and dreams. I did not dare allow myself to care about tomorrow. One never knew what tomorrow would bring. I looked at Kimberly and Kevin and how young they were at twenty-five and twenty-three, respectively. My heart ached for them with so many years ahead, filled with the challenge of integrating your death into their lives.

During the reception I was nudged from my brooding thoughts when Abba's "Dancing Queen" began to play. I remembered you on the dance floor during Aunt Elizabeth's wedding. You were with your cousin Erin, you were both in pale purple gowns, and you were dancing to this song. You were not quite seventeen. You loved "Dancing Queen" and told me, "I want it played at *my* wedding. All the women can move in circles around me, just like we did today." I looked into your sweetness and imagined you as a bride. One memory cascaded into another, and I remembered sitting in Janet's circle just eight months ago. When the sharing began, Michael turned to me and said, "I hear Abba's 'Dancing Queen.' I sense Kristin's presence; she comes to me and says she can more easily come to you since your intense grief has lifted."

The memory created a moment of peace amid the torrent of emotions unleashed by the wedding. I smiled and felt you move close, my dancing queen.

May 5, 2003:
Release

Over these months the basement became a sacred space. I was inspired to enter the darkness while a single candle burned and music played. I felt an urgency around my unclaimed, unexpressed, and fragmented pieces and allowed myself the luxury of being with them without judgment. There was release as I worked; there was a sense of liberation around my process. My defensive walls came down, and the energy that was in service to their upkeep was available to me in a more life enhancing way. I allowed what was inside of me to flow outside of me. I immersed myself in a field of screams for weeks, for months. I allowed a space for my unreleased scream as soundless sound moved through me. I felt Dad's scream, I felt Kimberly's scream, and I felt my own scream held in the energy of my creation. In a field of screams, I explored my broken and missing pieces and sensed my place in the lineage of mothers who had lost children. There was mercy.

May 11, 2003:
Mother's Day

I wanted to ignore this day and tried very hard to pretend that it was just another day. I was aware of Mother's Day falling on the eleventh, which seemed an added cruel twist of fate. And so I tried to focus on honoring my own mother. It had gotten easier to be around her as time passed. Perhaps I was finding a way to forgive myself. I took her out to lunch. As we ate, I was poignantly aware of the one who gave birth to me, and the one to whom I gave birth. I sat in the balance between the two, one living and one dead. It was all out of order, yet I ate and smiled. By the time desert arrived, intrusive thoughts seeped into my consciousness.

Just two years ago you wrote this in your diary.

> May 10, 2001: Mom loves me, and I feel better and I will talk about it with my therapist. After I get out of the bathtub, I will read and watch TV in the basement with the dog or paint. I will live in the moment. I want to love myself, to be able to walk into a room and be so confident and liberated. I have the worst horrible handwriting. I feel manic right now and tired, and I feel sad. I finally forgave myself for stealing. It was my way of releasing myself from materialism. I do see the light. I will pray every day, will at least try to turn myself from evil. I honor my father and mother. I have morals and number one, I love God the Father, the Son, Holy Spirit. Amen. I am happy.

Three days later you broke apart. As hard as I tried, I couldn't keep the memories from flooding in. The walls crumbled and there you were, two years ago, tossing my favorite wedding gift filled with Mother's Day flowers onto the kitchen floor. You woke up out of control. I watched you all morning getting more and more agitated. I tried to help. You called your therapist and went to your room. You came out of your room and followed me around the house, getting more and more verbally abusive. I did not feel safe in any room with you. There was no telling what you would pick up or what you would do. I was afraid of where it would lead. I went outside on the porch. You followed me outside and rolled around in the mulch. You screamed, "I will never see you again on any Mother's Day for the rest of your life." I wished I had known what you meant by those words, but I did not. I wondered if you were already contemplating your own death, or was it simply the ravings of a young woman gone mad.

It was Kevin's first day home from college. He had just gotten out of bed and entered the kitchen filled with broken glass. You had run out the back door. I screamed for Kevin to follow you. "Don't let her out of your sight, until we get help." He took off after you on foot.

On the phone, the police wanted to know if you were dangerous. "No, she's a little, one-hundred-pound girl, running." Is she on drugs? "No. She broke a vase, she's out of control and needs to go to the hospital." The police picked you up. I was so afraid of what you might do to yourself in that state. Would you throw yourself in front of an oncoming car? Would you run all the way to the bridge and jump? Suicide entered my mind once more. I could still see you sitting in the police car in front of our house, looking so little and helpless. The officer took Kevin aside and wanted to know if there was any abuse happening in the family. I watched him as he emphatically denied the insinuation.

We took you to the emergency room. You stuck your tongue out at us and made faces; you would not talk to us. You had a psychiatric evaluation. They strapped you to a gurney and took you by ambulance to a psychiatric institution for further evaluation. Fifteen hours later, you walked down the hall of the adolescent unit and turned and waved, as if you were going on vacation.

All of this moved endlessly through me. I couldn't stop it although I tried. In the moments when I was not conscious of the memories, I felt the aftershocks of the experience in my body. That day marked this day and every Mother's Day for the rest of my life.

They were treating you for depression. They continued to treat you for depression. I wondered if they were wrong. I wondered about another mood disorder. I wondered if you were suffering with a bipolar illness. I wanted to scream and never stop. Happy Mother's Day.

May 13, 2003:
Benediction

Collage #8: "Purple Tears"

I felt drawn to the color purple. I didn't know why, but it led me to lavender. It provided a healing place for May's reflections as I returned to your body again. Each time I seemed to open a new door and went a little deeper. There were not many words on this piece. Words were insufficient. Words only approached what was unspeakable.

Your whole body should be one massive bruise, but it is not. I enter the bruise; all that is broken is hidden beneath the skin. The faint fragrance of lavender oil fills the space, and I imagine you held in purple healing light. I want to fix it all. I want to cleanse your body and spirit of all the pain and suffering.

The lavender reminded me of the evening just before the formal viewing, after I spent the afternoon with you and Kimberly and I had applied your lipstick. We sat on the sofa next to your body, which remained on a gurney covered in a white sheet. We waited for the women to gather in the bowels of the funeral home. I invited family and friends. They entered a room that looked like an ordinary living room in someone's house, furnished with traditional furniture. Your dead body was the only thing that didn't fit. Just before we opened the doors, we placed Kimberly's blue silk scarf at your neck, to cover the scars of your autopsy. I was afraid of what I would see when the doors opened even though this was my private and unconventional way of saying good-bye. When the doors opened, I saw love.

I saw pain. I saw purple tears.

These women filled the room with candlelight and flowers. Some said prayers while others read poems. They held you and held me. Some wailed and cried from their brokenness; others stood in silent reverie. This was my real good-bye to you, a timeless ritual of intimacy. This was a way of being with you that allowed for emotions to spill out and be witnessed. We were underground. Tomorrow we would move from this space into the formality of what had become standard burial rites. This was a counterbalance to all of that; this was more raw and real. I wondered what it would have been like to have laid you out at home, surrounded by the things you loved. I will never know.

I enjoyed these weeks working in purple. My analytical mind could not understand how immersing myself in your broken body resulted in anything but further pain, but just the opposite happened: I softened and let go. I placed your purple, bruised hand into the frame of my creation again. I attached it to the upside-down figure dressed in feathers. I dressed you

in feathers like a bird, wishing to support you in your ascent into heaven.
I poured you out like lavender nail polish and watched you fall. You were
the young woman who took her own life, and you were the little school girl
dressed in purple. I reached out to touch the soft skin of your neck in a final
gesture of good-bye. I moved into a place where there were no words.

May 14, 2003:
Kiss the Rain

I stood in your room and played your favorite Billy Myers song, "Kiss the
Rain." We played it at your funeral. Its sound echoed through the still house.
I heard you singing along with the words, belting out the melody and refrain.
I heard you playing it over and over again. I remembered standing at the door
and singing with you in the months before you left for college. You looked
up from the spot on the floor where you lay, and you smiled.

I leafed through the pages of your journals and tried to make sense
of the evidence you left behind. You suffered for a long time. I did not
recognize the person you wrote about. I was aware of your times filled with
unhappiness, sadness, anger, frustration, jealousy, pain, and insecurities. I
accepted the full range of your emotions within the context of "normal."
Your darkness stood side by side with the light of your passion, playfulness,
kindness, strength, softness, depth, sensitivity, talents, and love. Your words
were terrifying. The contemplation of your pain was excruciating. There
was nothing normal about you. At what point did you move from growing
pains into mental illness? It didn't ease my suffering to place blame on
mental illness; it did not ease my guilt or my shame. It did not ease my
failure. I didn't see. I didn't know. I didn't understand. I couldn't hear what
you were saying even when you sang it to me. I fall to my knees and beg
forgiveness.

I am sorry.

Kiss the rain, 'cause I am trying to explain something's wrong.

Kiss the rain whenever you need me. Kiss the rain whenever
I'm gone.

October 11, 1994: I feel so young because I haven't had my period, my breasts are not growing. I have no friends. I'm just here. God help me.

February 14, 1997: I hate Valentine's Day so much. The mixer was the worst. My friends had no idea how sad I was. I cried and cried when I got home. I ate a lot of food. I felt so ugly and dumb.

August 18, 2000: I hate you, I hate you, I hate you, I hate you. I hate my voice. I'm ugly. I hate my handwriting. I'm scared to go back to school. Yes, I care about what other people think. I hate you, I hate you, I hate you. I am such an angry person. I miss my hamsters. I hate you. I hate myself. I have to act mature.

August 21, 2000: I hate always worrying about the way I look. It takes up too much of my energy. My compulsion to buy almost fills my insecurity of needing to look good. I hate Kim being the center of attention and everyone looking at her. I am jealous of her. I want what she wants. I want what she has. I hate my mother and father. I hate the way Kevin acts. I hate when he teases me. I am full of hate right now. I hate everyone. I hate my friends. I couldn't enjoy being sixteen. I always want to be older and feel more a part of things. I hate being the youngest. I feel so juvenile. Why am I eating so much? Why am I so hungry? I want to get away from everyone. I need to be famous. I am full of hate. I am tired. I am lonely. I hate this. This is my vacation. I want to get on with my life. I will live my life to the fullest potential. I will be the best. I need to be my own person. I am not crazy.

September 17, 2000: My portfolio college crap is driving me over the edge, and I'm too freaked out about everything. God, I feel so gross. I hate school. I hate myself. I hate my hair. I don't deserve what I want. I'm not good enough.

Kristin: April 26, 2001: I want to write, but I don't want to think about anything. I am feeling a little better, so who is Kristin Rita Strouse? Is she smart? I always had a pretty good report card, and I was definitely a hard worker. What is my favorite color? Pale yellow, because it is soft and calm and makes me happy. It's my soul color, and my mother wrapped me in it when she brought me home. I can't wait to get out of here. I can't even find my own handwriting. I want to become a doctor. Well, what about traveling and seeing the world?

June 17, 2001: I won't let myself fall.

I thought I knew you. I thought we were close. I thought we had a good relationship. I thought you were growing into yourself. I thought you had come to terms with your nose when you decided against having it "fixed." I thought you were embracing your beauty. I thought you had friends you enjoyed. I thought you were happy more days than you were not. I thought you had a normal relationship with food in terms of what and how much you ate. How could my thoughts about you have been so wrong?

I kiss you in the rain, Kristin. There is no way to atone for my failures.

May 20, 2003:
Sheila

I had spoken with Sheila every two weeks since your death. I cherished our time together because it steadied me. It was a natural extension of my inner work with her, even though it was by phone. I scheduled our session in the afternoon, after tennis. I took a shower and changed my clothes. I plumped up your pillows on your bed and pulled your yellow comforter with little white embroidered flowers over me, and I waited until one o'clock.

My whole body relaxed when I heard Sheila's voice. She said my name, and then there was silence as the space between us filled. It was as if we were together in the same room. I could feel her presence in the stillness, and I began to rest in it. I started to share the details of Mother's Day as well as my feelings. I stopped mid-sentence as I looked at your diary on the bed, the one I had opened to the worst pages. I could not speak. Tears began to form, and my whole body constricted in response to the memories of what you had written. Sheila did not intrude into what was happening. I could feel her take in a deep breath with me, and again there was quiet between us. My heart ached in its breaking open. She asked what was happening. I could not speak. She reminded me to breathe. She reminded me to make a space in my belly for the feelings that were arising. She allowed me to be in the place I was in. She did not try to make it better. She was in communion with me in the space where words were impossible. When I could speak, I did. I picked up your diary and began to read your words to her.

The sound of you hung in the space between us. Each word spoken dissolved something in me. Feeling, allowing, breathing, letting be, letting go and crying and feeling, allowing, breathing, letting be, letting go and crying. So it went until we were finished. There were no more spoken words between us.

May 29, 2003: Janet's Circle: Kristin's Story

The prompt for the evening at Janet's circle was, "You are in a place of learning and education." In my experience, I was taken by a monk in brown robes to a large room with rows of sturdy tables filled with ancient books. There were many people in this candlelit room; it was sacred and quiet. The walls and floor were made of stone. There was a massive stained-glass window that allowed light to pour in. The light warmed the space. I went up a set of spiral stairs and made my way to another room that overlooked the library. There was a fire blazing and several large soft chairs. On a table there was an open book. I was shown hundreds and thousands of names of people who were inspired by a book titled *Kristin's Story*. As I stood looking at the book, I received healing energy from those who were next to me. They offered me guidance and support. When we were finished, I was escorted out.

I wondered about my experience during my drive home. I had not considered publishing. My journals and images were private. The notion was overwhelming.

June 7, 2003:
Braided Doll

The spring showers gave way to early summer, and I didn't feel like making any more collages. I had grown tired of paper and wondered what it would be like to engage other materials. I heard of people making quilts from their child's clothing. It seemed like a healthy solution to the problem of what to do with personal items. There did not seem to be any clear-cut way through this minefield. I heard of one family who had friends come in and pack up their child's room and paint it; another family simply closed the door and left it as a shrine. I moved your things back into your room when FedEx delivered them to our doorstop, shortly after your funeral. Your room had been rearranged since then, in keeping with the natural evolution of change, just as Kimberly's and Kevin's rooms changed. I gave some of your clothing away. I sent them to India with a friend, to an orphanage.

I had been thinking about your clothes, the ones folded in your drawers. I had the notion of making a doll out of your black velvet shirt, a white T-shirt, and a gray cashmere sweater. I wanted to cut them into strips. I wanted to braid the three colors together.

As I worked on this doll, I remembered the Mother's Day poem you wrote me in 2001. You gave me a card after you were discharged from the hospital, after you had seemingly recovered yourself, returning to the Kristin I knew. You wrote,

> Separation
> Longing to stay a little girl
> Innocence
> Simplicity
> Love
> Hate
> The needing for more
> Not enough but you were enough
> Challenge
> Love myself and love you
> Balance of both worlds
> Black, white, look for the gray.

I heard you telling me to stay centered and stay balanced. I slipped my arm inside your sweater and felt connected with you. I wrapped my arms around myself, imagining your hug, right before I made the first cut. I was sweating and disturbed, cutting your gray sweater up and tearing your white T-shirt. I was destroying you in some odd way. I was having difficulty letting go. You wore the gray sweater with your gray pleated skirt at Christmas time. As I made the cuts, I felt you. I was attached to your clothing. I wanted to let go so that the pieces could become something else. It gave me an opportunity to move along the edges of another process in which form gave way to formlessness, which then gave way to form again. I do not know why, but I didn't find comfort here. It was very frustrating tearing, braiding, and sewing. Although I hadn't found peace in this process, I trusted that doll-making did what it was intended to do. The process of cutting and destroying had been surprisingly powerful. I went with the flow of it. I found myself sitting in the studio. I opened the doors and played music. I was comfortable here in this space. As I sewed button eyes on my braided doll, I sat and looked at the body of collage work I created.

June 15, 2003:
Cruise on the Mediterranean

We decided to go on a cruise with our friends, stopping at ports in Greece, Italy, Spain, and France. Thankfully, Father's Day was essentially passed over in the excitement of our departure. I had no expectations about this trip. I was sure our friends had high hopes that this would be a significant opportunity for healing, for getting away from it all. They had no idea what my daily experiences were like. I looked normal, but my deepest pains were hidden, revealed only in my art.

It was difficult to explain my inner world. When I tried, they listened. There was little they could offer, because the experience of your death separated us. Lately, when asked how I was doing, I said, "It's hard." My response was unenlightening. I had fallen victim to the very responses and catchphrases that had no meaning. I had momentarily given up.

I felt pressured by society, which seemed to place an endpoint to normal grieving. I felt that people turned away from grief after a certain point. There seemed to be a generalized lack of education that fostered gross insensitivity. I also felt that people simply could not handle so much protracted suffering. It became too much to bear and frightening in its scope. We did not have the luxury to walk away. Others went on with their lives. Death permanently altered the structure of out being. The waves of grief were relentless as they beat along the shore. The ocean did not alter its movement. Sometimes the waves were consuming, and sometimes the waves were small, almost imperceptible. There was no point fighting what was impossible to fight. I found myself outside our state room, looking over the balcony and into the vastness of my own grief.

At times I had shown my collages to family and friends; they got a glimpse of my inner world. I noticed they became quiet and tearful as they looked at what I had created. They moved toward my images to see the intricate pieces and imbedded words. They ran their fingers along the edges that defined me. They questioned me as to how this process helped. In their silence I sensed their discomfort and a lack of understanding. Some strongly disagreed with the creative path I had embraced, wondering if it might be more helpful to focus on something positive. In the end I knew they supported me no matter what. They were my lifeline and had not left me. I had not brought my magazines, scissors, or glue on the cruise. I wondered how I would endure these weeks without my process.

July 4, 2003:
Normandy, France

It was strange, revisiting some of the sites we visited together on our cruise in 2001, just before you died. Dad and I felt you walking alongside us much of the time. We again felt at home among the ruins. We especially loved Sorrento, Italy, and Pompeii.

I managed to carve out quiet time for myself. My physical body was affected by the simple presence of so many other people. When sensory overload set in, I excused myself. I hoped they did not think me rude. How does one explain the unexplainable?

I enjoyed sitting on the balcony at night alone. Out in the stillness, the stars in the night sky merged with the blackness of the ocean. There was no separation. I heard only the waves moving beneath me. I connected with the void in such a way that I could feel a pull into its depths and wondered if you felt it the night you sat on top of the roof. I wondered if the stars of the night merged with the lights of the city as you fell into the darkness. I felt I understood how easy it was for you to surrender yourself into the silence, if that is what you did. I guess I will never really know until I see you again.

We ended our trip in Normandy. I loved this place and felt complete among all the graves. Death wrapped its arms around me, and I was comforted in the embrace. Dad and I held hands and walked through the cemetery. Row after row of white gravestones created a backdrop to the fluttering American flags of red, white, and blue.

We ultimately enjoyed being together in new places, especially this one. It was healing. We were heading home, and I wondered what it would be like to step back into my life again.

August 21, 2003:
Leaving Home

It was August and back to school time. It was irritating to see all the back-to-school ads, and it was painful to witness mothers shopping with their daughters in preparation for college. It triggered all the memories I held of our last days together. I remembered how I opened the door to your room very quietly, came around the side of your bed, and snapped a picture of you sleeping. I was sure you heard me and allowed me this moment. You opened your eyes and smiled and invited me to tickle your back. I snuggled into bed with you on your last morning home and enjoyed our mother-daughter moment.

> August 21, 2001: Well, this day has finally come to me after almost eighteen years. This is my last night officially before I start my own life, my own separate space away from home, my own world. I have to get through this night and the next night. I feel jittery and excited and nervous. What will I miss? The green, animals, Sienna, taking baths, being quiet, waking up in my own big bed. I will miss being home. I will miss the

comfortable feeling of being under my mother's wing, because
I will be making my own decisions about money and things. I
hope I get along with my roommates and suitemates. I wonder
what they are doing right now. I can't wait to be settled and
moved in. I hope I travel in my life, like next summer.

August 24, 2003:
Mohonk Mountain House

We decided to spend a few days at Mohonk Mountain House. We started vacationing here when you were nine years old. I saw a picture of this magnificent retreat in a magazine and felt compelled to go, and so we did. On our first visit so many years ago, we stayed together in a fancy room on the top floor. It was a room with curved walls like a tower in a castle. I was appreciative of the times we spent in this paradise, sleeping with the windows opened, listening to crickets, sitting in gazebos, rock climbing, looking for bats, dancing wildly, and being together. Each memory broke my heart.

> *August 20–22, 1998: We arrived at Mohonk today. I'm so happy*
> *to be here. I couldn't ask for anything more.*

> *They asked me if I have a guy like fifty times, and I shook my*
> *head, though I wish I did. I love being here so much, my dream*
> *place, longing to be here, the Victorian mountain house, the*
> *smell, people, everything. I wish I had a boyfriend. I loved going*
> *caving, too: the experience of being down in the bowels of the*
> *earth, the smell, the candlelight, cooperation. I love the people*
> *here; it has been really fun.*

> *August 2, 2000: Dear Kim, I miss seeing your face. I'm lucky*
> *to have you as a sister. You are so wise, and you hold so much*
> *potential and talent. You inspire me to be a better person.*
> *Whenever I hear my music, I think of us in Arizona by the pool*
> *or having fun with the watercolors, and when I hear "Kiss the*

Rain," I think of you, too. I'm looking forward to spending time
with you at the beach and at Mohonk. We can tickle each other's
arms. I love you so much. I hope this letter brings you a little
sunshine amongst the clouds. Happy Birthday. Love.

On this August evening in 2003, before we headed home, the four of us
took out a boat. We drifted out into the lake and released some parts of you
into the water: your hair, a baby tooth, and a bit of your favorite sweater. You
loved this place, and so may you feel happy to be a part of it always. I did not
think we would ever return. It was too much joy and too much sorrow all
mixed together. I said good-bye to this sanctuary that we shared for so many
years. I let go into the water.

August 27, 2003:
My Birthday

I turned fifty-three today. I'd spent the past two years finding my way
through the maze of my mourning. I did not expect my life to turn out this
way. I remembered relaxing in the chair in our kitchen the evening of August
27, when we returned home from dropping you off at college. We'd spent five
days in New York getting you settled. We came home feeling good, proud,
and content. We had done it—you had done it. You were safely delivered to
the place of your dreams. You were in college in New York City. You were
on your way.

We were finally empty nesters. Dad and I returned to our beginnings,
just he and I. We had been through so much during the past year. We
helped you to the best of our ability. We took you to a good psychiatrist. We
provided good treatment for you. We were not afraid to do the hard things
when it came to placing you in the day hospital for three days in April, and
then the inpatient unit for three days in May. We thought we had moved
successfully through this family crisis. You were taking your meds, and you
were connected with a therapist in New York. We were confident that you
would be successful. We would continue to be there for you as we entered
new territory ourselves. Dad and I were looking forward to rediscovering
each other. I was looking forward to discovering what was next for me. I

had set myself aside professionally, in deference to the need of the family; now it was my time.

I had a degree in art therapy. I had completed my master's degree while I was pregnant with you. I loved the years I worked, though they were only a few. I was ultimately relieved to stay home and take care of the demands of my family. It had been a conscious choice. It was too much of a challenge to juggle the lives of three highly involved children. There was soccer, basketball, baseball, tennis, ballet, and art. It was Kevin's involvement in competitive tennis that did me in. I could not continue to ask for time off when he had tennis tournaments. I finally gave in. I knew I would return to what I loved. In the years between, I built on the foundation of my very traditional art therapy education.

I found other avenues to explore, nontraditional approaches to mental health. I joined a women's group, led by Sheila. We met several times a year, over long weekends. I investigated myself in that sacred space, in that Temenos. It ultimately prepared me for your death. The work invited me to be mindful and fully in the moment. I noticed my thoughts and my stories. I learned the value of carving out quiet time for myself. I sat in silence and reflected on my issues. I read and studied and worked on myself during those years when I was giving so much to my family. It offered me balance and filled the space that my professional life had taken up. I did not resent my decision because I found a way to continue to grow and learn.

When Kevin left for college, you became our only child. Those years were some of the happiest, when it was just you, Dad, and I. You had our full and undivided attention. You no longer had to compete with your sister or brother. It was hard being the youngest in a family of achievers, but you had met the challenge. You were not a shy and retiring child. You were outspoken and ready to defend yourself at the drop of a hat. You could be aggressive and impatient, all qualities of a type-A individual. We all felt the apple had not dropped too far from your father's tree. You took on your sister and brother. You joined Kimberly in her arena and took years of ballet. You joined Kevin on the tennis court and competed, too. Neither Kimberly nor Kevin could join you in your art world—that was all yours. Your art separated you from them. You stood alone in that exceptional light, and you loved that.

During those last years, we made it extra special. You enjoyed dinners, movies, sleepovers, shopping adventures, excursions to Rite Aid, and late-night outings for donuts. I gave everything I had. Dad gave everything he had, too. Arriving back home on the evening of my birthday felt significant, like a new beginning. It was my time. I had no idea what was before me. I planned to take it slow and discover my future. I planned to enjoy the autumn I loved so much.

I sat outside on the patio and reflected on the past two years. The first year I was numb to the world. This second emotionally laden year was spent in my studio creating images in an attempt to process your suicide and reclaim the fragments of myself. I saw the path I'd traveled more clearly. I was fifty-three today, and I still faced unknown territory.

We found this letter when your things came home from New York and you didn't. You had not mailed it.

> *August 27, 2001: Dear Mom and Dad, thank you for moving me in. I love it. It was easy to say good-bye. Happy fifty-first birthday. I wish I was there to celebrate with you. Hugs and kisses, and give Sienna a hug for me.*

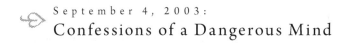

September 4, 2003:
Confessions of a Dangerous Mind

Collage #9: "What the Devil Is This?"

Your diagnosis weighed heavily on me all summer. Manic-depression, they now call it, Bipolar illness. I didn't understand. I couldn't come to grips with my own ignorance and stupidity. I was an art therapist and worked in a psychiatric institution for a brief time. I dealt with patients diagnosed with serious psychiatric illnesses. How could I have so misjudged you? Was it there, plain and simple? Over the course of your illness, I let go of anything I thought I knew. I was just a mother desperate to find help for her daughter. Intense fear and confusion, along with what I believe was misguided and incorrect evaluations of us and you, clouded the reality of what was unraveling. I disregarded my own inner knowing, deferring to others whom I respected and trusted. I was ultimately grossly disabled in my ability to navigate the territory of your evolving mental illness.

We listened to the social worker and psychiatrist. We took you to the best hospital, or so we thought. Were they wrong? Were you depressed? Were you suffering with a bipolar illness? Were you on the wrong medication? Were you receiving the wrong treatment? You were so young.

You said you would jump off a bridge, if you were to kill yourself. They said, "Oh, she would never do that. Don't pay attention to that comment; that's just attention-seeking behavior. Don't worry, that would never happen." They were right. You didn't jump off a bridge—you fell from a roof, fifteen stories to your death. What kind of unconscionable guidance is that, to tell your family to ignore you? It was their voice I heard that night while I was on the phone with you: "Don't pay attention to that." Had I known better, I would have asked Kimberly to keep you with her, to not take her eyes off you. I would have jumped in the car and driven to New York. I would have known that your suicidal comment was to be taken seriously. All suicidal comments should be taken seriously. You were deadly serious, and I missed it. There was no second chance.

They were all wrong. We were told you were very immature. We were led to believe you were choosing to act the way you were acting because you needed to separate from us. We were blamed. No one discussed the possibility that your behavior was connected with your biology. No one said that you were acting the way you were acting because you were suffering a biochemical imbalance. No one discussed your shoplifting incident, your sudden entrée into purging, your excessive spending, your $800 speeding ticket, your psychosis in May, the fluctuating insane and normal behavior interspersed with over-the-top aggression as classic symptoms of anything. In my opinion, costly mistakes were made that opened the door for your mental illness to take your life. We had no context in which to understand what was happening to you. This was insanity.

We did not understand the severity of what was happening, even with your brief hospitalizations. We could not process the reality of the previous months. We clung to the gifted, talented, and mature young woman we knew you were. You had been suffering for a long time, probably since middle school. A million apologies will not bring you back. I am a mother on a mission. Perhaps our story will help someone else. Perhaps our openness will save some other child. Perhaps we will make a difference through the Kristin Rita Strouse Foundation. Perhaps doesn't make it better.

What the devil is this? What the hell is going on? I try to understand your suffering. I paste you down onto the surface of my collage and can only imagine your agony. I move this way and that way with you, in an attempt to understand. My head explodes. One side is a manic burst of color, the other side a depressed mix of black and white. They say there is a fine line between pleasure and pain. Let me know when you find it.

You're dead, and we came to find out that we had a history of bipolar illness in the extended family that seeped through the branches of both family trees. Our immediate family had no history of mental illness. Dad and I were both flawed and fine; we were normal, whatever normal meant. I wished I had known about the family history. I wished I had known about the genetics. This silence served to kill you as much as the illness itself. I was murderously full of rage.

What the devil is this? What the hell is going on?

I would not be silent and secretive, like I was in the past, when your mental illness was exploding. I put aside my shame. This was our story. This was a confession of a rollercoaster ride that landed you six feet under.

Many people erroneously believe that nice and loving families don't have mental illnesses. They are wrong. These kinds of illnesses follow genetic lines through families, just like diabetes or heart disease or breast cancer. There is no shame in having these diseases. We have come out of the dark ages where other diseases are concerned. We are still in the dark ages when it comes to our understanding of mental illnesses and our acceptance of those who suffer. Early diagnosis and treatment can make all the difference; left unchecked, disaster ensues.

What the devil is this? What the hell is going on?

Not much was discussed or acknowledged within the family, not openly. That was a real pity because we had dedicated ourselves to mental health awareness, education, and suicide prevention. How could it be that those closest to us could feel so distant and removed? Of all the lives we touched, we wanted most to touch the lives of the family we loved. You were dead. Your mental illness destroyed you, destroyed all of us. Secrets were a part of our journey, and those secrets were a part of your suicide. Secrets and mental illness did not ultimately serve one another. We worried about what moved unseen in the currents that ran like a river beneath the family. We worried about secrets.

What the devil is this? What the hell is going on?

September 8, 2003:
Pulling Weeds

I drove by the cemetery and pulled weeds and trimmed. I kept scissors and a little brush in the trunk of the car so that I could stop by at any time and take care of your gravesite. I didn't mind going to the cemetery. It afforded me an opportunity to do something for you. It was an absurd notion since you're dead, and there really wasn't anything I could do for you. Dad brought me flowers, anticipating the arrival of the bad days. They wilted. I took off all the buds, put them in a plastic bag, and brought them to the cemetery with me. I scattered the petals over you. I stood alone and couldn't wrap my head around the fact that you were right below me. I sat on the ground.

I was rendered incapable of creating for most of the summer, except for "What the Devil Is This?" The suffering and pain I felt was mounting and accumulating. I had no energy. The second anniversary of your death was in full swing. I was stunned by my incapacity and sickened by the intensity. What happened to the difficult that was getting "better" over time? At least I noticed some "normal" days. Days I now called normal were ones in which I was not consumed by grief. There were no normal happy days or normal joy-filled days. That had not happened. I was on the lookout for some of those kinds of days. I was having bad dreams and felt like a volcano ready to explode. There was no clear, steady, upward movement to grief's journey. Just when I thought I had made some real progress, the rug got pulled out from under me with the September 11 anniversary. I felt like I was at the beginning again.

September 11, 2003:
Black Butterfly

On this second anniversary of September 11, I got up, got dressed, put in some wash, and cooked dinner. I had no energy to do anything else, so I sat outside in the garden, just like I did last year. The play of forest green across the lawn brought me to tears. Those colors took me into the earth as autumns light, tempered and stretched thin by the heat of the summer, were detected more by my body than my eyes. It was painful. I listened to the music of Krishna Das playing in the background. A large black butterfly with blue iridescent wings came and sat on my right foot. It stayed there for a long while and walked up my leg and rested on my knee. Eventually it flew away but then came back and rested on my other leg for a while before leaving for one of the butterfly bushes in the backyard.

There were times when I felt skeletal, as if I were living among the dead. The beauty of the iridescent butterfly reminded me I walked among the living. I felt your presence as tears rolled down my face, and I smiled.

The collective grief of this anniversary was palpable and only added another layer to my personal experience of loss. The pain in my body felt connected with the pain in every mother's body who had suffered a child's loss. I felt in alignment with something much larger than myself, a collective experience of sorrow that was beyond what words could express. The images and sounds of September 11 were part of my structure.

The terrorist attack must have taken a toll on you, in light of your growing internal disintegration. I was not surprised that the American Red Cross considered you a causality of September 11. You, as well as others who ended their own lives in New York, succumbed in a city devastated by loss.

I thought about the days following September 11, 2001, when Dad and I sat and shared over dinner. We talked of you and laughed because you had called each day, sometimes twice a day. We thought you sounded good. Dad said, "She's really on her way." It seemed that you were coping and making it through the first few weeks of college that were traditionally the toughest. You went to the movies with Kimberly and Joe one night. You had pizza with your sister on another evening. We were hopeful that you and Kimberly were in the process of establishing a closer relationship. On September 20 you sounded a little flat to us on the phone. We noticed it and did not discount it. I would see you in a few days on my visit to New York and Ground Zero.

September 23, 2003: Ground Zero

I remembered September 23, 2001, because our visit was brief. You said you had a lot of work to do. We walked to Union Square together and looked at the 9/11 memorial erected by loved ones. The ground was covered with flowers and notes. There were flags and candles and pictures of the missing everywhere. The area was filled with people grieving, people praying, and meditating. This once vibrant park was devoid of life; it had collapsed. I could feel the pervasive sadness of the place in my own body. The air I breathed and moved through seemed heavy. I snapped a picture of you standing in front of it all. You did not look at me; you looked off to your left. You did not smile, and your expression was serious and brooding. Your sunglasses were perched on top of your head over your hastily arranged hair, caught in a ponytail. You had on your jeans skirt and a red T-shirt you had cut up and pinned together with safety pins. I thought the shirt was an attempt on your part, as an aspiring fashion designer, to make a statement. I see it differently today. I see you barely held together by rows of safety pins, which stretched from your waist to just beneath your underarms on either side of your body. I did not know the picture would be my last image of you.

I also visited with Kimberly on September 23, 2001. She had the day off, so we did a little shopping in the West Village, where she lived. At the end of our visit, she wrote down directions, which guided me underground by subway toward Ground Zero.

I got off the subway at an unfamiliar stop and walked up the steps. I did not need to ask anyone which way to Ground Zero—it was evident. I followed the throng of people moving in one direction. There was no traffic because the streets were blocked off. People did not talk; the place was eerily silent. Everything was gray, still covered in ash. Small bits of debris, paper, or something were plastered to the windows, to the walls of the buildings, to the street and sidewalk. I moved through the space with others, a kind of death march toward the hazy pit where the sharp, lone pyramid of bent steel could be seen in the distance. The silence was deafening except for the sounds coming from Ground Zero, the voices of rescue workers mixed in with the sounds of equipment. I stood there, looked, and tried to take in the impossible.

I could not have left New York without going there to witness the gaping wound. The place was sacred, and I was glad I made the effort. I stayed as long as I could, leaving myself just enough time to take the subway uptown and make my way to the cross street near Times Square, where I boarded a bus back to Baltimore.

On September 28, 2001, you came home but went back to the city less than twenty-four hours later. You were infatuated with a young man you had met. I remembered Dad told you to slow down, but we realized we couldn't tell you anything. You seemed to be adjusting to college. That was the last time I saw you. I watched you turn and wave to me as you walked down the steps to the train. If only I had known.

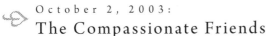

October 2, 2003:
The Compassionate Friends

I received a notice from the Compassionate Friends in Annapolis about an upcoming meeting. They are a worldwide organization that ministers to parents who have lost children. I had not considered attending their local meetings. I also had not considered sharing my collages with anyone outside family and friends. I hadn't considered working with others suffering from loss. However, a sudden impulse moved me past these notions. I printed a flyer, "The Art of Healing: Loss, Grief, and Grace" and sent it off, asking them to display my information. A week later I received a call from the Compassionate Friends facilitator saying, "Your work looks interesting." She wondered if I was willing to attend a chapter meeting and share my collages. I agreed and then spent the next week in agony over what I had done. I hated speaking in front of people. I drove myself crazy until finally I gave it up. I told myself that the images spoke for themselves; there was nothing to do besides share them. How difficult could it be to talk for fifteen minutes in front of a few people?

There were about seventy-five people in attendance. Once I got into my presentation, they cancelled their regular meeting and gave me the remaining hour and a half. My experience moved me out of what was personal and toward something universal. Many people stayed after and talked. They gathered around the tables where my images were propped up against the wall. They moved in close. They nodded and laughed as they took in the details, responding to our shared journey. The room felt alive.

People saw that collage offered a means to let out what was buried inside. They saw the potential of this process and understood that a creative process gave them permission to be with all their grief just the way it was, and that was healing. That's the power of art. That's the power of image. That's the power of art therapy, a creative modality for exploring oneself.

As I packed up my collages that evening, the director invited me to be a workshop presenter for the Compassionate Friends Regional Conference next year. She wanted to know if I could present my artwork in addition to offering participants the opportunity to make their own collages. I said yes before I gave it another thought.

October 3, 2003:
Sisters

Aunt Donna stopped by a few times with coffee, after getting your three cousins out the door to school. We sat in our pajamas like we did so many times in the early days of your death. It was a comfort to be with her then, as it was now. She knew there was nothing for her to do, nothing to fix, and so her presence was enough. She had traveled grief's journey having mourned the death of a husband and a still born baby.

Both my sisters supported me. They each experienced their own set of tribulations and were prepared to be with me in my moments. Aunt Elizabeth called often and listened. She was empathetic and tender. I looked forward to our intimate conversations. They weathered the storm of countless days and months with me. I wondered at their resolve in the face of so much sadness. They were there for me in so many simple ways. I felt them stepping close as your second anniversary moved in with crushing force. I needed my sisters, and they were there. Kimberly and

Kevin no longer had a sister with whom to share their lives. Thankfully, they had each other.

October 11, 2003:
Second Anniversary of Your Death

Kimberly and Kevin came home. I imagined that as the years went by, their lives would become more full and busy. We would not always be together for your anniversary, but for now we were. It was a beautiful day, and we spent it doing a lot of nothing. Kimberly suggested I make one of your favorite dinners. We had salmon, rice, broccoli, and blueberry pie. Father Ray came over. We sat in your room after we ate. Father Ray said mass, and Dad tried to stifle his sob.

As the sun set, the four of us sat in the backyard along the stone border of a garden, just beneath a large maple tree. We each cut a piece of our own hair, bound it together, and buried it under a five-sided stone. We sat quietly in a stillness that was saturated with two years of grieving. The sunset was magnificent, the kind of pink and blue sky you loved. I remembered the times when you asked me to stop the car so you could look at the colors. This evening, our quiet was broken by the sound of geese. We all turned our eyes upward. I counted eleven geese flying low, right above us.

October 14, 2003:
Yellow Dress Family and Friends

Last night was our second Yellow Dress Golf Classic. We raised over forty thousand dollars last year and expected to bring in over a hundred thousand this year. We were a voice for those who had lost someone to suicide and for those who had chosen to end their own lives. That accomplishment did not tip the scales against our sorrow. In the end you were still dead.

I looked out over a sea of faces, some old and some new. As I began to speak, many looked into their plates, not wanting to look at me. One dad fainted. His friends said he had smoked too many cigars. I thought he did what half the room would have liked to do. He fell to the floor in a panic. He fainted as a means of escaping the grief. Uncle Mike went to his side, took his pulse, and stayed with him until he regained consciousness. Our evening speakers, dinner, and auction continued amid the flurry. We did what we did, because we had to, and so last night the Kristin Rita Strouse Foundation thrived.

This morning I dragged in all the Yellow Dress Golf Classic boxes stacked in the garage from last night's event. I was in my nightgown and planned to stay that way all day. I remembered standing before a table in the center of the room last night. I looked into Joan's eyes and was drawn back in time to the afternoon I phoned to tell her you had died. She and Jon were away with Jan and John when I called. Joan slid along the cabinets in the kitchen as she fell to the ground; Jon went outside and threw up. The two couples drove home to be with us. I remembered their presence during the viewing. The four of them stood along the funeral parlor wall, giving us space and readying themselves for our journey together. They never left our side. I wasn't sure how they came to an understanding of how to be with us. I recalled that, just after the funeral, Joan came over. She sat stiffly on the ottoman in the kitchen and handed me a card. She said, "Read it later. I have written what I have been unable to say to you over these past days." She wrote, "We will be by your sides on every conceivable level through the years ahead to hold you, love you, and share with you this profound loss." We got into her bright blue VW beetle and drove off, taking care of everyday errands.

These friends found a way to be with us. It wasn't their actions that sustained us, for all the actions didn't change anything. It was their presence day after day and week after week. It was their capacity to listen. They managed to join us in the places we were. Others drifted out of our lives, and friends I had enjoyed disappeared. It was the price we paid in the trenches of our journey.

We all changed as a result of your death, perhaps in ways that made us softer around our edges. Things that didn't matter faded into the background of our lives.

October 27, 2003:
Your Twentieth Birthday

It was your birthday. I sat in your room and looked through your things. I couldn't seem to do anything else today. I was in an uncomfortable state of boredom, aware of an undercurrent of anxiety. It would have been a perfect day to create, but I was not in the mood. I had not been in the mood for some time. I found myself being mindful of my mood in the same way I was mindful of the words I spoke and the images I created. I gave myself permission to be as I was.

This watchful part of me had been strengthened throughout this ten-month creative process. It was the process that was the most important. It was the moment-by-moment meeting and allowing what was happening to just be, without struggling to make it different. There was relief in that practice. My healing continued.

October 31, 2003:
Halloween Golf

It was an unseasonably warm and beautiful day. Dad invited me to join him on the golf course. We realized it was a better way to spend the day than being caught up in memories of your favorite holiday. Dad decided to take up golf in light of the fact that our fundraiser for the Kristin Rita Strouse Foundation was a *golf* tournament.

I watched as he hit the little white ball. He played with his special one, the one with the Yellow Dress logo on it—a gift to the golfers at our event. He made me laugh. He was intense.

He talked to himself. He cheered himself on with a, "Now that's what I'm talking about." I held onto the handle on the cart's roof as we went around the curve and up the hill. He played a lot, even by himself. He focused for hours learning a new sport. This focus was his process. At the end of the day, he came home and was happy. It seemed to me that over the months, golf was doing for Dad what collage was doing for me. Our healing paths were different. I couldn't say that mine was better than his. His golf practice seemed to be working for him, and that was all that mattered. He didn't give me grief over the hours I spent in the studio with pieces of paper. I did not give him grief over the hours he spent hitting golf balls on the fairways and greens.

He putted. The ball went in, and he said, "Wait until the boys hear about this one."

November 30, 2003:
Explosion

Collage #10: "Rage: Code Red"

Survivors talk about being angry. I had not experienced it. I had not felt anger toward you, until my rage surfaced. It had been building. It was a little after the two-year anniversary, and something happened. I hated everything, hated everyone, hated myself—and worst of all, I hated you for what you had done. There was no logic to any of this, no reason; it just was.

I had taken a break from creating after I finished my collage in September. With tension rising, I willingly walked down the steps and rummaged through my magazines and folders. I had to bring some order to my vast collection of images. They were organized in categories, by color and symbol, in an overflowing filing box. I pulled out my folder marked red. This red was for anger, for rage. I spread my images out all over the floor and made my selections. I pasted an exquisite masked and robed icon right in the center of it all.

I am the queen of rage. I sit in a massive field of red. My anger arises like flames from a bottomless pit, and there is nothing to do but dive in completely. I feel the urge to scream at everyone, to have a fit in the grocery store, to yell at Dad, and to generally lower myself to the most base level of dysfunction.

On a dark and dismal afternoon, days into my process, I found an ad filled with question marks. I cut out those question marks and glued them down on both the right and left sides of my collage, along with some words.

I want to pull your hair out as I scream, "Why, why, why," like an insane monkey. I hold my stomach and remind myself that I am here in this body. I allow the coulds, shoulds, and would haves to explode out of my guts. There are many unanswered questions. How could you, Kristin? I take in my surroundings with eyes masked and darkened by death. I am in the underworld; the primitive part of myself has taken over. My thinking brain has given way; it's a matter of instinct and survival. My primal self takes care of only the bare necessities. I am supported by basic instincts that offer a sense of containment. My beating heart lies somewhere outside my body, exposed for the world to see.

Toward the end of November, I found this wonderful image of a woman in red, seated. I cut her out and placed her on a red leather wing-backed chair and then set it on fire.

I am in the fire and of the fire. I am totally consumed until there is nothing left but ash. I honor my rage and give it all its due. My right hand reaches for you, in your red dress. The energy of my rage pulsates out of the top of my head and engulfs all in its path. I am consumed in the fury.

When I walked up the steps and closed the door, I went into the real world where there was no place for rage like this. It took a lot of energy to hide my anger, to control what felt out of control. I was afraid it may break through onto some unsuspecting victim at any moment. I was aware of counterbalancing all of those feelings through my over-solicitous sweetness.

I reach for you, my little yellow bird, but it is too late—you are consumed by the flames of mental illness. You are dead.

> March 30, 2001. As I was passing the bridge, I thought of jumping off of it. Imagine how that would be, so easy, so quick. What is my impact on the class of 2001? Why don't people like me? I hate school. I can't wait to leave. Every day I think of college, the cruise, my future, and being better than my friends. I must show the world the real me, the honest me. I'm so lonely all by myself. I can't wait to be in New York. I feel so beautiful there.

December 5, 2003:
Gift to Myself

I attached little red bows to my latest collage and wrapped it up like a Christmas gift to myself. It was the gift of allowing myself to be seen and heard, no matter how dark and full of rage. The more space I allowed for the truth, the less power it had over me. I spent more time in the studio because I consciously wanted to release the rage within my body. I wanted to exhale it from myself with every breath. I didn't want to die from my intense emotions, from rage. My intention was to heal.

I particularly loved the torn edges around the dark figure at the top of "Rage: Code Red." I loved the light behind her that appeared to come through the crack. I loved that space that seemed held by the deep dark rose petals, a space out of which falls my love.

December 21, 2003:
Yellow Bird

Grandma, Kimberly, and I finished making the lasagna for Christmas. We were talking about you. We missed you. There was a loud thud; something hit the window in the kitchen. I had noticed birds hitting our windows since you died. It seemed to happen when you were in the conversation or in our thoughts. I made my way out the door. There was a small yellow bird on the ground below the window. It had broken its neck.

I remembered when Dad and I argued in his den over what he had written for your eulogy. I couldn't imagine him delivering that speech, but he was determined. I admired him for that. He wanted to make people comfortable and had included some levity in his remarks. I wouldn't have it. I wasn't interested in how other people felt. You were dead, and there was no room for levity as far as I was concerned. Our words crossed. There was a thud against the window, and we stopped, went over, and looked. There was a yellow bird on the ground. We looked at each other. Dad gave in to my needs and rewrote his comments. I was appreciative.

Birds, yes, lots of yellow birds. I remembered the little gray wren, too. It still sat on the branch outside the dining room window and fluttered against the pain.

December 22, 2003:
Castle

Collage #11: "The Wisdom"

I celebrated a year of image making. I took out all my collages and sat in front of them before I began my December creation. I sat in witness to myself. I felt that my journey had stripped me naked; I was exposed to the world. I didn't think twice about using the nude when I came across her.

I relax into the center of it all. My new self is born of breath. My breath is no longer shallow. My breath is no longer caught inside my aching lungs. I breathe freely, in light of the fact that my new self is held by death's screaming darkness and Botticelli's angels.

I collaged in a wonderful image of a castle. I tore it in half and placed it on either side of myself. I imagined the New York skyline dripping into the yellowed clouds surrounding my ruptured home. I was particularly pleased when I found the image of a woman standing in crucifix form.

I stand steady with my arms outstretched, balanced in the tension of opposites. I realize life is not this way or that way, but both ways. It's taken a long time for both my mind and heart to realize it. You took the road less traveled. In the book Radical Acceptance, *Tara Brach says, "The boundary of what you accept is the boundary of your love." I want a future filled with life, and so I must open completely to both your life and your death. My home is cracked yet standing. I intentionally engage the torn edges and cracks; they are everywhere in this piece. I fall in love with the cracks within myself. I fall in love with the light that comes from breaking open.*

Kimberly and Kevin were home. I wished I could make their homecoming easier. Kimberly couldn't sleep; she spent the early morning hours in your room, looking through your things. She put the clothes she's taken of yours away and replaced them with other things she wanted. She said it was like a ritual, a touching into you. For her, it brought order to the chaos of your death. It grounded her to the reality that you were not in the room next door to share the bathroom with her. She opened the medicine cabinet on your side of the double sinks and looked at the butterfly nail file and the little carved hand mirror you loved.

Kevin went into your room, too. I found him not long ago, holding some of your clothes. Between his sobs, he managed to get out, "I don't have anyone to play with. She used to follow me around." He said something about being your big brother. That emotional release was good for Kevin. On this visit, I noticed he took a leather bracelet of yours. I noticed him wearing it and was surprised it fit. He had lost a lot of weight since your death. He said he was just working hard. He had the yellow afghan from your bed with him. Kevin and Kimberly both seemed to find comfort in wrapping themselves in something of yours. Their cracks were different than mine. We each had a different set of demons inside.

This was my eleventh collage. It filtered through me, after "Field of Screams" and "Rage: Code Red." This collage felt different. I felt different after your two-year anniversary and a year of creating.

I have recently become conscious of the fact that we are born upside down. Of course I knew that, but it's taken on new meaning in light of the fact that I repeatedly play with your upside downness. I work and rework your falling. I wonder if I am finished touching this place. I find it an intriguing notion: the moment of your death, the moment of my death, and now my rebirth.

December 25, 2003:
Visiting You in the Moonlight

We stayed home this year and tried to get through the day as we experienced fluctuating degrees of sadness. None of the special dishes I cooked, none of the gifts, and none of the visiting seemed to matter. We were glad when the day was over and we could sit in our pajamas and watch *Seabiscuit* together. Your absence filled the room and moved Kevin to tears. He broke down over the fact that we had not visited your grave. It was getting close to midnight, and the cemetery was closed. Kevin got up and said he was going to visit you. Kim and I decided to join him. Dad was already falling asleep, and he couldn't imagine such an escapade.

We threw coats and boots on over our pajamas and drove around the corner with the radio playing Christmas music. The cemetery gates were closed, and so we found a darkened spot along the high fence where we thought we could climb over without getting caught. Kevin lifted us over and climbed over himself. We went running in the moonlight to your grave. We left you a Christmas cookie and a branch from the Christmas tree. We hugged, we cried, and we laughed at the possible headlines: "Family arrested on Christmas night breaking and entering a cemetery while in their pajamas, to visit their beloved, Kristin." It was well worth it and was the best part of our day.

four

forgiveness

January 17, 2004:
Everything I Need

Collage #12: "The Goldfish"

In Janet's circle we were offered the symbol of a fish. My fish was in a fishbowl and had everything it needed. It was filled with color and light, and it was graceful. My fish was like a jewel in the water, a diamond.

I was haunted by this simple experience and felt compelled to search through my collage folders for the Tiffany ad I had filed away. I spent my entire Christmas holiday consciously exploring, for the first time, an experience from Thursday's circle with my collage expression. I embraced that intention and opened to its possibility.

I place the fish at just the right angle on a thick, black, twenty-by-sixteen-inch paper. I want to create a bowl in which the fish has everything it needs. My environment includes water, land, and sky. I place small tile images around the fish. They are not right, so I remove them. It needs the look of glass. I want to create a feeling of movement and place large torn pieces of white paper around the fish. I find an image of broken glass, cut it up, and glue it on top of the pure white paper.

125

It's not at all what I imagined in my meditation—it's better. It's in the shape of a heart. I don't mean to create a heart, but when I step back and look, there it is. I like the layering that is happening. I use torn pieces of the fish's tail and place it into the colors of the water, land, and sky. The fish is now part of everything.

This collage was so beautiful. I decided to work on the black spaces, the in-between spaces. I found a black background with hints of turquoise specks—very subtle. I layered the black onto black. I loved the white torn edges and how they stood out against the rich black background. I had a sudden inspiration to use fabric from Kimberly's prom dress, which was black net with gold stars. It was perfect. The void now seemed to have depth and space within its own blackness.

I looked at the fish and had a feeling that it had become a bird. It was flying in the heavens and swimming in the deep. I had never heard of a fish-bird, but there she was.

Days after I thought I finished, I placed a photograph of you into this collage. I did it on a whim. I cut you up and placed you with the water, land and sky. The cutting was releasing. Placing you everywhere was releasing. This collage was different: I had not used any words. I was drawn more deeply into the spaces between the images. I felt myself resting there. I felt spacious and uncluttered by thought and emotion. I would love to be in this space all the time, but I'm not; I come and go. I considered my goldfish-bird and saw there was no separation between what was inside and what was outside. All was connected, all was one.

Here I am and here you are.

February 12, 2004: "So Do You Have Children?"

The bereavement group we attended after your death offered suggestions on how to handle awkward questions, such as: "How many children do you have?" I had to be prepared to meet strangers who did not know about your death. I found myself scanning the room in an attempt to stay away from anyone who may not know. I would have liked to avoid these situations at all costs, especially when feeling raw and tender. It was impossible, and the questions began.

"How many children do you have?" I hesitated and wondered about saying two. It would have been easier, but I couldn't and said three. I did try saying two a few times early on, and that was horrible. The pain of denying your life was far worse than the pain of explaining your death. The situation was compounded when someone I knew was standing right next to me, holding their breath, waiting, watching, and listening to the line of questioning. "How old are they?" My standard became, "Our oldest daughter is twenty-seven, we have a son who's twenty-four, and our youngest is forever seventeen. We lost our youngest daughter in October 2001." People looked shocked and uncomfortable. They mumbled words that conveyed their sorrow. I usually tried to change the topic or took the opportunity to leave and refresh my drink.

Most people said they were sorry and left it at that. Timing could be critical; one needed to react fast, especially around nosy and insensitive people. Some dove deeper. "How did she die?" You would think most people would know it's rude to inquire about the details of a child's death while noshing on crab balls, and yet it happened. My voice would drop to a whisper as I said, "She ended her own life." My quiet reply seemed to illicit a, "What did you say?" I revealed my own shame and discomfort through the quality of my own voice. I think they heard me but were shocked by the words that somehow needed to be spoken again. And so I repeated, "She ended her own life." I looked into their eyes and then shamefully looked away.

In the beginning, that usually ended the conversation because I often turned in tears. As time went by, I got stronger and found myself talking about the Kristin Rita Strouse Foundation and the work we were doing in support of mental health awareness, education, and suicide prevention. I took the opportunity to speak about grief and its ravages, instead of just saying, "I'm fine." I looked into their eyes and did not look away. It was not easy. I considered the lay of the land before every social event. It could be disconcerting when this happened at weddings, baby showers, Christmas parties, and birthday celebrations. Often these events were difficult to attend, anyway. People couldn't imagine what I went through at the happiest and most celebratory of times.

February 20, 2004:
Good Friday

I'd seen Monica for a massage every couple of weeks since your death. I found it helpful. Today as I slid under the covers on her table, I remembered another Friday, that 2002 Good Friday, just after you died. I remembered how tears streamed down the sides of my face as our session began. She cradled my head in her hands and moved my head gently side to side. I felt the snap of your head as you hit the concrete. It was three in the afternoon. She moved about my body; tears continued to fall as I continued to breathe. She moved her hands along the length of my leg, my leg whole and a moment later in pieces as I experienced your fracture. I wondered if she knew and sensed my experience. I wanted to end the session. It was so painful, so horrible, that I wanted to scream. I was afraid if I started to scream, I would never stop. My mind could not and would not wrap itself around the horror of your death, and so my body absorbed the horror for me. I could not stand it, and I went away, I went numb, and my unmet scream drifted off.

She paused, she knew. She asked me what I was feeling. I told her I felt your broken bones and wounds inside my own body. I told her it had happened before. She paused to allow the experience to be what it wanted to be. She was not afraid. I could feel her hands moving above the plane of my body, although my eyes were closed. She rested one hand on my belly; her other hand was over my heart. I could feel the heat in her hands, and my trembling body softened beneath her touch. She continued and lifted my left hand, moving along the bones of each finger. My skull, your fractured skull, my leg, your splintered femur, my hand, your bruised hand, my healing and your healing were linked together on that Good Friday. The matter of my body was released into a spacious, light-filled dimension that included you.

Over time what began as a shared experience between us on the massage table shifted to an experience that was more my own, more about my body. The experience of your fractured body and the story of your death gradually lifted from me. It did not take up residence inside me as it once did. I did not need an exorcism. I was not crazy. Grief was complicated, it was traumatic.

Imperfection

Collage #13: "Sudden Impact"

I was curious about what would emerge as my next collage, especially after my goldfish-bird. I thought I had turned the corner, and yet I came back to your body, to your fall, to the moment of your death. I had traveled this territory before. I did not have say about what I was drawn to. I stayed faithful to the integrity of my process and gave into the energy that moved and guided me. This collage revealed itself through my captivation of the beautiful nude, draped in pink. I contemplated you. I was there among the buildings, falling with you once again. I moved with you not in circles but in spirals, touching into places over and over but coming to them from a different place along my path. I repeated my visitations so that I could be free.

I want to hide the seams of the torn page and keep the perfect figure in perfection. I glue you down just right. I glue flowers on your body. I decide to move them, although the glue has dried. If I do it just right, I can always remove glued pieces, but not this time. I tear it. I tear you. I ruin everything.

It didn't turn out the way I wanted. Life didn't turn out the way I wanted, either. My emotions crescendoed out of proportion. This was about paper, yet I could not get hold of myself. I cried and I fell apart. You were torn, and it was my fault. I couldn't fix it and I couldn't fix you. I listened to the multiple meanings, turned off the lights, and went to bed.

When I woke in the morning, I was anxious over what I had ruined. That was an understatement. I spent days trying to fix what had been torn, but there was no way to fix it; it was what it was. I was driven to repair the flesh—I had to make it right. I used flesh from other images and glued it over the damaged places. I needed to cover the mistake. I was forced to add cracks and tears to your body in a way I had not envisioned. In the end, when all the dust settled, I liked the imperfection. It was real and honest. The imperfection gave it depth and interest. Light came through the cracks of your torn body; there was something beautiful there. I listened again to the multiple meanings.

My creative process offered an experience that turned into a teaching and healing opportunity. It was only my thoughts that labeled my torn image of you a mistake. As I let go, I discovered a gift. Through my creative process, I was forced to let go of perfection. Perfection was meaningless; life was messy and imperfect.

In finishing, I paste white doves across your broken body. They arise, and I imagine your spirit arising at the moment of your death. Hands reach for you. A few days later, I place a photograph of you into the collage. You look back at me, all dressed in white. You are standing by the kitchen door. We are on our way to your high school graduation. A moment later you burst into laughter, and a moment later you are gone. I scatter pink and yellow roses around you.

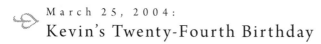

March 25, 2004: Kevin's Twenty-Fourth Birthday

We called your brother for his birthday. He said, "I'm fine," but his voice sounded thin and wispy. I hated the thought of him living in New York, blocks from where you died, but his degree in finance landed him a job on Wall Street. I wondered how he was really doing and what he kept hidden from us. I prayed for him every day and worried how your suicide took hold of him. He didn't like to talk about it. I listened to him crying, wishing he had known how much pain you were in, wishing he had been nicer to you. He was not open to being in therapy. He was an adult, and I couldn't make him talk or engage in a process that I felt was important. I could only love him and allow him to find his own way.

The last time he was home, he took one of your oil paintings back to New York and placed it on the mantel above his fireplace. He had your picture taped on the wall right in front of his desk. I asked if he was going out, and he said no, he was too tired. If you had not died, you would have been in your senior year of college; the three of you would have been in New York together. If you had not died, perhaps you would be going out for Kevin's birthday, celebrating like brothers and sisters do.

April 12, 2004: Alex

It was April 1998, and you came screaming into my bedroom. A lacrosse player had taken his own life. You had not known him personally, but he was friends with some of your friends. You crumpled on my bed in disbelief. I sat and cried with you as we talked about it. You could not understand how or why he would do such a thing. I remembered saying that the family's lives would never be the same, and offering a quiet prayer.

I never imagined that a few short years separated me from the same horror. I never imagined that I would meet Alex's mother, Grace, but I did. She said once, "My heart sometimes feels like it is made of shards of glass." I knew that feeling. Our lives ran parallel in many ways. We had lunches together and knew each other in the unspeakable places. I felt safe in her presence, as I did in the presence of all the mothers I met along the way who had lost children. It was funny how new people came into my life as others fell away.

I imagined you in heaven and liked imagining you with friends. I wondered who they were. I wondered if you and Alex knew each other, since Grace and I were friends. One evening after the sharing in Janet's circle, my circle-mate Ron turned to me and said, "I had a sense of Kristin; I saw her with a lacrosse stick in her hand." At the time Ron gave me the message, I didn't know what he meant and didn't make the association with Alex. I remembered thinking, *Kristin would have a paintbrush or tennis racket, not a lacrosse stick.* I thanked Ron and tucked the information into my memory.

As I drove home today, I suddenly made the association between you, Alex, and the lacrosse stick. I heard you say, "I was holding Alex's lacrosse stick. I was trying to tell you that we'd met." I smiled. I loved thinking that you knew each other, brought together by your shared journeys and brought together as your mothers shared lunch.

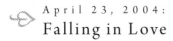 April 23, 2004:
Falling in Love

Collage #14: "Seen"

I was drawn back to the blacks and whites that were so prominent in my last collage. I began with the facade of a villa and staircase, and I built below it.

An ermine-cloaked woman makes her way up. I feel that I am the one climbing the stairs and imagine you near me. You gaze over what your death has created. A

large crack runs diagonally across your face and draws my eye down toward the
depths, where the stone-faced have only partially come back to life. A pair of eyes
form the middle ground; they are open to a world that is still upside down.

I had fallen in love with my collages and with the process of their creation. I loved the Madonna in the hair of the praying woman, I loved the sacred heart of Mary that appeared in the doorway, I loved the little child centered in the window of light, and I loved the woman in orange who ran into the mist. I loved the eyes of the mother; her tears were filled with a light that made its way deep into the recess of what was still petrified and cold. The mother's tears appeared on my cloak. I loved the light in this piece; it shimmered.

I sensed my distance from the early days of "Suffering," in the fact that I felt love at all. As I fell in love with the images I created, I realized I was falling in love with me. There seemed to be room for it. I sensed the impact of my creative process on my daily life, as joy and happiness seeped more deeply into my hours and days. In "In Our Hearts We Know," ShantiMayi said, "You will find what you seek in the center of your heart. We find this inner refuge when we are willing to lay down divisive inflexible conditions and identities that isolate ourselves, from our world and each other." I felt a shift and movement away from the need to engage the horrors of your death, and toward considerations of who I was now as a result of your death. My attachments to you and your death were loosening. I was looking inside myself, and that felt like a kind of heart wisdom.

May 6, 2004:
Gifts

My experience in Janet's circle ended with the appearance of an Asian man sitting on a red cushion. His hair was pulled back and he was dressed in gold. He told me to paint and write.

I have not considered painting. I got cold inside when I opened the tall, slender cabinet and looked at the antique milk tins filled with your brushes. I mixed them together with Grandpa's brushes so I couldn't tell one from the other; it was less painful that way. I mixed your paints together, too. I would like to learn to paint someday, but I have felt overwhelmed by the thought of it. I didn't have the courage to attempt something at which you were so skilled. I took the words of the Asian man to heart and took note of his encouragement to write. I had written down my circle experiences. I didn't know why I was driven to do that, I just did.

I had slowly transformed your studio into my refuge. I wished I had made the space more inviting and comfortable for you when you were alive. I replaced the long, metal conference tables you worked on with a large, square pine table from the European Antique Store. It was damaged and had a big crack along one edge. I liked it. I also bought a six-foot-long bookcase. The three open shelves held the books I treasured. My books found a home after being spread out all over the house. I created a kind of altar on the top shelf, filled with sacred knick knacks. There was a white swan, a pink stone heart, a Mary, a many-breasted Artemis, two snake goddesses, an Athena, a cross, some beads, a bird's nest with feathers, a snake skin, and your mass cards. I tore off a sleeve from your school uniform and tucked the candle from your funeral mass into the white cuff. There were several oriental rugs scattered about that were a bit used and faded. The space had been repainted a pale yellow with light turquoise accent walls. Your oil paintings were hung. I opened the windows a bit today. The Tibetan wind chimes moved, and there was music. I felt close to you.

May 15, 2004: The Compassionate Friends Regional Conference: Maryland

It was a large corner room. Tables were set up in the shape of a square, and two sets of windows let in light. I brought stacks of magazines and spread them out with glue sticks and scissors. I wondered if anyone would show up, but the room filled to capacity. I shared my story and my collages. I facilitated a room full of grieving parents through their own creative process of collage making. I provided them with the opportunity to bring into form images of their horrific journeys. It was fulfilling and rewarding.

I was proud of my own inner strength. I drew from a professional well that was quite deep and added my own personal and unique contributions that set this apart from anything I had done. Your death took me into another dimension with my work, weaving together the traditional, spiritual, and creative. The journey we shared, you and I, did not belong just to us; I was sure of that.

July 9–11, 2004:
The Bereaved Parents of the USA National Conference: Charleston, South Carolina

Someone from the Compassionate Friends Conference recommended me to another organization for parents who had lost children. I received an invitation from the Bereaved Parents of the USA to be a workshop presenter at their 2004 national conference in Charleston. Dad and I drove together and stayed at a charming inn on Charleston's waterfront. I found it mystifying to discover myself on a national stage with the opportunity to offer my work. It was intense, being in the presence of hundreds of grieving parents from around the country. My workshop was well received. Dad sat in on my presentation; he taped it and said he was proud. We met some amazing presenters, several of whom had written books about their experience of losing a child. We particularly liked Mitch Carmody's workshop and came home with his book, *Letters to My Son: A Journey through Grief.*

When I came home, nothing had changed and yet everything had changed. The opportunity to present at a national conference had opened something inside of me. Although I was not ready to gather other bereaved parents into a creative process on an ongoing basis, I realized it was simply a matter of time before I did. I wanted to continue with my own healing. I felt I needed more perspective. I knew I was on the right path for myself—now I sensed a future with others. I came home filled with hope, and that was a good feeling.

August 2, 2004:
Kimberly's Twenty-Seventh Birthday

Your sister turned twenty-seven today. She was the same age I was when I gave birth to her. We had never been to the Hamptons on Long Island. We thought it might be nice to get away and celebrate. She wanted to get out of the city, away from all of the memories of your death that often consumed her. I wished she did not live in New York, close to where you died. She moved from her apartment. She could not live in that space, a space she shared with you in the last hours of your life, a space where I talked with you on the phone just an hour before you died. Kevin lived there now. I wondered what effect that had on him. I wondered if he was disturbed by the events that took place there. He said he wasn't, but I wondered.

Kimberly filled herself with endless blame and self-recrimination. "Kristin was so dark, so blank, so hopeless and helpless that night. If only I had invited her to stay the night with me. I still see her turning to wave to me as she walked out of my life forever."

Kimberly continued to pour herself into Rita Project. I wondered why I never thought of it, but I didn't: she faced your death head-on, with a tool box filled with traditional therapy, art therapy, yoga, and meditation. She had years ahead of her and was determined to find a way into her own life, where your death would recede far enough into the background so that she could breathe in forgiveness for herself and for you. She loved you and missed you.

Today Kimberly met with a psychiatrist, who was exploring the possibility of inviting her and Rita Project to Ireland to present at the 3Ts Conference, "Suicide in Modern Ireland: New Dimensions, New Responses." It was astounding, witnessing Kimberly's life and its direction as a result of your death. If everything worked out, Kimberly and Rita Project would arrive in Ireland in the fall.

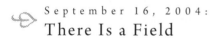 September 16, 2004:
There Is a Field

Collage #16: "Forgiveness"

I worked on this peace all summer. I opened the windows and French doors. I played music and enjoyed the longer days filled with sunlight. I began with the two women in the center, one in black and one in white. I placed them deep in the woods. During the final stages of working on this collage, I realize it was about forgiveness.

When I found the profile of a woman cloaked in black, I tore her out and thought of myself.

I gaze across the forest at you. Your eyes do not meet mine; they are downcast. I sense the sorrow in what you have done. I am filled with compassion for both of us. We meet in the middle ground, mother and daughter, black and white. I place myself at the moment of your death and allow myself the opportunity to be with you, to hold you once again and touch you. The horror has slipped away, and I feel compassion.

I have not used words in my collages for some time, and yet they found their way into this one. If one stood far away, one would miss them. They were embedded in the green, held by what grew and became forgiveness.

I adore the touches of white in the piece. You are in white and in the light. I adore the doves. I search for little white flowers and scatter them in the foliage. I experiment with the torn edges that appear white, only when torn in the right direction. The effect is other-worldly.

I remembered using doves in March's "Sudden Impact." I found the words, "I am timeless." I placed these same words into the field of my first collage, just underneath your body. I felt threads connecting this piece with past pieces and became aware of how intertwined my work was. My work transformed as I touched the same places; I transformed, too. Each collage prepared the way for the next. This summer I was in a place of forgiveness.

A few weeks after moving onto another collage, I found an image of a little ballerina dressed in white. I remember the photograph of you in your pink and blue tutu, posing in the family room right before one of your ballet recitals at Peabody Preparatory. You loved to dance and often spontaneously entertained me in the kitchen with a plié or chassé.

You sit on the edge and take it all in. I feel your presence, your participation in the forgiveness. I ask to be forgiven. I forgive you. We heal together. The poet Rumi wrote, "Out beyond any idea of wrongdoing or rightdoing, there is a field. I'll meet you there." Kristin, I meet you there in the green fields of forgiveness.

 December 8, 2004:
Paint the White Room Red

I wanted to move, Dad wanted to stay, and so we compromised. We redecorated the entire first floor with fresh paint and new furniture. I needed it to be different … and when it was, you were still dead. I thought it would be easy to toss out the blue leather sofa in the family room, filled with memories and sadness. When they came to take it away, I thought I would pass out. I cried as I ran my hands over the cushions on which we sat. I wanted to take it all back and say it was a mistake, but it was too late; I had to let go. It was difficult dealing with change of any kind, even though I initiated and looked forward to this change. I felt you in all of it. As I let go, I let go of you. All my hopes and dreams were swept out with my white living room. You would not be a beautiful, blushing bride in that room. There would be no gorgeous portrait of you in a wedding dress.

I painted the white room red.

This long process of redoing our home was really a process of redoing myself. I was aware of the subtleties and opened to it. In the end it was all interconnected with no separation between what happened inside myself and what happened in my outer life. The redoing process was pervasive. In the end I was happy with the way our new home looked. It felt lighter and opened a door to our future. There were no memories attached to these new rooms and new things. It was the same house, but the insides were different. My insides were different. We painted the pink dining room yellow, and that was the hardest thing of all to do. I let go of your favorite room and painted it your favorite color. Change and more change.

December 13, 2004:
Radical Acceptance

I had been reading Tara Brach's book *Radical Acceptance* over these holidays. Reading in itself was comforting, given the fact that I hadn't been able to concentrate and read for more than a year. I took in a few pages at a time and drank in every word as a prayer. She said, "Radical Acceptance is the willingness to experience ourselves and our life as it is." This was not a new concept to me, yet as I read her words, they touched me deeply. This was what I was doing in my collage making. Her words supported me and added another dose of credibility to the hours I spent in the studio. They reminded me that art making was healing, that being aware and awake in the moment was healing. When I entered my studio, I was peaceful no matter what I brought to the table. The more I touched what broke my heart, the more I released. I experienced a tender compassion that softened the raw edges of your death. This was soul medicine, because your suicide had desecrated my spirit.

I was drawn to the in-between spaces in my collage work. The space defined by what was torn, the emptiness, the void. The cracks allowed breadth. There was a lightness, and I rested there. My rational mind did not accept this paradox of resting in the dark void, however my heart sensed its healing properties. It was December, and I prepared myself for the holidays. Rumi's writings touched me. "The cure for the pain is in the pain." And so it goes.

December 25, 2004:
Christmas

I put up some garland in the kitchen and a few of my Lladro angels in the foyer. I would have been satisfied, but Kimberly and Kevin came home and wanted a tree. We drove to Valley View and decided on a small pine that could be planted in the yard after the holidays. We stopped by the cemetery on our way home and placed a wreath on your grave and Grandpa's grave. I couldn't bring myself to open the box of Christmas ornaments; the memories were too much. For now, we had a tree decorated with white lights and dragonfly ornaments that Aunt Donna surprised us with. As I placed a dragonfly on our Christmas tree, I remembered the dragonfly I placed on your heart in my very first collage.

I was glad we decided to stay home. I tried to cook as many of our favorite dishes as I could. In the end, I was overcome with exhaustion. I cracked under the pressure of trying to make it right, trying to make it good, trying to fix and save everyone from the pain that eventually seeped out of our hearts and moved all over the house. We all looked like deer in headlights while sitting around the dining room table, trying to have our usual Christmas Eve lasagna dinner last night. We looked even worse when we got up this morning, after not sleeping.

Grandma joined us as she always did. She became the center of our attention, and we seemed to find some relief in that. We sat with Grandma for a few pictures. In years past, we used to take rolls and rolls of pictures, but this year no one was in the mood. I don't know why we bothered—habit, I guessed. I couldn't stand to look at the thousands of pictures we had. I was able to look at pictures at the beginning. I don't know exactly when that changed, but it did. The family albums sat behind closed doors, next to the ones we took of you dead.

December 28, 2004:
Oh What Fun It Is …

Collage #17: "Holiday Spirit"

I worked on "Holiday Spirit" between Thanksgiving and Christmas, capturing the season, which was like a scab dislodged before its time, revealing an all too tender place. Working on this collage felt like a counter balance to the festive parties. I was able to enjoy some of them because I allowed myself the luxury of being with what was underneath it all, and that was a sense of loss, still your loss. In spite of my all too private feelings, I managed to bake cookies.

I was drawn to the deadness around the eyes and so cut myself out. Me holding Kristin, Kristin holding me, Kimberly holding Kristin, Kristin holding Kimberly, or me holding myself—what did it matter, it was all of us. The snow globe was upside down. Christmas was still upside down in many ways.

I hide the word "fragile" under the glitter of holiday ornaments. I hide my fragility so others will feel comfortable; after all, it's been three years.

In this collage I noted the fragments, the torn places, the upside downness, and the pain of it all. The regression was evident as I compared this collage with my most recent collages. The trees, the lights, the songs all moved through me like nails scratching along a chalkboard. TV was burdensome with its endless holiday commercials. The Christmas music was unsettling. The general hustle and bustle grated on my nerves. I tried to lean into it all and breathe. I knew I was healing if I just stayed present. I longed for Christmas to be happy again and trusted hard work would get me there.

I began this creative process in December 2002 with "Caution." The following year, during the holidays, I created "Rage: Code Red." There were no Christmas trees or ornament in either one of them. I felt I had made progress by the fact that I was playing with holiday images at all, even if they were upside down, broken to pieces and overlaid with buildings.

Amid it all, I find tenderness in the hands that are crossed over the young girl's chest. Once again I think of your hands. I love the barely noticeable profile of a girl with her hair blowing in the wind. You are always there, part of the background tapestry of my life. I place doves and peacocks with golden feathers into the sadness of this Holiday. I have started looking up the symbolism of images to which I am drawn. I uncover rich layers as I excavate and bring the treasures to the surface.

letting go

Amanda, Memory in Mexico

We spent a week in Mexico both for business and pleasure. It was a vacation that stood in sharp contrast to our first Mexican vacation, just after you died. I wasn't traumatized by the travel or by seeing families together. I wasn't traumatized by the reception we received on arrival, complete with Mimosas. I wasn't traumatized by the throngs of people that were with us. I wasn't traumatized this week. I enjoyed the beautiful surroundings. I read and relaxed and was ready to return home and resume my life, which was increasingly more demanding. I was involved with many normal things, things that I had put aside when you died.

On my last day of vacation, I sat with Dad in an open-air plaza and enjoyed a drink after shopping. Some college-aged students walked by and made me think of your high school classmate Amanda, killed in Mexico on March 16, 2004, during spring break.

I remembered how Kelly called and told me about Amanda's death. She asked me if I would go to the funeral with her. At first I hesitated, not knowing if I had the strength for it. It was only a few years after your death, and I still excused myself from funerals. Dad would go, and I would pass. I didn't know how he did it; I just knew I couldn't. It was the way we were, and we accepted that in each other. He derived his strength from being with others, even at a funeral. I derived my strength from solitude. In the end I said yes to Kelly, sensing this was important. We walked into the church together and stood beside each other during mass. I took everything in around me—the flowers, the music, the family, the former high school classmates, the teachers and administrators from your high school, and the coffin. I observed it all in a way I could not when it was you in the coffin. I reached for Kelly's hand, and we stood there in tears together. After the service people came up to me. I sensed they did not know what to say; my presence was a shocking reminder of your death.

Amanda's internment followed her church service. We drove to the cemetery where you were buried. We stood in view of your grave, just above and over, on the gentle slope of a hill. I pulled my black wrap around my shivering body. I shivered, though not from the cold or the wind. I shivered from the death. Kelly and I stood at the edge of where the mourners gathered. I continued to observe and bear witness to it all. I felt present to this moment in ways I had not been present during your funeral and burial. I was in shock then, protected from the bitter reality that came soon enough. I had forgotten a lot of it; there were large gaps in my memory. I stood next to Kelly and felt the missing pieces of my experience coming back into my consciousness through Amanda, through her death. As the service ended, the family turned to say good-byes. Amanda's mother spotted me and ran to me with her arms outstretched. I held my arms out to her, and together we fell to sitting on the ground. She screamed our children's names, "Amanda. Kristin." She choked out, "Our babies. Together. Two artists, painting in heaven." Her cry rolled over the hills and coalesced into a vortex of grief that mushroomed over stunned mourners. I received and acknowledged her in my embrace with murmured utterances of recognition that were more soothing sounds than formed words. Family and friends moved in quickly. I looked up and said, "It's all right; leave us, it's only grief." They would not listen. They were afraid of what they saw: two mothers on the ground, in grief, in tears. They scooped Amanda's mother from my arms and took her away, the palms of our hands sliding slowly from each other.

I got up and brushed the grass from my pants, wishing our moment together had been longer. People were afraid and did not want to bear witness to our suffering. They moved in quickly to separate us and abort a scene. How sad. How tragic for everyone that they could not withstand grief's passion. In some cultures it would have been accepted as perfectly natural for the bereaved to fall on the ground. The whole community might have joined in the outpouring and created a safe environment for the breaking open. Perhaps we have lost something along the way in our efforts to keep it neat and tidy.

I was glad I had gone to Amanda's funeral. Kelly and I walked over to your grave. I placed a single rose I had extracted from one of Amanda's floral arrangements and placed it on your grave. I covered my mouth with the wad of tissues I'd been carrying, stifling the sob I felt coming. I turned and hugged Kelly. A gust of wind warmed my ankles.

February 22, 2005:
SOS

A little over a year ago, I checked out local suicide survivors groups. I was helping out a friend who recently lost her mother to suicide, investigating support groups with her. I was not personally interested, remembering my uncomfortable and unenlightening experiences in the 2001 grief and bereavement course.

I was pleasantly surprised when I came across Judy and Paul at Survivors of Suicide (SOS). Perhaps I was in a more receptive place. Perhaps I felt more at home in a group for suicide survivors, where the particulars of our kind of loss were addressed. Meetings were twice a month at a local church, and I went on a pretty regular basis. Dad said, "I don't do groups; I'll stick with golf."

Judy and Paul were a few years ahead of me. I related to them as health care and religious professionals who lost a daughter to suicide. What I liked most about the meetings, besides the opportunity to be with other survivors, was the laughter. Paul had a sharp wit and a way of slicing right down to the core of things; it gave comic relief to what otherwise was gut wrenching.

People shared what was happening with them. The group did not tell anyone what to do; they listened and offered their own experiences as solace. I was not unnerved by participating in SOS. I felt I had some perspective and something to offer, especially when I shared what I was discovering through my creative process. It felt good to give back.

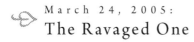

March 20, 2005:
The Yellow Dress

I entered the studio just like I had a hundred times, and I felt you there by the window, working on the painting of the yellow dress.

I remembered watching you put the finishing touches on the oil painting of a single yellow dress hanging on a hanger, the summer before you died. You were there by the windows, painting in the maroon University of Pennsylvania running shorts Kevin had given you. Your hair was caught up in a ponytail, high on your head, and you had casually wrapped the ends in a bun. Wisps stood out against the sun. Your light brown hair looked blonder in the light. You had a palette knife in your hand as you said, "Hold onto this painting, because one day it will be famous." When I looked at it I got a sinking feeling. The dress looked like it was fading away, it was disappearing. The art therapist in me was suddenly afraid. I pushed the feeling aside. You were smiling and happy. You were just exploring this yellow wedding dress, an image you had painted several times over the years. We laughed. Yes, I would hold onto your painting. You took your painting to college and hung it over your bed. It was now hung in the foyer. It was the first thing people saw when they came in the house.

This memory of you was sweet and tender. I did not cry; I just missed you.

March 24, 2005:
The Ravaged One

Collage #18: "Letting Go"

I spent the last two months on this collage. It took more time to finish because I spent less time in my studio. I was fine with that. This woman's image carried me through the winter and focused my attention inward.

I was drawn to the expression in her eyes, the curve of her hand at her breast, the tilt of her head and line of her neck. She was innocent and untouched, and she became my background. I imagined her sitting in a bed of flowers. She sat like that for weeks until I came across the one in the yellow dress.

I don't like her. I don't like what I see. I cut her out anyway. I wear a yellow dress. The ravaged part of me is poignantly evident, like an open wound. I need to pay attention. They say the body is the last to heal, that the trauma lives in the cells. They say that the death of a child takes at least ten years off your life. I was fifty-one when you died, so how much time do I have left? I paste another image of myself down. I sit with my back to the world and observe myself. I am all three parts: the innocent one, the ravaged one and the watchful one.

I left the collage as it was for a long time. Each time I looked at it, I was drawn to the empty black space behind the figures. My mind said it was finished; my heart knew otherwise. I wanted to fill the void at the same time I appreciated its emptiness. I found a ballerina and poodle, a boy and Labrador, and a child and a pen. I placed my children in the background, and the title of the piece became, "Letting Go."

You are the black-and-white fragments of my life as a mother. I release you. I long for you to move out of the field of my life, and yet there you are, like a dominating plaid, filling and almost overtaking my space. I glue gold stars over you in an effort to cover you up. Parts of you peer out at me as memories make me cry. I can smell your baby body; feel the touch of your hands as you reach for me, the dance, the game, the art of it all.

Letting go was a process that I was consumed with since your death. Your death added another layer to the normal process that parents experienced as their children grew up. I allowed myself the time and space to be with this. I placed my attention on letting go and had a sense of its transmutation in my body.

April 20–26, 2005:
Radical Acceptance Retreat with Tara Brach

Tara Brach's book *Radical Acceptance* became my trusted friend throughout the winter, and so when I discovered she was offering a silent retreat in

Albuquerque, New Mexico, I couldn't resist. I stood alone in my room and wondered what in the world I was doing. I had come to this Vipassana retreat to experience what Buddhists call mindfulness, to see clearly and to gain insight. I had come for the opportunity to hear Tara Brach speak her own words and to be in her presence.

The day began at 5:45 with sitting, walking, sitting, walking, Dharma talks in the late morning followed by more sitting, walking, sitting, walking. Afternoon Dharma talks followed by sitting, walking, sitting, walking. Evening Dharma talks followed by sheer exhaustion. I decided to tough it out because I was determined to discover what this experience could offer me. Tara Brach said, "It is the willingness to become still and pay attention to our experience, whatever it may be, that plants the seeds of Radical Acceptance. With time we develop the capacity to relate to our passing experiences, whether in meditation or daily life, with deep clarity and kindness." After three days I was nauseated, tired, confused, and defeated.

I took a walk around the grounds to be with what I was feeling. I wanted to sleep late. I wanted to read in the afternoon under a tree. I wanted some peace and quiet. I wanted to do what I wanted to do. I wanted to be happy. At the moment I acknowledged my feelings, I looked down and noticed a large, heart-shaped stone nestled in the dirt at my feet. This salmon gray heart stone fit perfectly in the palm of my hand. One side was smooth and lovely; the other side had an imperfection running down the middle. It had a deep flaw that seemed filled and mended to make it whole. The heart had two sides, and I held it.

I gave into the desires and needs of my body and slept, rested and read. I showed up for the Dharma talks but participated in the sitting and walking only when I could. I was tender and patient with myself. I wanted to be happy.

I loved when Tara shared my favorite passage: "The boundary of what you accept is the boundary of your love." I have wanted no boundaries to my love, and so I have allowed your death into my life completely. I took this and two other insights home with me. I realized the importance of my own physical body in my journey. I sensed my body needed extra care so that it would be strong enough to withstand the rigors of each day. The second gift was permission to completely embrace my own happiness. What a radical concept in light of these past few years. I had a right to live my life completely. I felt a shift inside me.

I noticed my longing and hoped my experience during this retreat had released me from a few more of grief's shackles. I was too often submerged just below the water line. I knew I had come a long way out of the depths. I also knew I had a ways to go.

It is with radical acceptance that I intentionally move away from your death, Kristin, and into myself and into my life.

May 8, 2005:
Mother's Day

I woke up and thought of Kimberly and Kevin today. I sat alone at the kitchen table with my cup of coffee and thought of you on another Mother's Day. I remembered your diary entry from that year. I got up and searched for it.

> *May 10, 1997: This morning I went to my art lesson from 9:30 till 12:00. I am doing a watercolor painting, and I was planning on giving it to my Mom tomorrow, but I'm nowhere near being done. Kevin and I went to the mall to get a present for my Mom. We picked out a statue of two angels. I think she will put it in the garden. I hope she likes it, because Kevin and I thought it was the best statue in the whole store.*

I placed the garden sculpture of the boy and girl angel at the top of the driveway, by the mailbox. Every time I came home, I thought of that Mother's Day in '97. I remembered holding it and feeling slightly uneasy. I wished the sculpture was of three angels. I remembered thinking I have three children, and so three angels should be in my garden. The gift was prophetic. I shuddered at the symbolism that wafted through my consciousness then, and I shuddered this morning at its memory. That day I pushed away the notion of three becoming two.

I read your words and smiled. In my memory your words of love sat side by side with your words of hate. I had the privilege of reading your words, captured in eight diaries written between 1994 and 2001. I read them when I could, when I had the strength. I wanted to understand. I took you in a little at a time before I was overcome with grief. You did not write consistently during those years; you wrote in fits and spurts. I never saw most of what you wrote until after your death. A current of sadness, anger, and self-loathing ran through your life. I now understood its depth and breadth; it infiltrated every aspect of your existence. I wished I had seen your diaries and had read them. I wished I had known. I wished I had been given the chance to help you. You obviously needed help long before things completely fell apart in your senior year. I did not know.

Do you take someone to see a psychiatrist because of what she has written in her diary? Do you take someone to see a psychiatrist who fights with her sister and brother? Do you take someone to see a psychiatrist who fights with her girlfriends one day and is best friends with them the next? Do you take someone to see a psychiatrist who is shy in her relationships with boys and longs for love? Do you take someone to see a psychiatrist when she hates herself one day and thinks she is hot the next? Do you take someone to see a psychiatrist because she hates her nose? I wished for answers.

We took you to see a psychiatrist when you were arrested for shoplifting. We took you to see a psychiatrist when we suspected you were purging and lost weight. We took you to see a psychiatrist when you couldn't sleep and began missing school. We took you to see a psychiatrist when you suddenly became verbally aggressive and out of control. We took you to see a psychiatrist when you were a danger to yourself. We took you to see a psychiatrist when you talked about worms coming out of the bottom of your feet, and when you told us that you knew the secrets of the universe. We took you to a psychiatrist who put you in a day hospital for three days. We took you to see a psychiatrist who put you on medication. We took you to see a psychiatrist who put you in an in-patient ward for three days. We took you to see a psychiatrist when you created a series of classically psychotic pastel drawings. We took you to see a psychiatrist. I wished for answers.

May 21, 2005:
You Should Have Graduated

It was May, and with it came Mother's Day and graduations. The advertisements were everywhere, and there was no way to avoid the reminders. Your friends from middle school and high school were graduating from college this May. I thought of them and wanted to cry; you should have graduated yesterday.

I couldn't help myself as I moved along an edge of pain-filled memories. I remembered middle school. I remembered how you got in the car and slammed the door shut. I knew you had a bad day and asked you if you wanted to talk about it. You said no. You told me how much you hated this girl and that girl. You told me they were not your friends—you called them bitches. You went to your room and slammed the door. I worried about you. Middle school had been so hard. I let you alone and gave you space. Dinner was difficult; you fought with Kimberly and Kevin. You were so angry. Kevin pushed his chair away and said, "Can't you do something with her?" I worried about your pain. I wondered if we should take you to see someone. Dad didn't want to have you seen because he was afraid you would be labeled. He was afraid you would get lost in a psychiatric abyss. I gave in. I did not have the courage to go it on my own. I was unsure and let it go. I would take care of it. I went to your room in the evening, and we sat and talked until there was nothing to say. I encouraged you. I loved you. I searched for your diary when you were gone. I read the horrible words you wrote. They made me afraid. I was afraid of what rage toward others could turn to when directed toward the self. I put your diary back; I did not like intruding on your privacy. I picked you up at school, and you got in the car. You seemed to have had a good day, and yet I wondered at the price of rejection.

That memory faded, and I found myself thinking about your college friends. I remembered the day we moved you into your room on the fifteenth floor; it was a warm sunny day, and we were happy. You loved your room, your yellow bedspread, your *Yellow Dress* oil painting, and most of all the spectacular view of the city. Just seven weeks later you walked down the hall and up a flight of steps to the roof. You sat on the ledge almost directly above your former room. I wondered if your roommates saw you fall. I wondered if *anyone* saw you fall. I wondered about their lives. I wondered if they ever thought of you. I wondered about your relationship with them. I wondered about the cumulative effect on you of unkind words and actions. I wondered at the repeated lacerations to your heart, woven through the fabric of your life from the time you were an adolescent to the moment of your suicide. I wondered at the price of rejection.

I wondered about the boys in your life. You never dated and yet longed for love. I wondered how these rejections touched you as yet another facet of the price we all paid.

> December 24, 1993: Dear Diary, There was a cute boy at church that looked and smiled at me; he was handsome!

> September 28, 1998: He hasn't called me. I'm really mad. I guess he doesn't like me at all. I want him to call me. I know he won't.

> July, 2000: Why aren't you attracted to me? Why don't you like me? Why is she better than me? Tell me. I want the truth. I lost you. You hurt me.

> August 23, 2000: When am I going to fall in love? I want a boyfriend. I want someone to love me. I want to have a relationship. I think of how ugly I am and how little I love myself; how sad, but that is the way I feel. I need to accept my ugliness. Should I get a nose job?

> October 17, 2000: Sex is built up to be the best thing on earth, and it better be. I look forward to it. I wonder who I'm gonna have sex with first?

> January 8, 2001. I want to love. I want a man in my life to fill my emptiness. I'm ugly and fat. Why don't guys think I'm pretty? Why don't they look at me? I'm so sad.

You longed to fit in, to find your place. You never felt you belonged. Where is the line between normal and abnormal? I thought you were normal, but I now see that your movement through the territory of becoming a woman was fraught with suffering, built on the foundation of a destructive self-concept. I was not privy to the depth of your self-loathing or to the insidious daily struggle you endured. You hid a lot.

I remembered when you told me about a middle school sleepover, years after the fact. The girls watched pornography that evening. You said, "I was shocked. I felt abused, almost raped by the images." The experience was unexpected, and you didn't know how to handle it. You were young and innocent. I wondered how it affected you. Why didn't you tell me when it happened? I wondered what else I did not know about. I wanted to be there for you. I thought I was there for you.

I wished I had another chance to talk to you, to help you, to encourage you. I wished our practical conversations and spiritual conversations had made a difference. Why couldn't you see beyond the moment that last night? Why didn't you give yourself a chance? Why didn't you realize the truth of who you were beyond any thought or form? All the wishes on all the stars in heaven will not bring you back. Have I deluded myself, thinking that one more conversation with you would have made it better? I have suffered over what could have been. Regret and guilt washed over me today.

The only place you seemed truly yourself was in your art. You had achieved your dream: you had made it to New York. You were on your way. What happened during those early weeks of college? What happened to your dream and the life you imagined as an artist? What happened when your work was critiqued? Did you simply give up as your grip on this world loosened? I wondered if that was the final straw, a final rejection that you could not come to terms with.

June 4, 2005:
Meaghan's Wedding

Today turned out to be one of the happiest days we've had since your death. We attended Meaghan's wedding. I wondered what this day would be like for us, watching someone so close to your age getting married, watching someone you drove to Notre Dame Preparatory with, watching someone who'd stir memories of all we'd lost with your death. I'd come to realize I could never really be sure how my heart would be on any given day, especially on special occasions. Today was filled with flowers, music, and candlelight. Today's wedding was wonderful in comparison to other weddings we'd attended since your death. It had been years since we'd had such a good time.

I did think of you. There was a place inside that held you and held this wedding at the same time. I noticed that. I felt some hope around Kimberly and Kevin's future. Hope felt wonderful, even if it was fleeting. I watched them struggle along their own healing paths and prayed every day for them. I couldn't fix their brokenness; they had to come to the fixing themselves in ways that made sense for them.

As I sat at the round table with our friends and watched the bride and groom dance, I could not help but think about that wedding in December 2002. I wished we could have gotten out of it, a wedding at Christmas just a year after your death. I was raw and barely held together. We walked in, and I wondered what we were doing. We did not belong. We had just completed our first Kristin Rita Strouse Foundation Yellow Dress Golf Classic. We had just marked the first anniversary of your death. We had just moved through the pain of Thanksgiving. We were bracing ourselves for Christmas. The timing of your death made September, October, November, and December a protracted and intense time of the year. There had been neither relief nor respite from the onslaught of grief since the season began. I wanted to go home. I picked up a drink and stood close to Dad by the table filled with flowers.

People came and talked with us. They were in a festive mood; this was a wonderful celebration, and it was Christmas. Their exuberance was overwhelming. I shifted my body weight onto my other foot as they chattered on endlessly about inconsequential things. Someone made an offhand comment about killing themselves over some stupid thing at their office. They repeated it and continued on, not realizing what they'd just said. I stood there and did not move. I couldn't imagine what I'd heard. How could someone make a comment like that in front of parents whose daughter killed herself a year ago? Were they stupid? Did they have any sense? I felt Dad pull himself up and stiffen beside me. I stood there and said nothing. A response began to take form inside my head: *I am sure you really don't mean what you just said. I am sure you were just kidding. Having lost Kristin to suicide, I know you wouldn't want anybody to suffer in the ways we have suffered.* The words stayed inside my head; I did not have the courage to speak them. People were rude about the things they said. I excused myself and went to the ladies room. I hoped one day I could speak what I kept inside. It was my duty. It was my responsibility to take moments like these and point out society's gross lack of understanding and compassion. I needed some time. I needed to get strong. I would speak out, just not that night. On that particular evening, it was just one of a few comments lacking in sensitivity. Stupid people made stupid comments. It took me over the edge.

This June wedding was different, four years later. This wedding marked a moment I would not forget. I knew the hours spent creating in my studio had made happiness possible. Time in its passage had been kind to me today. I was caressed by the energy of this marriage, which reminded me of my own inner journey, my own sacred marriage that included an ongoing redefinition of who I was. I was grateful for this day of celebration. Thank you for including us.

July 1–3, 2005:
The Compassionate Friends National Conference: Boston, Massachusetts

I decided to apply to the Compassionate Friends National Conference in Boston and was accepted. I was sharing my collage process in a workshop entitled "The Art of Compassion." Dad decided not to come with me. He supported me last year, as a first-time national presenter at the Bereaved Parents of the USA Conference in Charleston. I think the experience was overwhelming for him. It was overwhelming for me, too. We were so new to all of this. It was not easy to be around hundreds of parents from all over the country who had lost children. The grief was palpable. The compassion and understanding between everyone was undeniable. I had come a long way to attempt this national conference by myself.

I felt passionate about sharing my healing process, yet I was afraid to be here all alone. I spent some time in the bookstore last night, looking over the hundreds of books offered on grief, on survival, on healing. I was particularly drawn to a book titled *Dreaming Kevin*. I kept coming back to it, perhaps drawn to the name Kevin. I bought the book and tucked it in my suitcase for later.

Last year Dad and I went to the workshop offered by Mitch Carmody. He lost his son Kelly in 1987 and wrote a book entitled *Letters to My Son: A Journey through Grief*. It was a powerful presentation, and we both loved talking to Mitch afterward. When I walked into the TCF conference ballroom in Boston, it was filled with several thousand people. As I tried to find a place to sit, I saw Mitch in his red bandanna; he was here to present his "Letters to My Son" workshop. I made my way over to sit with him, and he introduced me to his friend and fellow presenter, Carla Blowey, author of *Dreaming Kevin: The Path to Healing*. We all sat together, and I felt an immediate connection to Carla. I went to her workshop and was captivated by her story, her dream, and her spiritual journey. She attended my workshop, and we shared hours together talking. Our conversations made me more aware of my collage work, circle work, dreams, and meditations. She encouraged me to consider a synthesis of the various ways I was exploring healing as a template for work with others. I listened and went home filled with ideas.

July 11, 2005: Fourth Yellow Dress Golf Classic

This was our fourth Yellow Dress Golf Classic. Our ever growing community of family and friends supported us. We stayed positive and focused on life, while addressing the serious issues of mental illness and suicide. We were proud to support the Johns Hopkins Medicine, Department of Psychiatry and Behavioral Sciences: Adolescent Depression Awareness Program; The American Foundation for Suicide Prevention's College Film Project, *The Truth about Suicide: Real Stories about Depression in College*; an art scholarship at your high school; and of course Rita Project.

Last year we showed *The Truth about Suicide: Real Stories about Depression in College*. It was a very emotional evening for everyone, especially because

Kimberly, Kevin, and Kristin were featured in the eighteen-minute teaching documentary. We gave copies to everyone. This year we went out of our way to soften the experience at the same time, embracing the educational opportunity that the event provided. We filled the room with yellow roses and offered a special gift to all participants. My friend Sandy custom-made ceramic hearts inscribed with "Be the One" as a reminder to "be the one to make the difference." People loved the gift. I was sure I would see them sitting on coffee tables and window ledges wherever I went. We were relieved when it was over.

July 19, 2005:
Winds of Change

Over the eleven remaining days of July, I sat under the trees in the backyard and read Carla's book, *Dreaming Kevin*. I knew it would be special after hearing her presentation in Boston. I was overcome by her prophetic dream alerting her to her son's death, and the spirited transmission that would occur for both mother and son. She shared her story with passion. Her healing journey involved finding her way into all the elements of her dream so that she could free herself from the guilt she harbored over Kevin's death. It was real and honest in its description of grief. I connected with her and her journey through grief as I read.

In the space between the pages I turned, I reflected on my retreat with Tara Brach, where I found the heart-shaped stone. I was reminded that I wanted to be happy. I considered Carla's words of encouragement to me; I couldn't separate myself from these notions once they grabbed hold of me.

Since your death, I was much more attuned to my feelings. I couldn't ignore things like I used to; I couldn't set myself aside. I didn't have the capacity. It was not about inner strength—I had no choice in it. It was the way it was. I did not have time for internal conversations, when my thoughts fought with what my gut told me. I did not have patience or the time to waste.

I felt moved by the winds of change. I was aware of a shift in energy around my current work. When you died, I let go of most of my private practice. I was in no condition to provide therapy for anyone, except for a few bereaved clients who somehow found their way to me. I continued to co-facilitate my women's circle with Mary. Mary and I had known each other for years, and our circle met once a month. I felt comfortable with it until recently, when the circle's responsibilities and structure began to weigh heavily on me. I felt out of alignment with its offerings. I wanted to let go in spite of the fact that it had been a place of transformation and healing for both Mary and I and the women who sat with us. It felt over. The doors that connected me with my former ways of working seemed to shut in my face. I felt a spark of excitement around the endings and new beginnings.

August 27, 2005:
Birthday in Maine

I woke up early in the morning and sat on the porch overlooking the water with a cup of coffee. I liked my instant coffee. Kimberly would tease me because it was not real coffee, but it sufficed and I was used to it. The lake was slate gray with a touch of pink from the morning sun reflected along ripples. The trees along the water's edges were reflected back, creating a lovely double border of right side up and upside down. You would have captured the view with a few brush strokes. I didn't feel a crushing pain in my chest like I had on other birthdays. Perhaps it was because we were together, here in Maine, sharing a charming cottage overlooking the water. I was thankful we were together. Our time as a family was precious. I was glad we came here, to someplace new, to someplace not filled with memories.

We brought Kimberly's birthday presents here and decided we would share our birthdays together. Dad and I heard Kimberly coming down the stairs and joined her in the living room. She sat on the green plaid sofa in her pajamas. A small pile of presents rested on the coffee table in front of her. She wanted to open her gifts with just Dad and I. She seemed undone. She held the antique rag doll she'd just opened and began to cry. I held her. The past few days had been difficult. The ravages of your suicide were evident. She was navigating her inner world the best way she could. Therapy usually helped; at other times, nothing helped. We did our best. I worried how the rest of the day would be—it was not even nine o'clock. Everyone else was sleeping.

We got ourselves together and proceeded. Today I turned fifty-five. It was a day of reflection in addition to a celebration as we climbed on rocks along the coast, visited a lighthouse, ate lobster rolls for lunch, and listened to classical music. It had been a summer of letting go, of change.

I was ready to embark down a new path. Meeting Carla in July only crystallized what I already knew deep inside. She brought me the needed measure of clarity that pushed me toward a decision from which there was no turning back. The notion that I could facilitate my own circle, shaped by my experience sitting in Janet's circle, bubbled up early this year and gathered strength through the spring and early summer. It did not appear as a whim, but rather a relentless knocking on my door until I finally acknowledged the guest's arrival. I was blessed with a few women who were willing to step into this offering and explore and grow together. When I returned home in September, I would begin my own circle with Pat, Mary, Lindi, Catherine, and Sabrina. I was excited. My circle, entitled Soul Gatherings, would meet in the space next to the studio.

September 14, 2005:
Butterfly Wings

Collage #19: "Transformation"

Vacation was wonderful. The ease I felt through August continued on into September, except around my last collage piece. I felt a particular tension and exhaustion as I move through this piece, as if I was done. I spent more time playing tennis and working in the garden than I did in my studio. I felt closer to the land these days. There was dirt underneath my fingernails. When I considered my work, I was tired of the raw edges. I was tired of so many pieces. I was tired of the complexity. I was tired of the territory I repeatedly moved over. I was tired and ready to move on.

I was anticipating the beginning of Soul Gatherings and equally excited about starting a once-a-month collage circle. I was enthused about change. When I considered it all, I realized everything I was doing was based on the fact of your death. I would not have gone to see Janet if you were alive. I would not have participated in her weekly circles for the past four and a half years if you were alive. I would not be creating collages if you were alive. I would not be a presenter at the Compassionate Friends National Conferences if you were alive. I would not have met Mitch Carmody and Carla Blowey if you were alive. There would not be any Kristin Rita Strouse Foundation or Rita Project if you were alive. What would I be doing if you were still alive?

In "Transformation" I worked with black and white roses and butterflies.

My left hand is covered in butterflies and partly covers my throat. I am held by my own questioning gaze. Butterflies form the edges; some are torn and broken, but mostly they are whole. I rise out of the ashes of your death. I play with eyes. I emerge out of the gritty field of my own face. One eye is open. One eye is hidden behind the wings of a butterfly. I am born, reborn, and transformed in a delicate field where blacks and whites blend into gray. A single blue butterfly catches my attention, and I paste it down. I feel movement away from your death. It's freeing.

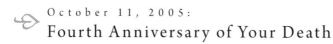

October 11, 2005:
Fourth Anniversary of Your Death

I slept in your bed last night as a way to feel close to you. I wished for a dream, but when I woke I had no memory of one. I was thankful I slept late and stayed for a long time in the comfort of your covers. I felt Sienna's warm little body along my spine; she stretched and licked my hand, nudging me to scratch her belly. None of that distracted my attention away from the fact that this was the fourth anniversary of your death. I felt my heart and slowly began to make note of my feelings. I felt watery and sensed that I was moving at a faster than normal speed inside. After all this time, after so much hard work, I was disappointed and shocked at the intensity of my grief.

I questioned the definition of healing. Had I been operating under some illusion? I realized a truth. There would always be moments when the terrors of your death were as real as any I could remember.

Later that afternoon, I pulled some of the petals off the yellow roses Dad gave me. I stopped by your grave and dropped them over you. There were already flowers there; someone had stopped and swept your marker clean for me. I felt nothing and everything as I stood over you and looked over the manicured greens. As the day moved forward, I felt a certain amount of reprieve. I made one of the dinners you loved. We lit a candle and I went to bed early, anticipating that tomorrow would be different.

December 8, 2005:
New House Dream

I slept in your room again last night. I loved sleeping in your bed, surrounded by your things. I did not share this secret with many people; they would not understand the peace I found wrapped in your covers. I had not dreamed of you for some time. This dream was tender: you came and gave me a Christmas gift.

In my dream, we were in a new house, in the family room. We were joined by Kimberly and Kevin, and we were all happy in this new place. We all looked at the portrait of the three of you, hanging on the fireplace. We knew you were dead and were sad. Then the house split open, and we were outside, where it was all green. There was a shallow stream running downhill. I saw you there resting under the water. I noticed your eyes were open and moving, and I could not believe it. You sat up out of the water, and we began talking. I told you I loved you. I held you. You were alive and beautiful. I called for Dad to come quickly—I wanted him to see you were alive, that you were back. You were not dead. I was relieved, and then I woke up.

I couldn't move and stayed in bed with my eyes closed, savoring the dream. I cried. I missed you so much. My dream stayed with me all day and felt restorative. I wondered if it was preparing me for December. I still disliked Christmas trees, Christmas music, and Christmas lights. I still was annoyed by holiday commercials. Parties were still stressful, with all the talking and excitement. Most of all I hated the word "still," as if one day I would get over your death. There was no getting over you. Although my feelings softened quite a bit over the years, the holidays *still* had the ability to dislodge me from the new normal days to which I clung. I didn't like these dark feelings. When I needed to, I cocooned myself inside and stayed as quiet and removed from it all as possible. January would be here soon.

December 18, 2005:
Sheila's Invitation

Sheila asked me to make a collage in honor of her Temenos Center. The healing, meditation, and personal growth community I participated in was celebrating its years of service. I was thrilled with her request, except for one thing: she wanted the collage on a five-by-eight-inch card. I couldn't imagine working small.

I considered this new form over the holidays, wondering if it was part of the endings and beginnings that had taken place over the past months. Temenos was a Greek word for "sacred space." I wondered if I was entering the new home of my recent dream, a sacred space of rebirth.

December 21, 2005:
Winter Solstice in New York City

Kimberly was not coming home for the holidays, and so we agreed to go to New York and celebrate with her for a few days. Mass transit was on strike, and we found ourselves walking a long distance in the cold to see the show for which we had tickets. It turned out to be a magical night, with all of us bundled up, laughing, and enjoying ourselves. I was surprised at my ability to be in New York with the lights and music. I was just so happy to be with Kimberly and Kevin, whom I missed desperately. I imagined you walking and laughing with us. It was a strange feeling; it did not break me.

We bought a spray of greens with a red ribbon on it and stopped by to place it on the spot where you died. I could not help myself as I looked up those fifteen stories. The harsh reality of your death came rushing in, as if waiting in the wings for just the right moment. I felt nothing and noticed how easily I had left myself. I noticed how wide the pendulum had swung in the past two days. Dad and I drove back to Baltimore in silence.

Ten more days until the new year.

December 25, 2005:
Hugs

Even though we had managed to have a surprisingly good time in New York, I was very apprehensive about Christmas Day itself. There had been no consistency, nothing dependable on which to rely. Each day was separate; I could not anticipate my feelings based on the preceding days. We put up a small live tree, some lights, and a few dragonfly ornaments. I made our favorite lasagna dinner for Christmas Eve. I made a ham, seafood casserole, and poppy seed cake for Christmas breakfast. I tried so hard to make it special. Still, your absence created a vacuum that nothing filled; even the gifts had no real meaning.

Kimberly made other plans, but Kevin was home. I realized that we were still finding our way through these holidays some four years after that first disastrous Christmas in Mexico, followed by an equally disastrous Christmas in Virginia. The level of discomfort was palpable, and I prayed for the hours to pass quickly. However, by early afternoon Dad sat in the kitchen with tears running down his face. Kimberly's absence had exacerbated our sense of loss. He was barely able to speak. He wanted to call his friend Jim, who had also lost his son to suicide. He finally called with encouragement and said, "I just need to talk; I need a hug." We sat and watched as their conversation brought more tears and nods and solace. We took a long walk to help get us through the rest of the day, which ended with dinner and sitting around the dining room table. The doorbell rang, and I went to the door. I could not imagine who would stop by on Christmas evening. There was Jim. He said, "I came over to give Doug that hug." We all cried our eyes out. Jim's visit gave us all the opportunity to talk about our grief rather than trying to make nice. What a perfect ending to one of the most miserable days of the year.

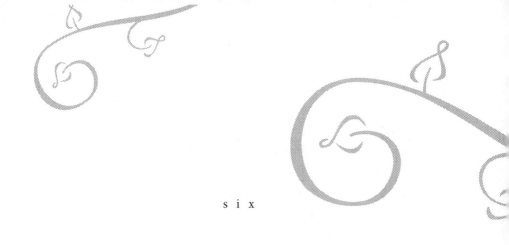

six

the scream

January 3, 2006:
Ease

There was some noticeable ease moving into January, unlike previous years.
The heartache of Christmas Eve and Christmas Day slowly faded. I was not
completely exhausted by September, October, November, and December.
Thankfully, I had strength in me after all. I was curious about what awaited
me this fifth year. Healing was hard work, and I felt resolute as I moved ahead.
I looked forward to the desolate days of winter and to staying inside, rather
than feeling overcome by the darkness like I was in the past. I had a pot of
soup cooking and could smell it all over the house, even in the studio.

January 5, 2006:
New Territory

Collage #21: "The Goddess"

I was ready to take on Sheila's request for a small collage, although the task
felt challenging. I assembled many images, sorted out what I was drawn to,
and discarded the rest. I noticed the resistance I felt. I was used to working

163

large. I noticed my fear and discomfort. I let it be with me as I engaged this new form. This small surface demanded focus. I worked quickly as I entered new territory.

I settled on a nude woman with a snake. I tore her out and positioned her so that she was held within the trunk and branches of a tree. I created a sacred space for her. I felt safe there, just like I felt safe in Sheila's circle. I was contained and protected. I tore apart an image of a mother and child, and I glued them down on the end points of an equilateral cross's vertical axis. I liked the shape of this cross as opposed to the traditional cross shapes I used in the past. It felt more balanced and less associated with suffering and crucifixion. In that space, I felt energy moving freely between us.

I finished in two days. It was extremely satisfying. I captured the moment succinctly and moved on to other important matters beyond my own paper play.

January 14, 2006:
Saint Thomas

We were in Saint Thomas for a week of relaxation combined with Dad's work. It was our annual winter getaway. I remembered our trip to West Palm Beach just fourteen weeks after your death: the warmth felt merciful but was not enough to sustain me. I felt chaotic in the face of what was normal. You killed yourself, and I was in Florida on business, on vacation, taking a time out. I felt insane—the world felt insane. I made no attempt to try to explain what was not explainable. I did not have the language yet.

Today I sat on the porch and watched the sunset without dark intrusive thoughts of you. I felt happy in the moment, and that was all I could ask for. I reached for the island magazine, tore out a few images, and laughed at myself. It was impossible to leaf through a magazine the same way I used to. I tore out what moved me. I placed my pile on the coffee table next to me and picked up the book in which I was engrossed.

Sheila, along with her request of a small collage, recommended *SoulCollage* by Seena B. Frost. I immersed myself in its pages. I said yes, yes, and yes to almost everything Seena wrote. It was powerful reading someone's writings that so eloquently described my own realizations, which

I'd gathered during years of creating my own collages. Although I loved her book, I was inclined to continue in my own comfortable ways. She offered a certain structure whose value I sensed, but I was entrenched in my own process. In my personal collage work, I arrived in the moment and allowed that moment to come into form.

January 19, 2006:
Where Am I with Your Death?

Collage #22: "Silver Death"

When I returned home from vacation, a question arose: "Where am I with your death?" I created my first collage in December 2002 and was curious how I would address your suicide four years into my collage practice. I took out some of my folders dedicated to color and settled into white and silver.

She almost shimmers. She is in a prayer-like position, eyes downcast and arms hidden within the folds of her dress. She is the one. She is pure energy. She is love and holds all of you, both your life and death. The bones are reflected in a mirror. I place the mirror along the front of her silver body. Death reaches her hand out beyond the mirror's frame and drops a red rose into the field.

Your death caused me to look at myself. Whatever I needed to see was reflected back to me. Any illusions I had were shattered in the process: illusions of myself as a mother, a therapist; illusions of pride; illusions that I knew anything; illusions of love, of faith, of trust, of right and wrong. The illusions were endless and painstaking.

Five years later, flesh appears on the hand of the skeleton. Life does come back slowly, bit by bit over a very long period of time. There you are with your bunny rabbit and angel wings. You have a wreath on your head, reminding me of the gold-beaded headband in which we buried you. You wore that headband to your graduation white dance, along with the white angel wings. You loved it. You were sweet and innocent then, and I am able to experience your sweet innocence still, even with your suicide. You are held in silver grace, your blood a rose.

After so many years of dealing with the torments of your shattered body, all broken and bleeding, it was a relief to see you angelic. In that moment, the images of your death appeared spiritual and peaceful.

Death never frightened me. I was drawn to the field of death and dying and fascinated by the process of letting go, especially after hearing a lecture given by Elizabeth Kübler-Ross at Johns Hopkins Hospital. I was in graduate school at the University of Maryland, taking a course in death education. I was impressed by this world-renowned expert and pioneer in the field. She shared drawings done by children suffering with terminal illnesses; those images demonstrated knowledge and acceptance of their ensuing death. The experience impressed me with life's mystery. All these years later, I saw it as a piece of my preparation for my own experiences of death and dying, even though I felt out of sync with the stages of grief, rooted in her work. All the reading in the world did not prepare one for death's reality. Direct experience is the master teacher. None of us escape life; none of us escape death.

January 20, 2006:
Who Am I?

Collage #23: "Golden Creatrix"

I finished "Silver Death" in an hour. The next day, after putting dinner in the oven, another question came into my consciousness: "Who am I?" I had not consciously created in response to a question in the past, yet here was another question, one that I surely engaged over the course of many years. It was as if my whole body asked the question.

I pulled out a bunch of magazines from the basket on the floor. I found a background with snowy branches and gold-filled light. I liked this image of Nicole Kidman dressed in red. I liked the position of her arms, and so I filled her hands with paint brush "swords."

I feel regal, powerful, and in command of my creative energies; they are at my disposal. I feel the solid foundation of rocks underneath my feet. A snake slithers from my artist's pallet, leaving behind the skin it shed. I bask in the light, and it feels good.

When I finished "Golden Creatrix," I brought it upstairs and put it by the sink. I looked at it while doing the dishes. I looked at the brush and powder image I placed behind myself. As I considered the disk of translucent powder, I remembered my ecstasy dream in December 2001. "I am holding a jar of translucent face powder." I made a connection between my dream and this collage and then made further connections with a book, *The Translucent Revolution* by Arjuna Ardagh. He defined translucent people as having "been affected so deeply by a moment of radical awakening that their relationship to who they are and what life is about has been permanently transformed." Your death marked this moment for me. He says translucent people "are not seekers, for they are more interested in the present moment than any future state. They are not followers, for their spirituality is more grounded in direct experience." I found my way into each moment of my journey through my collage practice. I, too, was not "interested in running away from anything or amputating any part of [my] experience." I ran toward it all, brandishing my scissors and glue.

I remembered my snake dream in January 2002. I wrote, "Snakes shed their skin. This dream awakened in me the notion that I was an initiate in a healing process that was multi layered and involved letting go." In the dream, I felt like the snake offered me its medicine when it attached itself to my left shoulder. I believed its medicine had come to me in the form of collage.

February 8, 2006:
Soul Gatherings

My Soul Gatherings circle had been sitting on Wednesday evenings since the beginning of September. Tonight was special. My prompt for the circle was, "You find yourself in water filled with light." In my experience I was in a river that was black, but the banks of the river were light filled. I noticed a slender woman dressed in blue with gold stars standing on a crescent moon. I stepped onto the moon with her, and we descended into the black water. The water became liquid silver, and we became silver. We traveled to the end of the river, which emptied into the universe. We were suspended in the heavens and took in energy that was there. The woman in blue began to paint. I began to paint. We released all our collaged paintings into the heavens, like so many stars. I was reminded, "You are an artist." I was told, "There are no walls around your studio; it is open." I then saw people standing in an endless line holding my creations. They tossed them into the heavens, and they became stars too.

Themes of silver and movement and of throwing and releasing objects into the heavens were part of the other women's experiences, too. As each woman shared, the individual experiences wove together into a collective tapestry of extraordinary beauty. I looked into the faces of two of the women who sat in circle with me; both were bereaved mothers. One was familiar with the work of the circle, having sat with Janet for a number of years. Her son Chris had been killed in a car accident. The other woman was new to sitting; I had met her at an SOS meeting. Her son Christopher had taken his life in January 2004. I now offered them what Janet offered me: a quiet place where their minds found rest and their hearts opened, a place where spirit and dream mixed, a place where there was healing. I felt a sense of satisfaction tonight. I turned off the lights in the studio and walked up the steps. I had a fleeting sense of you and Chris and Christopher as I closed the door. I slept better than I had in a long time.

February 11, 2006:
Taking My Pulse

Collage #24: "Blue Wisdom"
Collage #25: "Two Elephants"

A few weeks went by before I came back into the studio, and when I did, it was exciting. I created two collages in one week, an hour here and an hour there, and I was done. I found it practical to select one image and use it as a background. It was how I began. It was simple.

In "Blue Wisdom," water falls through a field of green trees. I think of a column of pure light and the experiences of healing that have come to me. I am lifted up. You are nowhere to be seen in this collage and yet you are everywhere.

My next collage, "Two Elephants," came out of an experience at Janet's. I still sat with Janet even though I had begun a circle of my own, because my time in Janet's circle was invaluable. In my experience there were two elephants. You were riding on top of one elephant; while the other elephant put its trunk down and lifted me onto its back. We rode down a path together and entered a cave. The elephant's flesh fell away, and there were only bones left. I stood on the elephant bones. I was on a grave site. The bones became liquid and filled an ink well. Someone said, "Write down the bones." I began to write on black paper and sang over the bones.

On my way home I kept hearing the words "Writing down the bones" repeated over and over again in my mind. I thought of Natalie Goldberg's book, *Writing Down the Bones;* I'd read it many years ago and loved it. When I got home, I searched for it, pulled it from the shelf, and took it to bed with me. I randomly opened it and read, "We must become writers who accept things as they are, come to love the details, and step forward with a yes on our lips so there can be no more noes in the world, noes that invalidate life and stop these details from continuing." She went on to say, "You must add the heat and energy of your heart accept what is and put down its truth." It was powerful, and I felt the urge to write and to create from my experience.

I cut out the elephants from the dry desert environment they are in and place them in a lush forest, underneath an illuminated tree house. I like the idea of moving them out of the wasteland and into an environment teeming with life. The elephants support my house. You stand on the roof of my house and release black and red butterflies from their cage. You are not in my house, in my space, but outside of what is mine. I imagine a fresh breeze moving through the rooms of my tree house, rooms that are open to life's breath and free from your constant presence. A single snake makes its way up a staff, reminding me of the medical symbol for healing, the caduceus. It rests beneath my home. The sun rises just behind your head.

My collage was separate from my circle experience. I did not worry about it; it was born from the fertile ground of elephants bones. As I looked at my creation, I remembered you loved elephants and had a collection of them. I brought them down to the studio and placed them on the bookshelf behind me. I was reminded of the Hindu elephant god Ganesha, worshiped for his ability to clear the path and remove obstacles.

February 15, 2006:
Grief Gifts

Collage #26: "Held"

I had lunch today with a group of ladies that got together socially every couple of months. We had all lost children. We were seated at a large table right in the middle of the restaurant, surrounded by unsuspecting others. We looked normal. Our conversations were anything but normal. This was a place where we could talk about the mystery of butterfly visits, yellow birds, finding pennies, seeing special numbers, and all the ways we felt our children move in close. We shared the difficulties that came up in the course of our everyday lives like birthdays, anniversaries, and holidays. We talked about ourselves and our grief journeys. I wondered if those who were seated close to us caught any bits of our conversations. I wondered if they noted the laughter as well as the tears.

Over the course of our lunches together, I sat with a mother who lost her son in a skiing accident, shortly after which her husband died of a brain tumor. I sat with a mother whose son committed suicide, a mother who lost her son in the Twin Towers, a mother whose only daughter was killed in a car accident in Spain, a mother whose daughter died in the Pan Am crash in Lockerby, a mother who lost a son to a freak head injury and blood clot, a child who happened to be a classmate of Kevin's when he was in middle school, and a mother whose son was struck by an intoxicated driver. We were survivors. We all had something to say even though each of our experiences were different. Those of us who were further along reached out and helped the new ones. That was how it worked: we were gifts to each other. I enjoyed sharing my meditative and creative processes with them. They were interested in what I was doing. This ladies lunch was special, and I felt uplifted when I returned home.

Perhaps it was the Valentine's season that took me into the red. Perhaps it was my time at lunch with so many courageous women. Perhaps it was the first image I came to when I dove into my files, for the hand holding red rose petals drew me in. I remembered opening the red folder in search of images as I explored rage in "Rage: Code Red." I found it interesting that I opened that same folder in search of love.

I cover my face in mesh and sparkling sequins. I am "Held." You see me and you don't see me. I feel protected as layers are peeled away, revealing a final, delicate inner core. My charcoaled eyes are exposed but my mouth is covered. Instead of the word "suicide" plastered on my forehead, two rag dolls rest in that space. One doll is black and one doll is white; they sit together. I am light and dark, right and wrong, alive and dead. I create and I destroy. It's all there, and I let it be as it is. There is stillness.

February 18, 2006:
Painting

Something happened this month, and that was my interest in the back of the small collages. I felt drawn into their emptiness. I felt the invitation to paint. It was a terrifying notion. I treaded into your territory, Kristin. Your paints and brushes sat behind the closet's closed doors, but I felt them calling. In a fit of courage, I pulled your tubes of paint out, placed my fingers on those tubes, and pressed, just like you had done years ago. I tentatively painted on a thin layer of silver. I don't know why, but then I placed my fingertips into your paint and rested my hand in it all. I touched it, left my mark. You literally rest in the palm of my hand. "Silver Death" is on the reverse side.

I had the whole day to myself, a Saturday with no obligations. I loved being in the studio with the morning light. I felt on a roll with my silver success and decided to continue. I lined up my other recent collages and continued to explore with your brushes and paint. The more I played, the more free I became. I moved from silver to gold. I experimented with symbols, obliterating one and adding another until I settled on the spiral for "Golden Creatrix." I wished you were here.

February 19, 2006:
Dripping

Collage #27: "Blood Rabbit"

During my painting process I had the notion of your blood and paint mixing together. It was not a disturbing notion but more a passing fancy. It came over me in the shower and while I drove to tennis; it came over me while

I was ironing and before bed. I finally had no choice and gave into what exerted itself on my consciousness. I entered the studio, and it took about ten minutes to complete "Blood Rabbit." I felt as though the entire image was downloaded like a dream.

Paint drips like blood into the form of a cross that releases a single rose into a field of red. You look out at me over your shoulder. Is that you or is that me? Am I the one being born out of all that blood? Are you the black rabbit looming just behind me? A single large red rose pushes its way into the frame. The blood becomes beautiful. Something releases inside of me as I allow the blood to become something else. The white on the right side of the collage seems to bring balance to the darkness. I like the movement in this piece; the paint flows.

On February 23, after lunch with a friend, I painted the back red. It took me hours to get the tone just right. It seemed flat and boring once it dried, and so I added a swirl of red right out of the tube. I then added a section of a black spiral in the upper corner. I had a sense of the path I moved along, and that was comforting. I was finding my way in the paint, in the mixing. I missed you and wished you were here to help me. You had such an amazing eye for color.

I loved watching you when I could. I would sneak down the steps to the basement to steal a quick glimpse of you. You always knew when I was lurking in the shadows, and you would stop for a break and invite me in. You liked to be alone with your work, and I always respected your needs around your creative life. I took what I could and savored the moments when you let me in.

Your paint sat on the floor at my feet. I was thankful for the spills and splatters of color that reminded me of you. I felt you as I ran my hands over the mess you made. You came to me in the paint. When I was done, the swirl of paint on the back side of this collage looked blood-like. I was drawn once again into the heartache of it all.

February 23, 2006:
Alchemical Colors

The colors that emerged in "Blood Rabbit" were black, red, and white. They were considered the three alchemical colors of transformation symbolically representing birth, life, and death. In *Women Who Run with the Wolves*, Clarissa Pinkola Estés said, "These colors also represent old ideas of descent, death, and rebirth—the black for dissolving of one's old values, the red for the sacrifice of preciously held illusions, and the white as the new light, the knowing that comes from having experienced the first two." She went on to say,

> Black is the color of mud, the fertile and the basic stuff into which ideas are sown. Yet black is also the color of death, the blackening of light.... It is also associated with that world between worlds.... Black is the color of descent. Black is a promise that you will soon know something you did not know before.... Red is the color of sacrifice, of rage, of murder, of being killed. Yet red is also the color of vibrant life, dynamic emotion, arousal, Eros, and desire. It is a color that is considered strong medicine for psychic malaise.... White is the color of the new, the pure, the pristine. It is also the color of soul free of the body, of spirit unencumbered by the physical. It is the color of the essential nourishment, mother's milk.

I also felt my connection to the Sumerian's myth of Inanna when I looked at "Blood Rabbit." Just like Inanna, I went into the underworld the moment you died and have traveled in its darkness. I was stripped bare and hung on a meat hook. It helped me through, knowing that in the end there was light.

In *Descent to the Goddess: A Way of Initiation for Women*, Sylvia Perera said, "The hardest descents are those to the primitive, uro-boric depths where we suffer what feels like total dismemberment.... These deepest descents lead to radical reorganization and transformation of the conscious personality. All descents provide entry into different levels of consciousness, and can enhance life creatively." There was something reassuring about knowing that others had gone before me. There would be others following me through this timeless dimension; perhaps my personal way through would be of service. I knew my creative process was in service to my healing and provided me the map I needed.

February 28, 2006:
Thank You

Four years ago today we met Dr. Kay Redfield Jamison. I did not know at the time that Kay Jamison was in the midst of her husband dying; he would die a few months after our meeting. Grief in many forms sat around the table of the Johns Hopkins Hospital, Tower Restaurant: the grief of a father, the grief of a sister, the grief of a mother, and the grief of a wife. She was in the midst of a living death while we were in the midst of the place she would step into, death in its final fixed form. We were unto ourselves, unaware of others around us. Grieving people seem to recognize one another, and so there was tenderness that day. We were thankful that she supported us as she moved through her own personal grief. She was a gift.

I was unsure of everything. In the weeks and months following our meeting with Dr. Jamison, when Kimberly questioned her dream and when I questioned our resolve, it was Dr. Jamison's words I recalled: "Yes, you can do it." Those precious moments moved Rita Project forward, out of the dimension of your sister's dreams, into the realm of possibility, and on toward reality. Five years later, Rita Project continued to offer open art studio services in New York City to those who had lost someone to suicide or had attempted suicide. Rita grew.

There are plans to open studios in Los Angeles and Baltimore. Fundraising benefits in support of Rita Project included readings from noted authors: Mariel Hemingway, *Finding My Balance: A Memoir*; Sarah Arvio, *Visits from the Seventh*; Maud Casey, *The Shape of Things to Come*; Nell Casey, *Unholy Ghost*; Edward Hirsch, *Lay Back the Darkness*; and Andrew Solomon, *The Noonday Demon*. In 2003, your sister introduced the documentary *The Truth about Suicide: Real Stories of Depression in College* for the American Foundation for Suicide Prevention's (AFSP) annual gala. Both she and Kevin appeared in the film. In addition, Kimberly served as a keynote speaker at the Johns Hopkins Medicine's Eighteenth Annual Mood Disorders Research/Education Symposium, as well as the Children's Mental Health Forum: Best Practices and Next Steps, sponsored by the Mental Health Association of New York City. Rita Project traveled to Dublin, Ireland, presenting workshops at the 3Ts Conference, "Suicide in Modern Ireland: New Dimensions, New Responses."

Kimberly was chosen New Yorker of the Week by NY1 News in a segment that included coverage of the Rita Studios NYC. Rita Project provided workshops in several New York City high schools, and in October it will travel to Oregon State University and provide suicide prevention education workshops. Kimberly continued on, devoted to the arts to help survivors of suicide. She made a difference. Rita, for truth, Rita for love, in your name, Kristin Rita.

March 12, 2006:
Signs of Spring

Collage #33: "Ascension"

I enjoyed the uplifting feeling of March as one season gave way to another, as winter let go into spring. It was not always the case. I remembered how I hated the light that broke my communion with the darkness of winter. I hated the crocus and the daffodils that pushed their way through. I remained dead and felt that deadness more severely as all around me grew. I couldn't help but reflect on your suffering, as your illness came to fullness during these same months. I wondered how painful a time it was for you, because you too had to endure the disparity between your internal darkness and the light of spring. It is no wonder there is an increase in the rate of suicides in the spring.

Today happier memories moved through me. I enjoyed the moment. My collage captured movement, change, and my feelings. I arose on a shaft of gold and moved toward a single large diamond sparkling with light. It felt like I was being moved by liquid gold. A field of diamonds supported my movement upward toward the larger diamond. My journey seemed located along the face of a sheered rock that was breaking up and becoming infused with shafts of light.

I appear naked, exposed, and vulnerable. I cover part of my face in my ascent. My eyes are barely visible; my neck is exposed.

I felt a lot of creative energy coming to me from the images on the paper. I discovered that diamonds were treasured for their healing properties; they removed toxins from the body. Diamonds were given to the one you love and stimulated unity and love for self and others. I liked this new self. I liked this process of discovering who I was as a consequence of your suicide.

March 26, 2006:
Home with Minuit

It was wonderful spending time in New York with Kimberly and Kevin. We celebrated Kevin's twenty-sixth birthday. We had dinner together in a little restaurant in the West Village. Kevin made time for us and returned to work after our visit. I worried about how hard he was working. I didn't think he was happy and sensed little joy around him.

I wished my children lived closer. It was difficult having them so far away. I missed the casual visits and relaxed Sunday dinners that other families shared. We were alone most of the time, which made the suffering around your death much more severe. I cherished these rare moments when we were together. I was also in the city to pick up Kimberly's toy poodle, Minuit. Kimberly was scheduled to leave the next day for a few months' work in California.

Kimberly slid her five-pound gray poodle through the car window and into my lap. She gave her one last kiss. I had agreed to watch Minuit during this time, however as I began to pull away, I said, "Kimberly, I feel nervous about this. What if something should happen to her? She is so little, and *I could not survive it.*"

Kimberly laughed and reassured me that nothing would happen. "She will be just fine."

I drove off with Minuit nestled in my lap while my heart skipped a beat. From the moment Kimberly laid eyes on Minuit, she felt she was special; she was sweet and precious and filled with puppy love. I felt a deep sense of responsibility as I brought her home. I wondered how old Sienna would react to this new addition.

April 13, 2006:
At My Waist

Collages: #34 "Corseted"

I was glad it rained today, for April's showers provided just the right excuse, a break in my routine. I was planning the Kristin Rita Strouse Foundation's Yellow Dress Golf Classic, which was two months away. We wanted to make it special. I was running around gathering auction items, working on table decorations and updating the information on our website. There was a lot to do. Today I took time for myself.

As I leafed through magazines, I realized I was not in the grasp of suffering like I was during the first year of creating. My collages were not grounded in the pain of your death. I understood what was apparent in the color, form, and content of my early creations; they seemed very straightforward. I was in the wound of your death.

My most recent collages were different. There was an air of mystery about them, meanings that seemed veiled and just beyond my grasp. I sat and witnessed the forms that seemed to be creating me, like this one. I could not resist this image.

I cannot take my eyes off the hand that covers the throat. I look off to the right with a pensive questioning expression. My eyes are charcoaled black like they were in "Once Upon a Time." I do not have the word "suicide" plastered on my forehead; instead I cover my head with an ornate black hat made of feathers and net. I appear delicate, perhaps fragile. A black cinched corset draws my attention; it forms the left side of my throat-clenching self.

I wondered at the meaning and had a sense of something tender emerging out of the thing that bound me. I found images of bent silver metal that went perfectly with the black bodice, producing a palate that moved softly through whites, grays, and blacks. I heard you inviting me once again to come into the middle ground and into the balancing light that is gray. I liked the interplay between the intricate fabric and the cold steel, which buckled under pressure. I wondered what had collapsed inside of me under the pressure of your death. Torn edges and cracks appeared, not too many but just enough to indicate the brokenness. A tell-tale bit of snake skin decorated the left bottom corner—snakes, symbolic of death and rebirth. I could have left it off, but it called to me, and I pasted it down.

I place a diamond and pearl broach at my waist, at my waste. I am awash in energy that makes me as cold as the steel before me. The hair on my arms stands at attention. I am struck by the play of words. I sit still and do not move. I place one hand over my belly and the other hand at my throat. A chill runs through me.

April 15, 2006:
In the Mail

Collage #35: "Yellow Bird Cage"

I walked down the driveway with the day's mail. The fragrance from the lilac bush caught my attention as well as the earth in our garden that was dark, moist, and fertile. I noticed my visceral response to its aliveness. I placed the mail on the countertop near the chips and scratches you created when you smacked your car keys down in a fit of rage, years ago. I felt alive today. I leafed through a store catalogue, a tantalizing treat I always looked forward to for the color and forms rather than the merchandise. A yellow bird cage caught my attention. I envisioned a yellow chair image, Van Gogh's *Bedroom at Arles* next to it. My day's work was done; dinner was ready to go in the oven. I had some time to myself. I was captivated by what just popped into my mind.

The bird cage and chair work well together. They invoke associations, and I sense you flying away, released from the cage of your mental illness, and me released from the suffering of your death. I look at the empty chair and feel into my own experience of emptiness that transformed over the past five years.

We went from five chairs to four chairs to three chairs to two chairs. We sat at the table with two chairs, and it was too much to bear. We placed a third chair at the table and formed a triangle; the apex remained empty.

April 17, 2006:
Van Gogh

The chair in "Yellow Bird Cage" was Van Gogh's chair, and it sparked memories of driving with you to Washington DC to enjoy the Van Gogh exhibition at the National Gallery together. We had such a wonderful day strolling through the exhibition rooms and experiencing his great works. You admired this painter for years and made a wonderful paper collage of his *Café Terrace at Night*. It was selected for your high school art show at Notre Dame Preparatory.

Over the years you painted several self-portraits in Van Gogh's style. I remembered looking at them and feeling an unsettling darkness coming to me through your strokes. You said, "I love his use of paint. I love the light, the color, the quick strokes he uses." I told myself that you were just copying what you admired. When I revisited this all again, I felt so desperate and deadly wrong. I missed what you were saying. You recognized something in him before your own mental illness emerged. We went to see Monet at the Walters Art Gallery. You did not copy Monet—you copied Van Gogh. You copied Van Gogh, and I could not see what was before my own eyes. I felt your souls converging. You were forever joined together in suicide. I imagined you and Vincent painting together on the other side, in the light. I played Josh Groban's "Vincent" and cried. I played it again and again and cried some more.

I came across a black rabbit and knew just where to place it. I had a box filled with little images, random cuttings that I knew I would use. I placed you on the chair and imagined you and Vincent together. I marked the space with yellow roses and offered a prayer for the both of you.

I fall and reach for you, but it is too late. I do not particularly like myself in this collage, but I have no choice: I am the one in the yellow dress.

I placed myself there in that exact spot, not somewhere else, and that was it. I did not like the expression on my face. I looked dead, and it reminded me of the moment I died when I received the call from the police that you were dead.

I do not like the bulging, strained curve of my neck. My neck is exposed as I tumble forward and reach for you. I take comfort in the fact that we are awash in yellow light.

April 21, 2006:
Lungs

Collage #36: "Green Crocodile"

I looked outside my kitchen window. Green was everywhere, and I was saturated with it. I was filled with its loving and compassionate light. All shades of green moved into the studio from the outside world and became the inspiration for my collage.

A crocodile weaves its way through a fern. Its imposing foot forms an umbrella canopy over my head. I cannot decide if the crocodile is there as protection, or if it is going to crush me. I stand on top of a coffin. A diamond tie cascades through the center of the collage and forms a crown for my head. I stand on the coffin's edge, on the midpoint of fern covered lungs.

I painted the back a soft green and added a bit of a yellow spiral in the lower right hand corner. I liked the splash of yellow; it drew me to the center of my journey.

There was an alligator in my walled garden dream in 2001, and I wondered about the connection. "There is a very large alligator sleeping just beneath the surface. As we continue to look, it becomes translucent. We begin to notice that there are some blue structures in the area of the heart. They look like rectangular boxes stacked one on top of another. We are afraid of disturbing the alligator. It begins to stir in the dark rich mud."

I got curious and decided to do some research on the symbolism of alligators. I discovered the alligator was symbolic of initiations, of endings and beginnings. The alligator was associated with primal, primitive energies that brought knowledge and wisdom. Knowledge and wisdom sounded appealing, however I had no interest in primal, primitive energies. I'd had enough heartaches over the years and welcomed the peace-filled days that tipped the scale toward normalcy each month.

I wondered about my dream, the reference to the blue boxes in the heart of the alligator. I associated boxes with gifts. Blue was the color I associated with the throat chakra, where the alligator's foot rested in this recent collage. I tucked this green alligator into the wooden box that held my small creations.

May 3, 2006:
Silhouette

Collage #40: "Clenched Heart"

The first week of May was easier this year. Mother's Day itself, with all the memories associated with it, still broke my heart. I sometimes hated turning the pages of the calendar because I knew that each month was peppered with its share of birthdays, anniversaries, and an ongoing assortment of holidays. I hated feeling clenched and bound by my sadness, even though those days were far fewer than they were at the beginning. I found myself leaning into all of it. It all mixed together, the dark dreary days along with bright colorful ones. This year marked five Mother's Days without you. It had gotten easier to endure. Dad said he would do anything I wanted. I sent him to play golf because I wanted to be alone. I didn't want to go out and be in the presence of families all celebrating Mother's Day. The fact that I was mother to Kimberly and Kevin had not offset my failures where you were concerned. I felt your death today. I couldn't help it, and so I went into my studio, free of distractions and obligations.

I found a profile done in black-and-white marble—at least, it looked like marble.

I feel cold inside, and so I relate to the coldness of the material. I remember how cold I was during the first weeks of your death. The cold is penetrating in its totality.

I remembered it eventually eased, yet I remained impervious. I worked on my stone self, chipping away pieces and hoping to reveal what was buried inside. I worked hard. I wanted to feel soft. I wanted to touch the one who loved her life and the world around her. I wanted her released completely. I related to the play of light and dark in the marble. My eye socket and mouth were black. Perhaps I had further to go than I imagined.

I placed a solid black silhouette along the cheek and neck of the marble background; they both looked away. In the center of the blackness, a fist arose and clenched a beating heart. I used three simple images.

Sometimes I still feel as if my heart is outside my body, raw and exposed for everyone to see, especially on days like these. I am glad these days are intermittent rather than pervasive. My collage is a perfect representation of how Mother's Day feels. I love it, and its creation has made the day so much easier to bear. It is real and honest.

May 18, 2006:
Wanting a Miracle

Aunt Elizabeth told me someone very special from India would be in the area. Sri Karunamayi was considered a holy woman, a living saint. I did not hesitate to take advantage of this rare opportunity. I was open to receiving healing in as many ways as I could; I never regretted taking advantage of the silent retreat with Tara Brach, or a week at Omega with Brian Weiss studying past-life regression. I really had no idea what I was getting into when I took on these healing adventures, but they turned out to be rich and transformative. Certainly my devotion to exploring my own healing through the creation of my collages was not quite mainstream, and so traveling to be in the presence of Sri Karunamayi was not really very much of a stretch.

I played my interclub tennis match with Kathy early in the morning, drove two hours, and then waited in line for four hours to have a few minutes with Sri Karunamayi. As I sat in the sacred space of this Hindu Temple, I watched hundreds of people write their longings on little white cards. They solemnly approach Sri Karunamayi, bowed their heads, and listened to the soft words she offered them. The energy in the room was potent, marked by the serious intentions of those who came before her. On my card I wrote, "Please bless my child, who is in spirit. Please ease the suffering of my loss. Please bless my work, so that I reach my full potential." She placed her hands on my head and said she would help with my grief.

As I left late in the afternoon, I wanted a miracle from Sri Karunamayi. I wanted her to make it better, whatever "better" was. I wanted to feel the entire weight of the past five years lifted from me. I wanted to wake up and feel something different. I wanted all the remaining darkness removed, and I wanted to be filled with light. I had been on a pilgrimage of healing, my path marked by traditional therapy, my creative process, meditations, dreams, and service to others. I still felt distanced from a place I imagined as healed, aware that just below the surface ran the torrent of your death.

I wanted a miracle and got a miracle. It was neither gentile nor kind. Was it a force of nature that dropped me back into the violent flow of grief and guilt? Was it coincidence? I should have been more careful and more precise in what I asked for. Miracles are funny that way.

May 23, 2006:
The Scream

It was quite an adjustment having two poodles. Sienna was seven years old and used to being the queen of the house. She had not done particularly well in sharing her space with this new little bundle of love. Minuit was sweet beyond compare and had brought us joy. My routine with the dogs was down to a science, gates and leashes in place, with my heightened concern easing as the days warmed.

It was such an exquisitely beautiful May afternoon, and I worked in the garden and read outside for a bit. The sky was a deep blue, just like the day you died. I was happy and heading for a shower before making dinner. Sienna and Minuit were in the kitchen together. I stepped over the gate and made my way toward the upstairs, and then I stopped and turned around to attend to Minuet's barking. She was calling to me in her most tender way, and I could not resist her plea to be with me upstairs. I scooped her up and, in a moment of joy and happiness, swung her into the air and brought her down for a kiss. I said, "Look, Minuit, you are flying," and again I swooped her in the air, and suddenly … she was falling.

Minuit was falling out of my hands and onto the cold marble floor. Minuit was falling right in front of your Yellow Dress painting at the foot of the stairs. Minuit was not moving. She lay on her side and did not move. I clutched her to my chest, pleading to God that she be all right. I felt her heart beating as I ran up the stairs, but she was not breathing. I collapsed on the floor at the foot of our bed, pleading once again, *God no.* Perhaps she knocked herself out; perhaps she had a seizure. She was not moving, she was not breathing. I breathed for her. I joined my mouth to her little mouth and released my breath into her body, and I screamed. I screamed and screamed as I fell into a million pieces. I called for you to help me. *Kristin, please help me, please, please help me.* I held Minuit. I held you, Kristin. I held her. I tried to save her, but deep inside I knew I could not save her. There was nothing I could do—she was dying. I fell completely into the horror of what was happening. I fell onto the bed with her and screamed. I clutched Minuit to my heart. I clutched you to my heart. I ran my fingers through her fur, through your hair. I kissed her and pleaded and pleaded for a miracle. I felt her heart slowing. I felt your heart slowing. I felt her heart slowing right next to mine. I screamed and screamed. Her little heart stopped. She was warm in my arms as she left her body. You were warm in my arms as you left your body. I do not know why, but I ran to your room, Kristin, and stood screaming while my own warm urine ran down my legs. I screamed a scream of death, a scream that had been waiting to rise out of the earth through me all these years: the scream of the mother for her child.

I called Dad. By the time he arrived, I had moved through the whole house cradling Minuit and sobbing. He joined me in the bedroom and collapsed on the bed himself, crying and broken. We screamed together, embracing and falling together into a grief so pervasive that we disappeared for a time. We had descended into the bowels of the underworld. We cried for Minuit, we cried for you, and we cried for ourselves. We cried now in ways we had not cried when you died. We cried and dropped into hell.

Shortly after Dad arrived, Grandma and Aunt Donna came into this mad house. They had no idea how to help a screaming Sharon carrying a dead dog around the house. They told me to stop and to get a hold of myself. They were gripped with fear while I was deeply aware that what was happening was much bigger than Minuit. I turned my eyes upon them and said, "I will not be quiet, I am going to scream as much as I want. I never screamed when Kristin died. I am screaming now, and there is nothing you can do to stop me. There is nothing you can do to help me."

They were sucked into a vortex of grief, desperate to control what could not be controlled. In fact, they served as the voice I needed to hear in order to speak my truth, not only to them but to all the countless others that make up the face of our society, which struggles in its inability to bear witness to death's ravages. For a very brief moment we stood in frozen silence. I could feel energy entering my heart and the hearts of everyone there, connecting and weaving together experiences of your death that had been missing or cut off, as well as opening to the moment just as it was. I could feel the completed tapestry of grief coming into form as we all stood there in the kitchen. My mom and sister were with me to finally witness the agony that I silently bore myself that early morning when we learned of your death. Something very deep within all of us shifted, connecting Minuit and you. I felt like I was floating in timeless space. I felt our hearts breaking open yet enveloped in love.

Within moments of my experience with my mother and sister, my friend Adhikari came in the door. I somehow knew that I would need her pure presence and had called her to come and be with me. I knew I would need someone who was not afraid and someone who knew the territory into which I had descended. She did not say anything, because there were no words in the face of this other death. She opened her arms and held me close. Minuit's dead body rested between our two beating hearts. We stood in the exact spot that I had picked up her little limp body, just at the foot of the stairs, beneath the painting of your Yellow Dress. Adhikari was calm and quiet. She did not try to fix what could not be fixed. She did not tell me to be quiet or to take hold of myself. She entered into the space of my grief and was there with me.

We walked upstairs and lay on the bed together. Adhikari encircled me as Minuit lay on my chest. That simple gesture of embrace said everything: "I touch you in this untouchable place, I am not afraid to be with you in the darkness." I continued to cry as grief overtook my heart. Dad, Grandma, and Aunt Donna sat quietly at the foot of the bed. I lay there and began to allow the words to take form that would give expression to the realizations that were coming to me around this death and your death. She fell. You fell. She fell out of my own hands. You fell beyond my reach as mother. Minuit gave me the opportunity to hold her as she died. As I held her, I felt as though I was holding you. I felt as though I was being given the opportunity to be with you in your death. There was nothing I could do to save her, and there was nothing I could have done to save you. I was given the opportunity to scream my scream that had been silenced in the traumatic moment of hearing of your death. This little gray poodle gave me the opportunity to be whole in a way that I could not, had I not experienced and re-experienced death in its totality.

Death arrives when it arrives; it does not care about what is happening. Pure joy can turn to pure sorrow in an instant, and suddenly the world shifts. People have a hard enough time with "normal" deaths, so it is no wonder the effect that sudden shocking deaths have. These particular kinds of loss frighten people, and that fear takes them into places in which they shut down and become ineffectual as compassionate helpers. Death marks an ending of life as one has always known it and opens the door to the unknown. It dissolves all form and casts one into timeless space. I am not too sure that modern society has done a very good job with helping those who find themselves held within death's grasp.

May 24, 2006:
Telling Kim

I couldn't sleep. I got out of bed and went downstairs to the family room until daybreak. I turned on the fire in the fireplace and sat in its reflection, wrapped in a blanket on the sofa. I watched the minutes pass. We waited until noontime, a reasonable hour to call Kimberly in Los Angeles. Dad and I agonized over how to tell her. At one point I considered taking a flight out there to tell her in person. As the phone rang, I slid out of myself as I had before, when I told Kimberly of your death and held her as she screamed. My voice was a whisper and cracked as I said her name. I emptied myself of Minuit's death. Kimberly listened quietly. In a moment of silence, I braced for her response. She was calm and compassionate. She was more concerned for me than anything. "Mom, I'm so sorry, it's okay, it was an accident." We talked, and I continued to cry as she soothed and reassured me. I was relieved when I hung up. I was appreciative of her understanding. I went upstairs, pulled the shades down, and got under the covers.

June 2, 2006:
The Yellow Dress

I felt the same as I did in the weeks after your death, because Minuit had taken me back there again. All the feelings I prayed I'd never experience again surfaced. I couldn't do anything but what was required, and then I just sat. The world was too painful again. I had no skin—I was just energy moving. There was a difference, and that was my level of awareness and realization about what was happening. It was a completely normal response to trauma and grief. I was not terrified like I used to be. It would pass; I just didn't know how long it would take. I intended to be as open to my feelings as I could. I realized I had been given the opportunity to revisit grief and to continue to mend what was broken. I was given the opportunity to go very deep. I had that crushing pain in my chest, as if my heart had been removed. There was an empty space through which my breath moved in and out. It was not my lungs that breathed, but my whole body was breath moving through and around every piece of myself. I asked Sri Karunamayi for a healing miracle, but I never thought it would come to me like it did.

Minuit's death came just weeks before our fifth Yellow Dress Golf Classic for the Kristin Rita Strouse Foundation. This was always a stressful time. With Minuit's death, it felt more highly charged. I wondered what the five-year anniversary would be like. I had the notion that after committing so much of myself to healing, this would be easy. I never anticipated any of this.

Since rendered incapable again, enmeshed with your death, I was even more grateful for my studio space. I was busy making special center pieces for the event tables this year. I took a picture of your yellow dress painting, made thirty copies, and glued them on small canvases. I added a thin layer of clear acrylic paint. I spent time with each of the images, creating brushstrokes to give the feel that each was a miniature original. My hand mimicked the movement of your hand over and over again. I could not help but feel the impression of an owl beneath my fingertips. I always thought the bodice of your dress painting had an owl-like appearance. Yes, your yellow dress definitely had an owl-like appearance.

I will place your *Yellow Dress* on miniature pine easels. Together with some yellow flowers, they will make a statement and secure your presence in the hearts of those who attend our event.

June 5, 2006:
Stillpoint

I arrived in Manchester, New Hampshire, in a fragile condition for the fourth and final module of training at the Stillpoint School of Integrative Life Healing. This year I gifted myself with personal study in an area I was interested in: energy healing. I notified Meredith, the director, teacher, and mentor, of my condition. I shared what happened to Minuit. She listened, which gave me comfort.

This morning she privately spoke to me about sharing my story with about seventy-five students and faculty. Meredith said, "I will stand right next to you. Whatever you say will be enough." My heart began to beat quickly in recognition of what was being asked of me. I was being given the opportunity to openly talk about your fall, Minuit's fall, my scream, and the interweaving of time and circumstances that offered healing. I agreed.

She called me to her side, and I felt her support. My voice quivered at the beginning. Steady, steady, steady, and my story flowed. There was complete silence as tears fell. I shared it all. I shared more than I could have imagined, and in the end there was stillness. When I finished, Meredith took a silver chain with a silver heart on it from around her neck, and she placed it over my head. Everyone in the room stood and began clapping. I opened my heart completely in public. I spoke my truth. Gifts come in a variety of packages.

June 12, 2006:
Fifth Yellow Dress Golf Classic

I wore a yellow dress and a gold and diamond yellow dress pin that we designed and had made. People commented on what I wore and said I was *the* yellow dress. Dad and I had worked tirelessly to make a difference personally and to raise funds for the programs we continued to support. At times the magnitude of our effort overwhelmed us; at other times it felt effortless. It was always humbling, especially when we were able to comfort and advise someone who called us in desperation over problems they were having with a child. I wondered how our sharing impacted the families that called. Often we never heard from them again. No matter if they were one-time encounters or ongoing conversations, we continued to be an open book, a resource for anyone in need for any question, at any time. Hopefully someone would benefit from what we learned from our journey with you, through the horror and confusion of your mental illness. Hopefully they would find their way through. I often felt you in the wings, ushering people toward us and facilitating the connections.

This year we had a live tree at the event and invited those who had lost someone to suicide to tie a yellow heart on it. By the end of the evening there were over thirty yellow hearts on the tree. It was a staggering visual and an intense reminder of how many of us were touched by this all too silent and shame-filled thing called suicide.

When I looked at the family portrait of the four of us in front of your *Yellow Dress,* it was a bizarre snapshot of your absence. We stood there all smiles, while inside a multitude of stories moved unseen within each of us.

We funded a special program at your high school and hoped that Dr. Lisa Machoian's lecture on her book, *The Disappearing Girl: Learning the Language of Teenage Depression,* would provide a compelling opportunity for the students to learn about mental illness. We awarded the annual scholarship in your name to a deserving junior at your high school, one continuing on with her artistic training. We continued to support the Department of Psychiatry and Behavioral Sciences at Johns Hopkins Medicine, through the Adolescent Depression Awareness Program (ADAP). Dr. Karen L. Swartz had done an amazing job as director of this school-based curriculum that she envisioned as a national program, filling the much-needed gap in traditional health education. To date, ADAP's message, "Depression is a serious and treatable medical illness," had impacted eight thousand students. I had no doubt that ADAP's message had saved lives.

Tonight we honored your sister Kimberly and Rita Project. We showed a film of Rita Project's offerings for survivors in New York City, documented when Kimberly was named person of the week. Over the years we heard many personal accounts from those who attended the weekly open art studio. Rita Project had made a difference in their lives. Several survivors said they would not have made it through had it not been for Rita Project and its creative approach to the many faces of suicide. I was proud of Kimberly and the path she chose as a result of your death. She faced your suicide head-on, determined to celebrate life.

June 24, 2006:
Recovery

Collage #42: "Gift Boxes"
Collage #43: "Buddha"

I spent the rest of June in a recovery mode, which included hours of reflection over the past five years. I was unable to push pause, to push eject, to change the story that continued to play endlessly. Unanswerable questions churned inside, the whys rising again to the surface, as well as the need for purpose, mixed with the desire to make sense of it all. A mind could only watch so much before it got exhausted, and so I was exhausted. Once I finished repacking all the KRSF boxes and putting them away for next year, I withdrew into quiet comfort and focused on the status of my heart. I searched for an image of a bound heart, lost somewhere in my filing system.

I find my heart broken into a million pieces and glue it down. A diamond cross marks the center point and offers its blessing to the breaking open. I close my eyes in this place of reverie. I hold my head up high and expose my opened throat, which releases what was silent. Silver boxes tied with delicate red ribbons cascade along the right side of my body. I cut out the words "all about fall" and scatter them among the ashes.

It captured my experience of the past month, of Minuit's death and of your death. I felt clarity as I considered the image before me. I embraced the gifts that came through your death and breathed a prayer of gratitude for all of it. I was not the same as I once was. It seemed I had become a better version of who I was. Your suicide has exacted a terrible price; I choose to reframe that price in terms of love: a gift of grief.

I played tennis with my friends. I worked in the garden. I continued on with my life as it was before being taken to my knees with Minuit's death. I looked the same on the outside, however I was aware of myself again in ways I had not been for some time. There was another "before and after" that defined this self I was growing into. Minuit marked that before and after. The tasks of daily living were mere notations on a list of things to do. My primary concern was to carve out time in the studio again. I dropped in, because there was nowhere else to rest.

I found this wonderful image of a stone Buddha and placed it on a background that was mostly dark except for a single piece of paper that twisted and turned in the light. I tore the Buddha in half and placed a portion of its body within the body of a faceless woman who turned and faced me. A shaft of the paper's light entered the top of her head. A single figure draped in saffron peered into a rock's crevice that was cracked and crusted over.

A monk takes possession of the middle ground between the Buddha and the faceless woman. There is a red-tipped paintbrush, bathed in a shard of triangular light, in the right-hand corner of the collage. I step back and absorb this collage as an indicator of where I am now. I am particularly drawn to the page of light that enters the woman's head. I am seriously considering the possibility of writing, taking it just one page at a time. The possibility feels off in the distance; it's there, though. I see it.

July 14–16, 2006: The Compassionate Friends National Conference: Dearborn, Michigan

By early July I gathered my strength, anticipating the Compassionate Friends National Conference in Dearborn, Michigan. I always liked getting to the conference a day early so that I could get myself settled, check out my room, and make sure I had everything I needed. I was sitting in the lobby and reading through the conference brochure, marking the workshops I wanted to attend. I especially wanted to go hear Bill Guggenheim's presentation on after-death communication. I was curious, especially in light of my own ongoing conversations with you. They were comforting, whether they were imagined or real.

A man came over and sat in the seat opposite me. I knew he was there for the conference because he was carrying a conference goodie bag just like mine. People are open and friendly at these conferences. We all know why we are here, and there is an instant bond that forms around our shared experiences of losing a child. We began talking, and I said I was interested in the Bill Guggenheim workshop. He smiled and said, "I am Bill Guggenheim." Each conference had presented a synchronicity and introduced me to someone amazing, someone interesting who encouraged me. I enjoyed meeting Bill and picked up his book, *Hello from Heaven*, at the bookstore.

I spent the next few hours talking with parents from around the country; they were casual yet intimate conversations with strangers gathered in the hotel lobby. I waited for Carla to arrive, who was presenting, too, and we spent our evening over dinner, talking our hearts out. I spoke about Minuit and my scream. I showed her some of my small collages. She listened. I felt supported and held by her kind words and inspired to consider writing. She assured me I had a book inside, just waiting in the wings until I was ready. She urged me to begin and trust that my story would emerge effortlessly, because it was a story that needed to be shared with others. She suggested that I focus on my images; they would be the fertile ground of my beginning.

During the following days I presented "Using Art to Heal: Suicide Survivorship" and "A Dialogue with your Brother or Sister Using Collage." I attended a variety of workshops and felt enriched when I arrived home.

Before I knew it, the summer passed. August was a few days away, and with it the anticipated march toward September and October. I wondered how the fall would be.

August 2, 2006:
Phone Call

The phone rang in the middle of the night. My eyes flew open, and the sound terrified me until I heard Dad say, "Wrong number." I could not get back to sleep, reminded of how the phone ringing in those first two years would startle me and begin a cascade of body memories that I associated with your suicide. I could not get back to sleep and lay in the darkness until light shone under the blinds in our bedroom. It was Kimberly's birthday.

We waited until evening to call your sister in New York. When I put the phone down, I realized that I spoke with Kimberly over the same hours I spoke to you for the very last time. I remember you called me from Kimberly's apartment around 8:00 p.m. We talked for about an hour that night, before you left and walked back to your dorm. You said, "I am not doing well. I want to come home." I listened. I encouraged you. I was firm. You said, "I feel like jumping."

I said, "Oh Kristin, come on, what does that mean? Don't say that." It simply did not register that you were saying, *I want to die. I am going to leave here and go to the roof of my dorm and die.* I remember offering words of support, listening and reflecting feelings back to you. I remembered the social worker at the hospital's words, "Oh! She would never do that—that's just attention-seeking behavior. Don't worry, that would never happen."

We discussed my coming up that weekend. I asked what your plans were for the next day. You said, "I have to go to the museum and do some research for the paper I am writing." I felt unsettled and worried when I got off the phone, yet felt I did the best I could under the circumstances. I was not with you; I could not see you. I thought I would see you over the weekend and take it from there, except you died a few hours later.

I hated phone calls. A deadly thing occurred in that space between us. More than hating phones and phone calls, I hated myself for not understanding, for not hearing what you were trying to tell me. I went to bed that night saying a prayer. I asked the Blessed Mother to wrap her arms around you. I surrendered you to her care. Four hours later the phone rang, and life as I knew it ended.

You went to Kimberly's apartment that evening. Her boyfriend, Joseph, was there, too. He took a whole roll of pictures of you talking with Kimberly and of you talking with me. When I saw the images he took of you, I shut down completely. I flew out of my body as I was drawn into the despair in your dark eyes. I looked at those pictures once, and once was enough. I imagined them hanging in a New York gallery, an exquisite example of one perched on the edge of life, an evocative testament to the tragedy of your death, to the ravages of mental illness.

You left Kimberly's apartment and stopped on the corner to wave to her as she leaned out her open, second-story window. More than likely you walked the most familiar and direct route down the avenue to your dorm. You found someone's wallet just outside and stopped at the front desk to turn it in. How thoughtful, for someone about to end their own life. You went to your room and left your coat. Would things have been different if just one of your roommates had been there? You took the elevator to the fifteenth floor. You walked a short way down the hall and up a set of steps, and you pushed open the door to the roof. We knew from the security report that you left the roof and went back to the roof again. You sat on the ledge for a long period, enough time for the sweat from your hands and the seat of your pants to leave marks on that ledge. Your body was found by a student's boyfriend who walked into the garden at the back of your dorm. He saw you lying gracefully on that slab of concrete, just beyond the entrance to the patio. He came close and saw your blood.

I wished I could go back to that evening's phone call. All the wishes in the world will not change what is. I move between the should haves, could haves, and would haves. They are intertwined with, "I did the best I could at the time." Guilt washed over me once again.

Today was your sisters twenty-ninth birthday.

September 11, 2006: Fifth Anniversary of 9/11

I played tennis this morning and then went home and curled up with Sienna on the big green chair in the kitchen. I was stronger and steadier and had the capacity to watch the programs on 9/11. I was interested in their fifth anniversary, my fifth anniversary, and the threads that wove between us. I was not traumatized by the images or the memories. When Dad came home, we sat together throughout the evening. I was struck by the stories of transformation shared by the victims' families, especially the children. I felt strong kinship with their journeys. I felt their stories of loss as mirrors to my own story of loss. I recognized something spiritual running like a thread of gold through those who had the courage to speak. The journey through grief was long and hard, and I felt empowered by that truth, so eloquently captured. I felt a sense of gratitude for the tender and courageous coverage of this tragic moment in our country's history. I remembered that day, and visiting the site of the attack. I was able to allow all of it to move through me without going numb, without falling apart.

October 11, 2006: Fifth Anniversary of Your Death

I wanted this fifth anniversary to be significantly easier. I felt entitled and clung to that desire for months until finally surrendering it as an illusion I'd constructed because I wanted it that way. I was disappointed by my mood that changed on a dime as your anniversary drew near. It did not matter that I had worked hard to heal and screamed my scream. When October arrived, it brought with it the fall. Each day of this October, I struggled. I was unable to take comfort in the fact that August and September were remarkably "normal," because when grief arrived, it arrived in full force. It swept in not like the initial hurricane, but a slow-moving, insipid disturbance, one with characteristics that were familiar. Today I felt worn out and angry.

There was tension between Dad and me. We had not felt that between us for a long time. Thank God for the understanding we had in giving each other the space we needed to get through. Today, no measure of quiet mind and no measure of success on the greens was enough to sway the rising tide of grief. We were on edge.

At a certain level, I found myself expecting little from anyone. That way there were no disappointments; after all, this was our journey and not theirs. Over time the attention to our sorrow had dwindled, as it naturally should. I could always count on our closest friends and our family to remember … except this year a lot of family forgot the day you died. Perhaps I could have reconciled this if it had been any other year, but this five-year mark was so significant for us that I simply assumed everyone would acknowledge it, especially our family, our own blood. I was wrong. The day came and went. Some remembered with calls and cards, and some simply went on with their lives with no particular thought of this day. Dad and I were crushed as the sharp point of grief's knife dove deeper into our hearts. It was a rude awakening to realize that life does go on, and in some ways it beckoned us to move into our own lives more fully.

Parallel to my dark mood was a river of gratitude for the early years, which were behind us, filled with the suffering and raw experiences so deeply associated with your death. I looked forward to my future and hoped that we would continue to heal, individually and as a family. I thought of you today, Kristin.

 October 14, 2006:
Grand Canyon

Our friends invited us to their wonderful home in Arizona. I thought it would be a good idea to get away and celebrate our survival. They could not have been more loving and generous with us, offering us an opportunity to be in the splendor of the desert and red rocks. However, I could not extricate myself from the place of my dark descent. During our travels I took in the breath-taking scenery. I felt in communion with the outer landscape, my own inner landscape a reflection of rushing water, shirred red rock, and canyons cut and worn away by a steady force. I was the play of shadow that moved over the mountains. I was both light and dark, fluid and impervious, joy and sorrow.

October 11 stayed with me as the impact of the past five years exerted itself. I was not myself. Dad was not himself, either. The stress of your anniversary and the stress between us escalated.

In Arizona, I found myself thinking about the family vacation we took to Sedona when you were eight years old. Our experience at the Dude Ranch took up residence in my mind and would not give me any peace. I saw you hanging onto the horse for dear life, as it galloped around the ring with you on its side. This was not exactly what I had in mind when we planned this restful getaway. It seemed to move from bad to worse.

I do not know what we were thinking when we planned a trip to the Grand Canyon. I felt terrified as we approached the rim. I could not go any further. A fear of falling erupted inside of me. I felt sick and dizzy and wanted to run from the place. I had to find a way to control myself and not ruin the day with our friends. I was quiet and strange, unable to access the middle ground within myself. Dad was unable to accept my mood, impatient and angered with what was between us. He jokingly nudged me toward the edge. It was too much, and I stood away from him, by myself. I was too far gone to find the stillness in this majestic place that broke me open. Your death and my imagined experience of your falling filled every cell in my being. There was nothing I could do.

I felt like I descended into the empty space of the canyon and floated within this huge opening in the earth. The mix of beauty and horror moved through me, reminding me of the ever-unfolding journey I was on. I felt much more prepared than I was at the beginning. I approached these experiences as unending opportunities for healing. I knew that there would be times like these when I simply had to open to it all and breathe. I knew there would be times when my capacity to handle life events would wax and wane. It was part of this ongoing journey.

I hoped I was able to hide my inner torments and that our friends did not suspect. If they did, I prayed they would forgive me. My grief was overwhelming and complex, and it took time. It was a sad commentary on the place I was in.

October 23, 2006:
Tattoos

Collage #47: "Reborn"

The seeds for this collage were planted in the last days of August, as my birthday approached. The fall entered me with the changing light, and I asked once again, "Who am I?" I found this yellow-hued woman with tattoos on her body. I loved the tribal markings that set her apart. Your death permanently scarred me and marked me as other, a mother of a child who ended her own life.

Instead of tattooing the word "suicide" on my forehead, I tattoo my art on my body. I am my art. I am my own creation.

The V-shaped space between the brushes called for something special. In my box of little images, I found a Madonna and Child set against a yellow background. Before I glued the Madonna down, I mulled over which was the top of the collage and which was the bottom; it could go either way. I oriented the paintbrushes and tattooed woman upside down. When I looked at my collage, I had the sensation that she was being born out of her art work.

When others looked at this piece, they asked me why I placed the Madonna and Child upside down. I said, "I haven't—you have." I sensed in that a natural discomfort in having the main figure upside down and falling. I understood that primal fear.

I place a bouquet of red roses underneath the Madonna's feet and along the bodice of the tattooed woman. I touch the blood again, and there are roses. I cover the woman's opened chest and offer a blessing to her lungs, as they release grief. I imagine us together again, mother and child.

November 15, 2006:
A Perfect Fall

Collage #49: "Paradox"

Aunt Gale and Uncle Fred invited us to Louisville for Dad's birthday. We had
not visited them since before your death. Next to our bed was a picture of you
and your cousin Abby. We did a lot of nothing, as families who are intimate with
each other do. We raked leaves in their yard and enjoyed freshly baked chocolate
chip cookies in the evening. We laughed and created memories far removed
from home. It was a nice celebration of Dad's birthday. Our weekend gave us a
good start to November; things had eased from October's downturn, and we
returned to our new normal. I wondered about the impending holidays in light
of this current happiness.

*I do not set out to capture life's paradox; it manifests in the image. The hands
that pull and the hands that hold form the focal point of this collage. I place red roses
and a cross to mark the space where both exist side by side. Tears in the form of paint
fall from my eyes and into my chest, which had been split in two with your death. My
blue eye is completely open and engaged with life. Red softened to pink as I am both
torn apart and held at the same time. My spiritual self rests.*

Life happens, all of it. Our recent trip to the Grand Canyon was a perfect
example of an experience that contained awe and majesty at the same time it
ripped me apart.

December 18, 2006:
Armful of Greens

I spent a few days in New York, just before Christmas. I shopped with Kimberly
and Kevin, and we walked arm in arm in the West Village and along Fifth Avenue.
I enjoyed my time with them. I enjoyed the city and the holiday decorations. You
were here amid it all. I could feel you under the surface, but we did not mention
you. Before I left New York, I walked to your dorm with an armful of greens.
I went to the garden where your body was found and placed the greens in the
large planter that sat over the concrete slab. I did not stay; a few moments were
all I needed. You were not there. I noticed the garden had become shabby and
old. I moved an errant bench back in place around a table and said good-bye.

part II

thriving

Tenth Anniversary of Kristin's Death

In the early days, right after Kristin's suicide, I was told by survivors, "In time, there will be healing." I was not reassured by that thought. I couldn't image myself or my future in the face of her violent death. Ten years later I had a different perspective. There *was* healing, a healing shaped by the choices I made. Each day was up to me. My rational mind directed me at first. Eventually my heart opened to a journey that made healing possible.

I considered the years from a contemplative place, for today marked the tenth anniversary of Kristin's death. Douglas and I decided to spend the anniversary away. The Lodge at Woodloch proved the perfect retreat: golf and spa, replete with meditation and watercolor classes. The entire year had been a time of reflection, revisiting, and remembering.

This was our time to celebrate each other and the life we shared with Kristin. Before we left, Douglas and I took a walk through the woods and stood by the lake, whose edge was filled with moss green lily pads. The Poconos were beautiful, the autumn light exquisite. I looked at the color of the trees that marked our drive through the mountains and felt deeply nourished by the beauty of change. I closed my eyes on the way home and moved into a timeless, dreamy dimension as my thoughts lingered over the past ten years, which seemed divided into part one and part two.

The first five years through grief's labyrinth were years of significant transformation. I checked out a grief and bereavement group and participated in traditional modalities of treatment, which provided the initial support I needed. I worked on the Kristin Rita Strouse Foundation, raised money, and raised awareness. I joined Janet's circle and exposed myself to altered states of consciousness. I conversed with Kristin and took special note of night and day dreams. I immersed myself in the world of meditation and mindfulness practices. I listened to my inner art therapist's guidance and stepped into a creative vortex, the world of collage. My creative process defined me and my subsequent work in ways I never imagined. I filled my healing toolbox with personal experiences and shared what I discovered with others. I moved on to a national stage with my professional work. I screamed my scream and let go. The barren tree, shocked and defoliated of feelings, finally came back to life. I survived.

I had a sense of gratitude that those early years were behind me. When I considered the second five years, part two of my journey, I was filled with the mystery woven through my life. The sixth, seventh, and tenth years were especially significant, and I savored those key moments. They seemed to be of particular importance, a bridge to another deeper understanding and integration of Kristin's suicide. My life had meaning again. I thrived.

the bridge

January 21, 2007:
Sundays in Paradise

I was on my way to Puerto Rico with Douglas. I wanted to take a good book with me, and so I drove into historic Hampden, to Breathe Books. On this Sunday, I walked toward my favorite bookstore and glanced across the street at the shop, Watermelon Sugar. I could not help but remember all the mornings I dropped Kristin off on that corner as she knocked on the door to a nearby walkup apartment on the second floor. She had arrived for her private painting lessons with two faculty members from the Maryland Institute College of Art. Kristin met Stacey and Bob in 1997, when she took Painting I with them. She was the youngest student in a class of college students and adults. At the end of the semester, they invited her to paint with them on Sundays, and so began a long and wonderful relationship.

I noticed that my thoughts were of Kristin's life rather than her mental illness and death. I savored each memory, because it had not always been that way. She was more than her suicide. She had experiences that were rich and wonderful. It was a pleasure to remember how special she was.

Kristin loved Sundays. No matter what happened during her week, she was always ready and longing for her time with Stacey and Bob. She never missed her lesson for any reason—it was a priority. She dressed in what would become her standard paint clothes: comfortable jeans, tank tops, T-shirts, and cardigans. She kept her paints in a large blue plastic paint box that opened easily to display all her paints on several shelves. She kept her brushes in a coffee tin, wrapped with blue and white floral contact paper. On her way out the door, she grabbed her large red tote bag, which was filled with the rest of her materials. I remembered how Kristin dropped into the seat next to me and put on the radio, and away we went, rain or shine. She painted with Stacey for hours. Bob played classical music while he made Sunday brunch. It was never an ordinary brunch, always something that Kristin raved about, whether it was the homemade bread, special dressing for the salad, sauce on the fish, or homemade dessert. During lunch they talked with her about art and music, literature and philosophy. After lunch Kristin and Stacey painted into the afternoon. I looked forward to picking her up. When she came out the door with all her art materials in hand, she always had a huge smile on her face.

She shared what she ate first, wondering why I didn't cook wonderful things like Bob cooked. Then she shared parts of her conversations with them, ending with what her day of painting had been like. Over the years she developed her talent. They guided her when she began to consider colleges. They helped her select her portfolio, which was difficult because she had so much work from which to draw. They celebrated with her when she received her acceptance at one of the best art schools in the country, and they grieved with me at her grave. During her Sundays with them, she lived the life of an artist. They provided her with an extraordinary experience during her most formative years.

It was Stacey's wedding dress that Kristin painted. It hung on a hanger in Stacey's studio, and Kristin worked on it Sunday after Sunday. That painting became the source for other renditions of her dress during the summer before Kristin left for college, during the summer right before she died. Our foundation's yellow dress logo came from those Sundays with Stacey and Bob. When Kristin died, they grieved as artists.

They produced a body of work in Kristin's memory, and it was exhibited at Goucher College's Rosenberg Gallery from January 14 through March 1, 2002. It was called "Splitting and Binding." The brochure that accompanied the exhibition said,

This work is about loss and healing, a cycle that we all repeat for as long as we live. For Stacey and Bob it's their attempt as artists to make sense of the chaos they've felt resulting from events both personal and public. Specifically the work deals with the loss of a student they worked with for many years, a young woman who died in New York exactly one month after the September 11th attack. The taking of her own life was, like all self inflicted deaths, complex; but the troubling events in New York City, her new hometown, didn't encourage her to keep living.

A death call is always shocking no matter if sudden or long expected. And the death of a young person trumps all other final notices. When a loved one dies we're adrift in a cloud of emotions and images that slip or scream in our minds refusing to slow down long enough for us to settle them into anything sensible. Our thoughts lead us through a fun house filled with clocks instead of mirrors. Each timepiece set to a different moment, a random year, all discordant ticking, and each memory clanging like an alarm clock gone wrong. We look for ways to find order amidst this chaos so we can make plain our pain and suffering, better to share with others in hope of finding some small measure of release.

Death brings an immediate split from the living flesh of another and forces us to be forever bound to both their memory and the ache that ebbs and flows but never disappears until we leave this earth. We are split apart and we must weave together these pieces and become whole again if we are to heal. Art is certainly one of the tools used by every human society to bind up wounds and move on with life. It's also a way to honor the beloved dead. We make a mark to recognize the indentation those who've gone on make upon our lives and souls.

When "Splitting and Binding" opened, I walked through the gallery with Stacey and Bob. I looked deeply into the pieces they created in Kristin's honor, in an attempt to make sense of her death. I looked into their eyes, and there was pain. Our time together that afternoon was quiet, because there was so little to say. Kristin was dead. The images spoke for them and moved us.

November 11, 1996:"Dear Diary, Today I went to art class and I started another Mary Cassatt pastel.

February 1, 1997: Dear Diary, Today I had my art lesson, and I finished drawing my Ballerina by Degas. I drew it in grays and whites and blacks only, and it turned out pretty good.

March 20, 1997: Dear Diary Today was a good day. Art Class was fun because we are doing watercolor. Watercolor is one of my favorite media. Mom said when I was really little, I would just pick up a pencil or crayon, and I would draw for hours.

April 23–24, 1997: Dear Diary, My favorite class is art and my drawing is looking better each day because I am going into detail. I'm really taking my time. This summer I hope to take a drawing class.

June 18, 1997: Tonight was Fine Arts Night. I am sad my picture for the cover was not picked. My Mom and Dad got me three white roses, and they are beautiful. I hope I get a chance to draw them before they die, so I can remember them forever.

June 19, 1997: The art class was really good. I drew fire and ice along with dilemma and transformation. I'm not done with transformation, and I haven't even started resolution. I love everybody in our class. When our teacher was looking at our

*pictures, he looked at mine for a long time. He put his hand
across my drawings to listen to the picture.*

*June 20, 1997: Today was our last art class. We worked in black
and white paint, and I let go. I loved this whole week. I shall miss
my friends. I hope they live a happy, safe life.*

As I made my way up the steps to Breathe Books, I thought of Kristin
and I thought of them. I had not kept in contact with Stacey and Bob, but I
thought of them often. I thought of all Kristin's happiness on Sundays. For
her, it was a bit like being in paradise. I had Kristin's yellow dress paintings. I
had Kristin's blue paint box. I had Kristin's coffee tin, filled with her brushes.
I had Kristin's red tote bag. I wished I had Kristin rather than those things.
On this Sunday, I was filled with happy memories of Kristin as opposed to
other not-so-happy memories of her. The happy and sad memories had their
place and often sat side by side in my consciousness. There was space for
both. I smiled at the clerk as I walked in the door. I inquired about a book
someone recommended.

May 13, 2007:
Mother's Day

We took Grandma out to lunch for Mother's Day. I noticed how much easier
it was for me to pay attention to her and enjoy the day as a celebration of my
motherhood, too. When I came home, I went upstairs to our bedroom and
opened the middle drawer of my dresser. I took out the stack of cards and
letters Kristin had written to me.

*May 1993: Happy Mother's Day! Every year has been a better
and more growing experience between you and me. I'm glad I'm
able to share my thoughts with you. You are everything that I
would want a mother to be!*

*May 1995: For thirteen years of my life, you have given me the
world. I'm growing older with you, and the past will stay the*

past because the future is what you make of it. Think of me and capture the moment. Look back on the memories and you should be fulfilled. Now and forever you will be my very special mother.

May 1999: You stand by me; your love has made me what I am today. The laughs we had, the cries when anger broke, the moments of silence we shared have nourished my soul. I hope you realize how special you are to me. I learn from you. I learn with you. You are many things to me, but most of all I see you as a Mom who will love me no matter what. That is a good feeling to have. "The soul should always stand ajar, ready to welcome the ecstatic experience." —Emily Dickinson.

May 2001: Mom: Wow what a year it has been. You have been stretched past limits you never knew you had and have grown so much. I am so happy to look back and think you were with me through it all. I truly feel like myself again. I don't know where I would have ended up. Thank you. Love, Kristin.

I was glad I kept her cards. They were treasures. I separated hers out from the rest and wrapped them in special handmade paper with gold feathers on it. I tucked them away a few weeks after she died. For some reason I was able to read through them periodically during the first year. I think it was because I was still in shock. After a time I could not even open the drawer to look at them, for fear I would dissolve. This Mother's Day stood out. I savored all Kristin's love.

As I looked up from reading my cards, I had the fleeting memory of Kristin bouncing into my bedroom and planting a kiss on my cheek before she raced out with her girlfriends. I remembered her taking one last look in the mirror as she approvingly moved out of its reflection in a pair of tight jeans and a silver sequined top. I remembered how many times the pull-out sofas in the basement were filled with Kristin's girlfriends, sleeping over after an evening out. I remembered Kristin waking up in her pink lace camisole and plaid boxers, her hair in a ponytail. I remembered getting bagels and donuts for the girls in the morning and helping to gather their things as their mothers came and picked them up. I remembered the laughter and so many happy times.

June 11, 2007:
Sixth Yellow Dress Golf Classic

Our Sixth Yellow Dress Golf Classic was a good day. We raised over ninety thousand dollars, which pushed us over the half a million mark of money raised for programs that supported mental health. We took advantage of our captive audience and highlighted the work we funded at Johns Hopkins. Dr. Karen Swartz, assistant professor at Johns Hopkins Medicine and the director of Clinical and Educational Programs at Johns Hopkins Mood Disorders Center, spoke about the Adolescent Depression Awareness Program. This program had been taught to 8,716 students in two states, Maryland and Oklahoma. It was a comfort knowing we had made a difference. On the cover of this year's program, just above the image of Kristin's yellow dress, we wrote, "Hope … the Gift of Miracles."

July 20–22, 2007:
The Compassionate Friends National Conference: Oklahoma City, Oklahoma

On my stopover in Chicago, I struck up a conversation with the lady in a straw hat who was sitting next to me. She was going to Oklahoma City, too, and was a workshop presenter and author. Marie Levine wrote *First You Die* after the death of her only child. I smiled at the synchronicity of this meeting and made note of the numerous authors I'd met over the years.

I facilitated my collage workshop, "The Art of Healing: Loss, Grief and Grace" and presented, "Wisdom Bowls: The Inner Journey of Healing" for the first time. It was a guided imagery and meditation workshop, and I was pleased with its debut

On the afternoon of my last day, I walked up a quiet street toward the Oklahoma City Memorial. I walked among the memorial chairs and sat by the reflecting pool. This was a blessed place. I sat and considered my conference experience, noticing how each year had built on the other. I noticed how much stronger I was and how much more I had to share. I was able to offer a greater perspective because I was much further down the road in my own healing. It was deeply moving to be with so many parents who had lost a child, and to conclude my weekend in a place filled with the spirit of so many who died on April 19, 1995.

July 24, 2007:
Rest

Collage #56: "Lavender Elephant"

I came home from the Compassionate Friends conference and gave myself a few days of rest. I read in the garden just off the studio, where I planted lavender. Perhaps it was the smell of the lavender while I read that moved me. I reached over and broke off a tiny bundle and crushed it between my fingers, and I breathed Kristin in. I was taken back to my moments alone with her, when I anointed her body with lavender oil and said my good-byes. Those memories lead to musings, and I imagined myself in a field of lavender. The image within me was so compelling that I put down my book and walked through the doors to the studio in search of lavender images.

In my field of lavender, I place lavender eyes in the sky and encircle them with an amethyst-encrusted swan. It seems so dreamlike and captures the feelings I have as I rest in the totality of my summer.

It took the remainder of that afternoon to cut, glue, and put it together. It sat like that for a few weeks until I opened an old magazine and came across this image of a dead elephant. It haunted me, and I instantly knew it belonged in the field of lavender. When I placed her there, the whole collage transformed, as if it had been waiting for this symbolic image of Kristin to arrive. I placed a small, fluttering blue bird just above her decaying, stiff body.

I looked at the color of that collage and couldn't help taking out "Purple Tears." I placed them side by side, lavender, bruises, and tears. All my experiences around Kristin's broken body felt condensed within the body of that elephant. I had a sense of laying Kristin to rest in a field of lavender. It felt as if enough time had gone by to let go.

Strangely, I watch Kristin from above, one eye encircled by the body of a swan. The swan's beautiful, curving neck seems to form a bridge between two worlds, the one above and the one below. I love the symbolism of that and feel our connection through this beautiful bird. A single pear-shaped amethyst drops from the swan's beak, like a teardrop from heaven.

When I considered what I was letting go of, I realized I was not letting go of Kristin—in fact I felt closer to her than I ever had. My relationship with Kristin had shifted over time, from a corporeal one to a spiritual one, from loving her in her physical presence to loving her in her physical absence.

My ability to love again seemed shaped by the two processes I embraced. I reconstructed our bond each time I sat in circle with Janet and then with those who sat with me. I opened myself to another dimension. I experienced healing and sensed Kristin's presence as I moved between worlds. I also reconstructed our bond each time I descended into the stillness of my studio. As I looked back, I sensed the debris of Kristin's suicide in the traumatic details of her fall, in her bruised and broken body, and in her blood—they were intertwined with the trauma of her mental illness. I reconstructed our bond by wading through the violence. Collaging allowed me to touch into the debris that tainted and destroyed our relationship. I allowed it in. I touched it and moved into it. I released it and did not turn away. It allowed me to recreate my life narrative in the face of her death. It took time, and it took work.

I felt like the swan. I was connected to heaven and earth.

July 30, 2007:
Hershey Kiss

As July came to a close, I opened the cabinet over my desk in the kitchen and reached into the straw basket filled with candies. I thought of Kristin. I thought of the candies she loved, the Hershey Kisses, the Skittles, and the Jolly Ranchers. I popped a chocolate kiss in my mouth and thought of her and Douglas. I remembered they went to Hershey Park together on July 30, 1992. It was a ritual, something they both looked forward to each summer.

Kristin got to decide how they would spend the day. She made a wish list, which included going to the amusement park. They got up early and stopped at McDonald's for breakfast as they drove north toward Pennsylvania. They spent the whole day together, going from ride to ride. They got soaked on the water slide. She made Douglas go on it more than once. Kristin was glad she'd packed a change of clothes. She had her face painted with the image of a white unicorn. They had dinner together and topped it off by going to the toy store in the evening, where Douglas bought a Madame Alexander doll for her collection. It was their special time together. I remembered all the beautiful notes Kristin wrote on Father's Days and birthdays.

> June 17, 2001: I love that you are dedicated to your family. We are number one to you, which is very important. You work so hard at everything. Life is dark, light, good, bad, weak, and strong. We are the Scorpios, the fighters. We are two peas in a pod. Your studies in psychology have definitely been put to good use by this terrible seventeen-year-old. Whoever saw it coming? Well, I needed to grow up, so I did what I did, what I needed to do, and you were there for me, and I won't forget that. Happy Father's Day.

I wondered if Douglas thought about those special days he carved out with each child. They were long gone, ghosts of winter, spring, summer, and fall. I hoped those memories came to him on the golf course as he continued with his healing process, his practice, his silent way through.

August 3, 2007:
Show Me the Reason

Tonight, our song played as I drove home. I often heard this song on special days—an anniversary, a birthday, a holiday. As I listened, I was reminded of all the evenings I picked Kristin up from her art classes at the Maryland Institute College of Art. They were magical evenings. She would pop into the car, enthused and eager to share what she had learned. Invariably the Backstreet Boys came on, and we'd turn up the volume and listen to "Show

Me the Meaning of Being Lonely." I would cry and she would laugh. Its words haunted me tonight as they often did, but I did not cry. "Show me the meaning of being lonely. Is this the feeling I need to walk with? Tell me why, I can't be there where you are? There's something missing from my heart."

I only listened to certain music during the first year, because the harmony and beauty of sound was more than my heart could bear. I was drawn to songs that connected me with Kristin, like the song we shared, the one about being lonely. I bought *The Backstreet Boys: The Hits—Chapter One* soon after Kristin died. I played it so much that I wore it out and had to buy another one. I imagined Kristin speaking to me through their words. I heard her voice and sensed her presence in many of the melodies. I felt a sense of peace. The stars and moon were out. Kristin would have loved it.

September 8, 2007:
The Diamond

I had been looking forward to this wedding for some time. I noticed that the happy anticipation of special moments had returned; it felt good to look forward to something, whereas in the past I did not dare look forward to anything because the future held little promise. Dad's extended family gathered for this Long Island celebration at an elegant turn-of-the-century chateau. The ceremony took place in the formal gardens, followed by cocktails served in wood-paneled rooms. As we began dinner in the main ballroom, Dad's cousin Sue discovered that her three-carat diamond had fallen out of her ring. The whole table began looking on the floor. No diamond. She and her husband Bobby left to search the facility.

While eating, I alternately considered the impossibility of anyone finding that diamond, that needle in a haystack, and the possibility of someone finding it. I excused myself as they cleared away my dinner plate, giving into a persistent thought: "Go and find it." My rational mind tried to discount what I was being urged to consider. I decided to listen to my inner voice, and I asked for Kristin's help. For a half hour or more, I made my way through various rooms. I noticed lots of little specks of things on the floor, but I did not bend down to investigate what they were. I kept moving from one room to another. I was very still inside when suddenly I heard, "There, pick that up." I did not have my glasses on but reached down and felt something solid. I brought it closer to my eyes and saw the pear-shaped stone glisten in the light. I knew I had found Sue's diamond.

Bobby and Sue couldn't believe it. I myself could hardly believe it. The good news traveled from wedding guest to wedding guest. I found myself repeating, "I really didn't do anything. I just listened."

I listened that night as I had been listening for years. I had listened to an inner voice that invited me into my creative process. I had listened to my body wisdom, which directed me into the depths of my grief. I had listened and understood that the only way out of hell was to walk through it. I had listened to and embraced the mystery of my journey, and I was guided. I found diamonds along the way.

There was nothing much to say. The experience spoke for itself.

September 12, 2007: Wings

Collage #60: "The Book"

The anniversary of September 11 came and went. I found myself honoring the day, remembering and feeling a kinship with all those remembering, too. I paused and took notice. I was not overcome; I was not pulled into the past, aware of a great push forward. I felt myself amid unwritten pages, and so I created an image of my book. In that piece, an open book sprouted like wings from my bent back.

You are upside down; I am right side up. I have fallen with you endless times, and I am tired of falling. I have fallen with you in order to stop falling. I long for some closure and sense the suffering in that longing. There is no end point to this healing process, for death cannot be undone. I want to feel myself rooted to this earth and to the truth of my life now. I want to be in the present and in this moment, not tied to the past. You have receded into the background of my life. I bow to you. I honor our journey and acknowledge you as teacher. We are deeply connected.

I did not see it at first. It only came to me later as I looked more closely. The image in my collage of Kristin's face was almost identical to the actual image shown to us by the police woman in the morgue. Kristin's face was shrouded. That was our first glimpse of her, dead. We sat at a round metal table. The uniformed woman placed two Polaroids of her face on the table. I prayed that it would not be her face we saw, but it was. At the beginning I cried tears of blood from my eyes, mourning her. Now my tears fell like roses from me. I was bent in prayer over her. I thanked her.

September 24, 2007:
Storyteller Writer

I began to write on my mother's birthday. My story was born through my mother's body, my body, and Kristin's body. It is a story about the realization of my most primal fear as mother, the loss of my child. On that day I felt embraced by all women, past, present, and future. I felt the presence of a lineage that moved in to support the sharing of my story. My story was not personal or special, because it had been told before and would continue to be told. It was about life, death, and rebirth.

I had wondered at what moment I would begin, because the notion of writing had pressed on me most of the spring and summer. I remained unmoved and overwhelmed by the sheer number of images I'd created over the past five years. I struggled with my own fears and insecurities about the writing process. At the same time I trusted I would write when I was moved to write, in the same way I was moved to create. I wondered if it would it be a special day or an ordinary day, like the day Kristin died. I did not pick the day. The day picked me, and so I began as my story effortlessly flowed from me. The impulse was pure, clear, and undeniable. I began to write. I sat free and open as my fingers moved along the keyboard.

October 10, 2007:
Blackbird

I pulled out my journals and calendars and began to gather all that was available to me. I wondered what I might find. I came across one of my earliest circle experiences with Janet, written on January 13, 2002. I had completely forgotten what I'd written in my small red leather book, embossed with two angels. It was given to me by Gale and Fred on the day they left, the day after Kristin's funeral.

I wrote, "I walk down a labyrinth and into the darkness, into hell. I am in a million pieces, shadow pieces of myself. I am accompanied by a single blackbird, but one blackbird is not enough, and soon I am joined by an entire flock. Each blackbird carries a lantern with light, and that light fills the black space of the labyrinth. When it is time, each blackbird takes a piece of my broken shadow self into the light and carries it out of the darkness. We fly together. One blackbird stays on my shoulder to remind me of its presence."

In the collage I completed last week, in honor of Kristin's sixth anniversary, a winged white rabbit ascends into the light. It's escorted by a turquoise dragonfly and gold seahorse. Some part of me urged me to keep the image of the blackbird perched on my rabbit ear. I noticed its presence and made the significant connection after reading the blackbird entry in my journal. Considering my discovery, I felt gratitude for the blackbirds sitting in the trees outside the studio and family room. The blackbirds kept alive the promise that things would get better. Their caws were a consistent presence, often noted in spite of the circle memory that faded into the distant past. Sitting in Janet's circle, connected with spirit in an altered state of consciousness, I was given the template through.

The symbol, image, and physical presence of blackbirds felt like velvet threads woven into the fabric of my healing. Today, I took in my 2002 circle experience as a kind of prophetic prayer filled dream. I was told that healing takes time and happens when the time is right. I retrieved the pieces of myself in the pieces of paper I glued down. I saw the blackbirds as guides who assisted me with my shadow pieces and supported my movement from darkness into light.

I was overcome with the impact of this journal discovery as I began the research process for my book. Others may have taken it as mere coincidence. That did not matter. It also did not matter to me whether my blackbird experience came to me from another dimension, or whether it arose from my unconscious mind. The power and significance of it was undeniably meaningful to me, and I felt embraced by mystery.

My experiences in Janet's circle were often experiences that were beyond my capacity to explain or describe. Douglas would ask how circle was, and I would often find myself trying to explain what was unexplainable. Words paled in the face of experiences that rearrange my very matter with exquisite tenderness.

October 11, 2007:
Sixth Anniversary of Kristin's Death

I woke at 2:30 a.m. and wandered through the house, looking out the windows into the night sky. If I could have willed Kristin back into her body, I would have. I imagined her walking through the darkened backyard and returning to us. My magical thinking had a certain place in my journey because it offered moments of solace, where a part of me entered another reality, a moment where I floated in a suspension of denial. I set reality aside for an instant. Even a small, fleeting moment like that offered comfort in the darkness. Like a shooting star, it was gone; magical thinking and reality collided once again. Those moments of peace left their mark—it was a part of the process. Magical thinking was different from experiences of mystery, like yellow birds flying into windows or special songs at special moments, noticing the number eleven an inordinate number of times or seeing Kristin's initials on a license plate. Those experiences linked Kristin and me. They were moments when I connected with Kristin not by way of her physical body, but by way of her spirit. They were moments of grace. I believed they came to me from another dimension as gifts from the other side. They reminded me that life continued after the physical form died.

I finally went back to sleep, but on waking in the morning, I was filled with Kristin's loss—not like I was during the first year, but I was filled nonetheless with a penetrating sadness. I knew there was nothing to do but just be. I sat outside under the trees, as I did in those very first days and weeks following her death. I was quiet. Nature was reassuring once again.

We had our friends Jim and Dottie over for dinner. They lost their son, Nicky, and so we shared our sorrows. We could be ourselves with each other in ways that we couldn't be with others. Author Marie Levine called those who had not suffered the loss of a child the "uninitiated." I liked the label. The uninitiated would never really know. I was glad they didn't know; I would not wish it on anyone.

The death of a child permanently altered things. Death did that. A child's death did that in specific ways that separated it out from other deaths like the death of a parent, or the death of a spouse, or the death of a sibling. The initiated were aware of the subtleties. Suicide offered gifts of guilt, shame, stigma, and anger. I opened those packages, took a look at what was inside, and worked with them. I didn't discard the contents or lock them away behind a door. I wanted a fully lived life. I owed it to myself, Douglas, and my surviving children. I owed it to Kristin. I owed it.

In his book *Life after Death*, Deepak Chopra said, "There is no time, for I am beyond death. Time is a field of gain and loss. As long as you are in time, it is an illusion to think that you can prevent loss, which is just another word for change." I lived in a field of constant change, and like tall grass I moved with the wind until the storm was over and then returned to my center, to what was real. Chopra says, "Death cannot touch what is real. The trappings of existence can fall away at any time; the essence will always remain. And that essence is you."

October 14, 2007:
Faith

I felt particularly reflective of my life today. The intensity of this time of year beckoned me into an introspective state. At the end of the day, I laid in bed with my covers pulled around me. Just before sleep, I gave thanks for my beliefs, my faith. I was born from my Irish heritage, born from my girlhood experiences sitting around the dining room table and listening to my father and his friends talking about life, about philosophy. I gave thanks for my growth that rested on that foundation, growth born from years of reading and personal experiences of mindfulness as I tried to embrace each moment fully. I had unwavering faith not in the religious sense of the word like my father, but in the spiritual sense of the word. I had an eclectic set of beliefs, woven together from a wide range of traditions, distilled in its essence as love.

I believed in God. I believed in God's love and compassion. I believed in order and purpose. I believed in the interconnectedness of all living things. I believed I was put on this earth for a reason. I believed Kristin was put on this earth for a reason. I believed our lives intertwined for a reason. I believed in free will. I believed that life was about lessons and growth. I believed in the afterlife. I believed I would see Kristin again. My spirituality was a part of my moment-to-moment existence and was evident in my artwork, when I placed the words "I am timeless" into my first collage.

My beliefs were my core. My faith was strong and woven like a golden thread into the tapestry of my life's work. It was all I had when I learned of Kristin's death and fractured into a million pieces. My faith was challenged and tested; it remained steady and served me. It provided a structure and context in which I made sense and found meaning in both Kristin's life and death, and ultimately in my own life again. It supported my trauma work.

Over the years I had discussions with survivors: ones steeped in beliefs and faiths of all kinds, and ones with little or no beliefs and faiths of any kind. I sensed the different paths these sets of survivors moved along. The ones with little or no beliefs and faiths seemed to fall into two categories, those who shut the door emphatically to any further discussions, and those who seemed to waver a little. Many of those who embraced life's finality appeared content in the natural order of birth and death and allowed their grieving process to rest on that matter-of-fact foundation. Those who seemed to waver a little in their philosophical beliefs often asked me how they could come by faith. They wanted to believe that consciousness continued after the physical death of the body; unsure, they appeared tormented by the notion that their loved one was in the ground or turned to ash. I often sensed this second categories' struggle with purpose, because they railed against the randomness and senselessness of their losses. If I could have given beliefs and faith away I would have, for their journeys had particularly difficult challenges steeped in fear and desperate longing for connection. I observed these journeys from a place of non-judgment. In the end I could only share my experiences. In the end I could only be myself.

With survivors who had beliefs and faiths similar to my own, the tapestry of our shared journeys were woven with layers of meaning and purpose. The journeys we traveled seemed rooted in a spirituality based on free will and our souls' desire to experience life in order to grow. We considered our lives as co-creations with those we traveled, both in body and spirit. We embraced ourselves as spiritual beings gathering experiences in a physical existence.

I processed my journey with Kristin from this spiritual perspective; it steadied me in the face of so much horror. Having a strong set of beliefs and faith did not give me a free ticket through my grief. The work remained—it was what I came here to do, and there was no getting around it. It challenged me to consider my part and Kristin's part in the life we had agreed to share. In my heart there was room for the unanswered and unfathomable, for the mystery of life was profound. In the end I came back to myself, and to how I faced Kristin's death. I noticed the choices I made along the way and the doors that opened to me as a result of those choices. I felt Kristin's presence in it all. I felt supported by God's grace, even in my darkest hours.

 November 3, 2007:
Charcoaled Eyes

Collage #63: "Wild-Eyed Writer"

In the first weeks of writing, where words poured from me, I found myself enveloped in an energy to which I was unaccustomed. I could only write for short periods of time, an hour here or there. It was an intense process, and I was adjusting to it. I was moving from the unspeakable to the spoken. My body was not used to sitting, my hand not used to the keyboard. So far the intensity seemed to be the only difference, as the similarities between writing and creating collages were striking. I had no preconceived ideas; I just showed up and sat at the computer. My thoughts and feelings moved through me. I felt in sacred space as I sat in the family room, just like I felt in sacred space in my studio. I noticed I was spending more time writing than I was creating collages. I wondered if one creative process was being replaced by another.

I took all my collages out of storage in the basement and placed them in sequence around the family room so that I could easily look at them. Over the years I had developed a kind of practice that involved talking with my images, often out loud. As I listened to myself describing my process and what I saw, the words glided through my consciousness. In doing so, their meaning expanded, illuminated, and surprisingly supported what was happening day to day. I felt there was no separation between my process and my life; one informed the other. It was like conducting a translation. I made meaningful associations. I was thankful I had titled and dated my collages. I do not know what propelled me to do that, because I had no idea that when I began, that I would create for years.

This "Wild-eyed Writer" was born when I found an image of a diamond-encrusted pen. I remembered how much Kristin loved pens and pencils; she collected them wherever we went and had a whole desk drawer filled with those treasures. We buried her with a few of her favorites tucked between her bruised and all too stiff fingers. Kristin would have loved this one.

When I first see her, I think she's enchanted, with her wild white hair and charcoaled silver eyes. She seems serious, contemplative, and mysterious. She holds the pen firmly in her hand and does not seem bothered by the weight of it. The pen's tip touches the middle of an open book with wings. You join me in your yellow dress, gracefully floating in front of me. In my mind, you release a completed bound book from your fingertips and sign it with a kiss.

In a previous collage, my eyes were charcoaled black. I recognized those eyes of death, from as far back as February 2003 in collage #3, "Once Upon a Time." I had my entire body of work sitting in front of me. It was easy to see the connections. I was consciously searching for them now, whereas in the past I simply sat in the reflection of my images.

In that early piece, my dark and brooding eyes looked out from beneath the "suicide" I had plastered on my forehead. What a merciful way of alerting everyone to my status in the underworld—a horrifying vision, even to myself. Others were not privy to my internal world, and perhaps that was the very worst of all, carrying what was invisible.

Years later, my eyes were charcoaled still but with a dusting of silver that brought light. I viewed the world in a precious way as a result of Kristin's death, a grief gift of sorts. When she died, my world turned upside down—I turned upside down. From that 180-degree rotation, I viewed life differently, and my perspective was altered. In "Wild-eyed Writer" I was drawn in by my charcoaled silver eyes. I was reminded of my healing journey, and I sensed something beautiful there.

I noticed that my hair was completely white, wild, and untamed, a telltale vestige from the early days of total dismemberment. It stood on end in wisps from all the pulling, an unkempt mass of tangles that said old and ancient. It captured a truth filled experience and pulled it forward in time, a physical mutation unseen by others but nonetheless real. She was wild. I loved her tangled hair.

I loved Kristin's hair and cut a long piece of it off just before they closed the casket. I hated cutting it but knew she would understand that I had to have a piece of her with me that I could touch. I placed it with a cutting from her bunkaleena and put them in a round clear plastic case, along with a silk butterfly, in the cabinet in our bathroom. I passed by it every morning. I used to notice it every day; now it was just there, along with my books, carved Buddha, candles, crosses, and a few cards.

November 22, 2007:
Thanksgiving

Kimberly and Kevin came home, and so for the very first time, just the four of us celebrated Thanksgiving. It felt really good; we needed that quiet. We needed the time alone to just be together and heal. Strange that it took us seven years to allow for that degree of self-care during one of the most stressful times of the year. We were happy in ways we had not been happy before. We laughed and cried together. Kristin was a part of our day, a single burning candle on the dining room table. All our energy was available to ourselves, for the walls of protection that had been necessary during past Thanksgivings were eliminated today. This was the first time we did not disintegrate in total exhaustion and tears by the end of the evening, going to bed early as a means to find some relief.

As I cleaned up the dishes, I reflected on all of the Thanksgivings and was aware that no combination of family celebration mattered, because the suffering was there, and there wasn't any way around it. We had to go through it. For fifteen years we were host to both sides of the family with a sit-down dinner for fifty or more, with two turkeys and more side dishes than one could imagine. I could not conceive of providing such a huge Thanksgiving just six weeks after your death, and so I let it all go. Our family tradition broke apart, as well as the traditions of the entire extended family.

This was a particularly powerful Thanksgiving. It churned up resting sediment, and I found myself considering family gatherings as well as gatherings in general. Beyond the sun that streamed through casement windows, beyond the tables graced with platters of abundance, beyond the laughter and exuberant conversations, there was the unspoken. No one mentioned Kristin anymore. In fact, people rarely asked us, "How are you doing?" I wondered if they thought we were all better after a number of years. I wondered if they had forgotten Kristin. Maybe family and friends would like to forget her, because her death had brought a lot of pain. I was sure that seeing us must have brought it all back. I was aware of a dance we did together, especially as the years went on. We engaged in the silence, it separated us from the truth. They wanted it to be better, and sometimes it was and sometimes it was not. There was compassion in acknowledging what was. Kristin was dead.

It took an enormous amount of time, years and years for the pain to ease. Perhaps they were caught in fear, in erroneous beliefs, like those beliefs that allotted six months to a year for normal grieving, or beliefs that one gets over it and moves on. I am angry that society does not understand the depth and breadth of suffering that a bereaved parent experiences. And I am angry that bereavement theories do little to correct that lack of understanding. I also realized that the bereaved community did a disservice to society in hiding and smoothing over the truth of their own suffering. One was never the same; it was a matter of working through the trauma, discovering a new self, and finding a way to meaningfully fit back into life again. Healing was lifelong.

It was Thanksgiving evening. I folded my black and white dishtowel over a few drying pans. This particular holiday allowed for remembering and perhaps a restructuring of holidays based on our evolving needs. I was glad we stayed home. When it was all said and done, our family was our family. They loved us and we loved them. Life was imperfect.

December 5, 2007:
Raw Edges

I left "Wild-eyed Writer" unfinished for a long time, because I could not come to grips with cutting it from the surface of the page and into its five-by-eight-inch format. I loved the wild white hair and diamond pen that extended beyond the boundaries. One evening, on a whim, I cut the collage out. The second I finished cutting, I hated it and noticed all the emotions and judgments rising within me. I was angry and upset that I had not let it be what it wanted to be as it broke from the traditional format to which I had grown accustomed. The words "broke from tradition" resonated inside me. My healing journey had not exactly been a traditional one. My process with this collage seemed to be giving me permission to break rules. I stayed alert and wondered about deeper meanings.

I impatiently threw away all the pieces and scraps; they sat in the trash for weeks as I moved on with other things. I placed the "Wild-eyed Writer" before me as I continued to write, and I observed the continued unease I felt. Finally I rooted through the trash for the pieces, but I couldn't find them until I dumped the trash all over the studio floor and meticulously searched. They were crumpled; I ironed them. I placed what I could find around the edges of the already completed collage and glued it all down on black construction paper. I tore it off and glued it all on white construction paper. I tore it off, only to glue it back on white paper again. I played with this wild one, dancing with her and asking what she wanted from me.

In the end, my "Wild-eyed Writer" settled down onto a nine-by-twelve-inch piece of heavy white watercolor paper. I positioned her off center and glued the found scraps from the trash around the borders. The edges and pieces formed an incomplete frame. The edges were raw. It was the rawness that made it real and interesting. The edges were not neat and perfect; some pieces were missing, and they would always be that way. I had been immersed in this collage's unfolding process for a long time. I noticed how it coincided with my writing practice.

As I considered this collage, my attention was drawn to what spilled out of the frame, to the edges. I had dumped the trash out on the floor and meticulously searched for the lost pieces. I listened to an inner voice say, "Do not be afraid; root around in the trash, go right to those places, to those edges, for that is what is real. There is beauty in the truth, in what's torn." My creations spoke to me as much as I spoke about them and to them as I wrote. In that moment I fell in love again with the edges of my grief journey.

Support came to me as one creative process informed the other. I had spent most of my days with images, not words. I had a limited familiarity with grief and bereavement literature, mostly from my days in graduate school. I had no idea what was currently in the literature from a theoretical and research point of view, both in the field of art therapy and grief and bereavement. I had no desire to delve into these academic worlds.

I was aware of the extensive body of work written by survivors, powerful and evocative accounts of personal courage and survival. I had read some but not much. I was content in the world I had created for myself. I was focused on my own healing process. I existed in a bubble unto myself.

The creative process around "Wild-eyed Writer" served as a teaching. It told me to have courage, because my creative journey broke from traditional paths of healing, and my writing beckoned me deeper still. I was encouraged to root around in the trash of my life. I had no real clear sense about where I was going or the shape of my story. I continued to feel into unknown territory. I was wildly writing, and that was all I knew. I was sharing my images and it was as simple as that. I felt supported and encouraged.

My sisters asked if writing was a cathartic experience. They seemed surprised to hear that it was not. I created in a refined and expansive emptiness and now wrote in that same emptiness. The creative process opened the door to altered states of consciousness; art making and writing were powerful vehicles where I showed up and was present. It was more like being in prayer that anything else. The words continued to move through me. I wondered if I could have written about my grief from the beginning, from the early mourning of Kristin's death. I sensed that I could not. The unspeakable needed its due before I wrote. I had no language for Kristin's fall, her bruised body and her blood. I moved in spirals and through layers. I loved the process. I looked at this recent image of myself, this "Wild-eyed Writer." I looked at the other images of myself, created over the course of the last six years. I felt inspired.

December 12, 2007:
Circle of Snow and Light

My own spiritual development circle had met every Wednesday since September 2005. Soul Gatherings had become a sacred time where I felt supported and guided. Our meditation tonight began with an image of falling snow. In my experience I sat in a winter garden, and snow was falling. Each snowflake passed through my body, taking away my grief and remitting it to the earth. Like an image in a snow globe, I was upside down and right side up. I was tossed this way and that way at the same time I was healed by snow and light. I rested in this sacred space with the sound of angels singing the Gloria. Each cell within me responded to the harmony. I sat with gifts in red boxes at my feet. The red reminded me of blood, of the root chakra that supported me and kept me grounded. An angel moved forward and wrapped her wings around me for protection, while another offered me her wings so that I could soar to the heavens. I was not alone; Kristin was right by my side. Tears dropped from my closed eyes as my experience came to an end, the midline of my fuchsia shirt a few shades darker.

I tucked "Snow and Light" inside my heart and knew that in the coming days I would cherish this healing experience.

In ten days we would board a plane for Saint Lucia. We would spend the holidays in a tropical paradise by ourselves. We would end this year missing our children still.

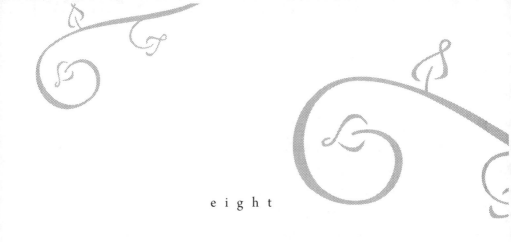

eight

making meaning

January 1, 2008:
Full Moon

We ushered in the new year with mixed feelings. We spent the holidays alone in Saint Lucia. According to the Wikipedia, free encyclopedia, "Lucy's Latin name *Lucia* shares a root (*luc-*) with the Latin word for light, *lux*. In Lucy is said, the way of light."

Kimberly and Kevin spent the holidays together in Los Angeles. Love made the separation and breaking apart of Christmas possible; without love change is impossible. I had come to terms with most of the 364 days of the year, except Christmas. Christmas memories served as lightning rods into the depths of my evolving journey. It seemed that Kristin's death demanded complete surrender, in the process of rebirth. My attachment to our previous Christmas traditions had loosened; Saint Lucia had played its part. Things changed. Perhaps we were in the right place, after all. Letting go and moving with the flow of life was a process.

January 10, 2008:
Medicine

In my dream I was bitten by a huge snake. I was unafraid as I observed its large fangs penetrating my skin and pumping venom into my left calf. An observing part of me was aware and took note. I listened to my inner voice saying, "This dream is important and should be recorded upon wakening." I was filled with its mystery as I woke and moved through my day.

I remembered another snake dream, from January 23, 2002. In that dream I was in my unfinished basement crawling over snakes. I removed an inner white robe and saw that snakes covered my body. One had bitten me on my left shoulder. I was not afraid.

I experienced my two snake dreams as bookends, to these seven years around grief's labyrinth. I was fascinated by these dreams. I became a sleuth of sorts: I did research, I googled, I looked things up. I found meaning in the symbolism.

In my dreams I had been bitten on my left shoulder and on my left calf. I wondered about right vs. left. In Jung's book *Man and His Symbols*, Marie-Louise van Franz said, "The right side [is] the side where things become conscious … while left signifies the sphere of unadapted, unconscious reactions." The left side is also the side of the heart, the side of love.

I remembered sensing that the snake's venom was medicine rather than poison. I sensed that my unconscious literally and symbolically received medicine, so it could release into consciousness what needed healing.

I remembered that I removed layers of clothing in my dream. In my creative process I let go into my images and shed what was not needed, just like a snake. I thought of these dreams and of my grief journey. I was aware of snake images in my collage work. I did not know exactly when the image first appeared, until I searched and found a snake in December 2003's collage #11: "The Wisdom."

A large green snake makes its way down the trunk of a tree that appears cut in half. An open book sits like an ornament, marking the snake's descent.

I looked at that tree cut in half and felt myself cut in half by Kristin's death. I glued it there, an open book, in 2003. At that time I focused on myself as the open book, the nude exposed by the trauma of suicide. The open book now took on more meaning, especially in light of the fact that I was writing.

Snake: symbol of transformation. Its image appeared in other collages with an unusual concentration of them in 2006, in the months prior to Minuit's death and my scream.

March 14, 2008:
Rebirth

Collage #73: "Awakening"

Sarasota, Florida, with my girlfriends was wonderful, a real getaway with tennis in the morning and afternoon. A few years ago, I would never have considered going away, knowing it would have been too stressful. I would not have had the ability to be with others over an extended period in such close quarters. As time moved forward, I was once again able to participate in the fullness of life.

When I came home, I found a flower image photographed on black paper. It was compelling. I instantly saw buds emerging from a body; I also knew what body I wanted to use. In March of 2003 I created collage #5, "I'd Rather Die." I used many images from an ad that was quite popular during that time. In my mind, the resemblance between those images and Kristin was striking. I found them extremely evocative as I made my way into her brokenness. I saved extras of those images and made copies of certain ones I loved. There she was. In five minutes, "Awakening" was complete.

You rest with your hands over your heart. The most beautiful buds in various stages of opening emerge from your body. It is so simple and so beautiful. I notice the placement of the buds along your torso and sense their blessing. I paint the back and edges of this collage black. I color copy two of the buds and glue them onto the painted surface in the lower right-hand corner. In the quiet I hear, "Once there were three, now there are two." It moves over me like a soft breeze. I feel a sense of tranquility as I take in the image before me.

I placed "Awakening" next to "I'd Rather Die" and sat quietly before them. I created this current collage using an image I used five years ago. I noticed my treatment of Kristin's dead body, and the changes over time. As I considered the entire body of my work, I noticed my continued movement over her falling, brokenness, and blood. Today buds emerged from her stilled form. Death and birth were intertwined in this image.

March 17, 2008:
Curious

I was curious about how my images of Kristin's death transformed over the years. I returned to my first collage in December 2002, "Caution," and noted how I imagined her flying and falling at the same time. *You are perched atop a building, spreading your wings and wanting to fly away.* I imagined her falling a short distance as I repositioned the grounds proximity to the top of the building. The black paper held the paradox. I tentatively approached Kristin's brokenness in the fully clothed figure resting at the base of a cathedral's spire. *A large black and blue hand rests on your abdomen.* After creating my first collage, I moved more fully into the horror of it all—her fall, her brokenness and blood.

In January 2003, collage #2: "Madness," I played with Kristin's dead body several times within the same piece. Her body was dressed and formal in its lifelessness. Blood took the form of tears—but my tears.

In February 2003, collage #4: "Suffering," I immersed myself in Kristin's destruction. I moved from an initial symbolic floral treatment of blood, to a graphic pooling representation. Twice, I placed her falling body into the frame of my journey through hell. I entered into it all and found release as I let go of what consumed my imagination.

In March 2003, collage #5: "I'd Rather Die," I laid Kristin out repeatedly, too many times to count, in order to come to grips with the fact she was dead. Mercifully, blood took the form of red rose petals.

In March 2003, collage #6: "Grand Illusion," I played with the notion of Kristin's impermanence. I played along the edge of the living and dead. *She gazes at me upside down, not once but three times. I paste "fly" into the right hand corner of this collage, and I imagine her ascension.*

In April 2003, collage #7: "Field of Screams," the intensity of Kristin's death seemed to reach a crescendo. Black and blue images mixed with skulls.

Kristin was upside down and falling; she was in flames as I explored *"How the bottom fell out."*

In April 2003, collage #8: "Purple Tears," I moved completely into the black and blue, into the bruise. Kristin fell like a river of purple nail polish.

I engaged other aspects of Kristin's suicide over the next year, her mental illness, my rage, myself, and my spiritual beliefs. I returned to the themes of her falling, brokenness, and blood in March 2004, when I created collage #13: "Sudden Impact." In that piece, Kristin's body was draped in a red braid and covered with red flowers while hands reached up to support her fall. Spirit, in the form of white doves, was released from Kristin's ribcage. Blood transformed to something visually more palpable and less violent. I imagined Kristin held and supported in the moment of her death and created an image that would visually align me with my hearts longing. Her body, although torn and broken, appeared beautiful and at rest.

In September 2004 collage #16: "Forgiveness," I met Kristin in the middle ground. Mother and daughter were held in a compassionate forest of green light. There were no images or references to falling and blood. Kristin was dressed in white; she was light. I held her and sensed healing.

In December 2004, collage #17: "Holiday Spirit," references to falling were predominately captured in the buildings that were upside down with a veiled white figure falling, almost unnoticed in the background. Blackened eyes were the soft tell-tale references to the bruises. I sensed change.

Another year went by before I returned to Kristin. I consciously asked, "Where am I with your death?" In January 2006, collage #22: "Silver Death," Kristin's life and death was held in shimmering silver energy. There was a feeling of compassion as I imagined the presence of Kuan Yin, the goddess of mercy. I pasted down a winged Kristin with a bunny rabbit and red rose. After so many years of dealing with the torments of her shattered body, it was a relief to see her angelic. That image of Kristin's death appeared spiritual and peaceful. Images of her violent death transformed and allowed for a more peace filled integration of Kristin's suicide.

In February 2006, collage #27: "Blood Rabbit," Kristin's blood was symbolically represented by dripping paint. Red roses were scattered about. One small rose fell discretely from the edge of a red cross.

I spent a lot of time telling the story, revisiting the moment of Kristin's death. I was unaware of any conscious fixation concerning the event. I did not ruminate over it during my waking hours. It came up unconsciously, through my association with the images that found me. I stepped aside and allowed what was happening to happen, usually surprised that I once again returned to falling, to Kristin's body, to blood, to that moment.

My experience was that the storytelling was restorative, as I revisited the narrative of Kristin's violent death. I felt energized rather than depleted as I created; it was always a tender revisiting. The creative texture was an energy field, a compassionate and safe container for the pieces of horror to arrange themselves and then arrange themselves again. There was a humanness to the process, a nurturing quality that belied reason. I created and felt resilient.

Mutually exclusive and contradictory elements, inherent in Kristin's violent death, were contained on paper: she was alive and dead, she was falling and flying, she was broken and whole, she was bleeding and beautiful. The paper was a space for images that were irrational because grief was irrational and did not make sense. Kristin's suicide did not make sense, and so I played in it and found my way through.

I noticed that my attention moved fluidly back and forth, oscillating between creating into the horrific details and considering design elements such as line, color, and form. I engaged both my right and left brain. My movement between horrific details and design was unconscious and only became conscious as I moved into a place of reflection over my process. Eventually the horror lost its power and strength. My fingers no longer needed to feel into images of Kristin's death. There was more light than darkness; I had a different perspective.

I noticed how I took care of Kristin in the present moment and gave myself the opportunity to be with her in her dying. I moved with ease through time. Image stimulated memory, and one memory connected with another memory. Often the door opened to memories of Kristin's life in addition to her death; they mixed together. At the end of an hour, at the end of a day, in the end I felt better.

My visual diary seemed to support the efficacy of the process.

March 25, 2008:
Kevin's Birthday

I came in from tennis, and the phone was ringing. I stood in the kitchen by my desk with my coat on and heard Kevin's voice. I sat and suddenly felt sad; he was calling me before I had had the chance to call him on his birthday. I offered my usual, "Hi, bebop." I did not hear his usual, "Hi, bebop," in response. I knew something was wrong as I heard myself saying happy birthday anyway. For some reason I asked where he was—although I expected him to say he was at work, somewhere inside of me, I knew otherwise.

I heard Kevin saying, "I'm home sitting on my bed, with a box of things from my office. They let me go this morning. They let me go on my birthday." I imagined him sitting in his apartment, where Kristin had been with Kimberly just a few hours before her death. I sensed Kristin sitting on the bed with her brother, arms around his shoulder as we realized his days on Wall Street had come to an end. I wondered if he felt her draw near to him.

I heard our breath move together out of our bodies. There was a stillness that seemed to gather around us, although he was in New York and I was in Baltimore. Out of the silence came the details of the morning that answered the why and how of it all. He knew it was coming, because financial institutions were experiencing shake-ups of every variety. He had weathered a few storms, but not this one. Out of the silence also came the realization that this was the most amazing birthday gift he had ever received.

We talked about the moment as an opportunity to explore other possibilities. He was not happy on Wall Street, had never really been happy there. He described it as a soul-less pit, one devoid of purpose and meaning beyond the accumulation of wealth. He wanted to make a difference. I wondered how long he might have spent immersed in a job that crushed his spirit. I felt life in motion, moving Kevin forward and into the unknown. We laughed, although I suspected that tears were an equal part of Kevin's experience. He was going to take some time for himself. I wondered what was in store for him.

April 12, 2008:
Erin's Wedding

Today was Erin's wedding. I remembered how I eased into the chair in the kitchen and held the receiver casually, listening to my sister Elizabeth say she had good news. I noticed her hesitation as she almost whispered, "Erin's engaged." If she had been with me, she would have seen my face flush and tears well up in my eyes. She could not see my shock as I slumped in my seat and crossed my legs tight. I refused to cry and to give into the moment. This was my sister's moment, and I wanted to be happy for her and for Erin. I cried after I hung up.

From the moment Erin got engaged, I wondered how I would feel on this wedding day. We had been to so many weddings in the years since Kristin's death. The days preceding any big occasion were the days in which the grief work got accomplished. Each experience was different. This one was of particular importance because I had memories of Kristin and Erin together from the time they were babies. They were the same age. They were favorite cousins and were glued to each other at every family gathering. We had so many pictures of them in each other's arms, laughing. I remembered them standing in the family room at Easter with their arms around each other. That picture by the sofa was the last of them together before Kristin died. Kristin would have been in Erin's wedding, and Erin would have been in Kristin's.

Today I grabbed hold of myself and took another look in the mirror before leaving our hotel, hoping that all the months of considering this wedding would allow me the reprieve for which I prayed. I realized I had no control and feared what I was feeling on the inside would ooze out and everyone would see it. I placed makeup in my purse and added a few extra tissues. I got in the car with Douglas and Kevin.

On the way to church, I reflected on how Erin's wedding asked me to find my balance within states of joy for her and intense states of sorrow over Kristin. I felt the staggering weight of loss in the fact that Kristin would not know love, not be engaged, not have a bridal shower, not shop for a wedding dress, not walk down the aisle with her father, not say "I do," and not have a first dance. I noticed how my grief over all other losses crept in and found rest on the foundation of Kristin's death. Her death magnified life's normal challenges a thousandfold and required more from me. With this ritual, this passage, this coming of age, I revisited the well of grief, descending into the abyss of Kristin's suicide—an abyss that held all my losses past, present, and future. I placed my attention on my feelings and let them be.

I started to get very hot when we turned into the church parking lot. We got out of the car and did not look at each other. The moment was sensitive. I sat quietly in the church and then stood. I looked at Erin as she walked down the aisle with Keith, and I was able to breathe in the exquisite joy of the moment. I breathed in love and felt that love holding all I had been through in the preceding months. I stood with my hands folded on the pew in front of me. Douglas moved his hand just close enough to touch my pinky finger, as if holding my hand in that moment would dissolve us both. I listened to the music and knew I would never hear it for Kristin. I felt nothing in that moment ... and I felt everything.

I was proud I made it through the wedding ceremony. I did not dissolve. I was able to smile and to be happy and cry at the same time. Elizabeth, Keith, Donna, Mike, and Mom were all vigilant in their tenderness. During the reception, the cousins enveloped Kevin and made him laugh. They sat at a table together. I glanced over at them on occasion but mostly kept my eyes to myself. It was enough hearing their voices and noticing the ones that were missing. No one could have done more on this wedding day.

Watching the first dance was not easy. I felt my family's eyes on me, gauging my reaction and ready to move close, to reassure. In order to keep steady, I watched but did not see. I felt my soft self being replaced by something else, something hard and unyieldingly cold. Douglas and I got up and joined the rest of the family. I felt Kristin sweep by as we danced. I moved through the day without collapsing as I stayed in the moment as best I could. I moved through this wedding portal. I was on the other side of something and was relieved.

Life's circumstances came and went, arose and fell back into the ocean of life like waves. They crested and crashed onto shore. Kristin was always somewhere in the landscape. In the beginning there was Kristin and only Kristin; her death consumed me for several years. I had only to look back at my earlier collages to remember my grief. I lived and breathed it, and I was glad that I had found my way through it.

Today was an opportunity, and I took stock of myself. I had come a long way. I would not get over Kristin's death—there was no finish line, no end point. There was a lot of peace in embracing the way of it and knowing that my grief was normal. There would be other life events, other weddings, other birthdays, and other anniversaries. I would continue to meet what arose in my life.

April 15, 2008:
Out and About

We sat in our seats high above the audience and readied ourselves for the program. I remembered how Douglas and I enjoyed author Frank McCourt last month. The Speakers Series at the Meyerhoff was one of the things we looked forward to. We never would have considered season tickets to anything during the early years of our recovery; it would have been too difficult getting out, there were too many people, we were too exhausted, we couldn't think, and we couldn't sit still. We were in a different place now.

We both loved hearing Frank McCourt share the story of his life, captured in the pages of *Angela's Ashes*. I resonated with the pain and with the storytelling. I admired his process. I was glad to be out and about, to be a part of the ordinary. I was aware of how much in the flow of life I was again, the weekend wedding a thing of the past. Since we returned home, there had been lunch with a friend and the Twenty-second Annual Mood Disorders Research/Education Symposium, presented by Johns Hopkins Medicine. I relaxed and smiled as the lights dimmed.

May 11, 2008:
Mother's Day Celebration

Collage #71: "The Dance"

Today I celebrated myself in addition to celebrating my mother. After our traditional lunch, I took the afternoon off and wrote. I was in deep layers of communion with the energy and content of my images as I wrote in the family room. My collages were out of storage, my favorite one next to me: the one I created this past February. I examined it and moved fluidly through time and observed my metamorphosis. I had recreated myself, had re-imaged myself.

It is a good February, and so when I see her, she beckons me. She seems to embody the light I am feeling, even though it's the middle of winter. I float above pink hydrangeas in a soft green woodland. I dance a dance of joy in this space with you. Multicolored jewels fall from the sky and surround my moving body.

I created a frame for this collage with the leftover pieces, just like I had with "Wild-eyed Writer" in October 2007. The technique offered me a sense of control. I chose what stayed in the center and what moved to the edge.

I find you on the edge. You seem to be completing a headstand at the same time I have the distinct impression you have fallen from the heavens. I return to your fall again. I allow the unspeakable, unfathomable, and impossible in, but it's not at my center. A portion of your dress swishes by me and is the only reminder of your presence.

A small dragon sculpture marked the place where Kristin touched this earth. She lived in a dimension that was separate from me and yet was not. I saw that she took up space in the outer edge of my life.

As I considered this collage, I saw that our dance together was ultimately one of beauty. I was sure I never would have used those words during the early years of our dance, when I was gripped in the horror of her suicide. I was mystified by my creation and what it said to me. I created "The Dance" right before Valentine's Day. I was ready for it to be a celebration of love rather than one of heartbreak.

As I turned and placed "The Dance" back into its rightful sequence, I noticed the pink dogwoods in bloom on the back patio. I remembered Kristin sitting under them and opening her graduation gift from us. We gave her a string of pearls.

May 23, 2008:
Minuit's Anniversary

Today was the second anniversary of Minuit's death and my scream. I had it marked on my calendar so I would not forget. I wanted to honor her memory, for it was a pivotal moment that connected past and present, a transformative moment that still touched my heart.

The evocative images might have gone unnoticed for a while, but eventually I would have seen them. I would have seen what related to my scream, to my primal letting go. The images had been there right from the beginning. My consciousness had placed the appropriate forms right in front of me so that I could observe the missing piece. I sensed that my spirit engaged what my physical body was incapable of handling. I found my creative process quite extraordinary, because it moved me closer to a moment that was ultimately beyond my control: Minuit's fall.

- January 2003, collage #2: "Madness"—a monkey opened its mouth, revealed its teeth, and screamed.
- February 2003, collage #3: "Once Upon a Time"—I dripped like water over another part of myself that clutched at my own throat. One self rested inside another self like Russian dolls stacked one inside another. Invisible parts screamed a scream that was heard and not head.
- April 2003, collage #7: "Field of Screams"—pure sound emanated off the page; it screamed.
- November 2003, collage #10: "Rage: Code Red"—I wanted to pull Kristin's hair out as I screamed why, why, why, like an insane monkey.
- December 2003, collage #11: "The Wisdom"—I breathed freely, in light of the fact that my new self was held by death's screaming darkness and Botticelli's angels.
- July 2005, collage #19: "Transformation"—My left hand was covered in butterflies and partly covered my throat.

The subtle references did not end there but carried through even as my collage work significantly changed in 2006. I scrutinized each collage and searched for other times when I was drawn to my body and to my waiting scream. The three collages preceding Minuit's death on May 23, 2006, were shockingly significant.

- April 2006, collage #34: "Corseted"—I couldn't take my eyes off the hand that covered my throat.
- April 2006, collage #35: "Yellow Bird Cage"—I did not like the bulging, strained curve of my neck. My neck was exposed.
- April 2006, collage #36: "Green Crocodile"—I stood on the coffin's edge, on the midpoint of fern covered lungs.

As I revisited those images, I saw them in a different light, because their significance remained veiled, even within my own awareness as I was creating. I had noticed my screams absence from the night we received the phone call, when I watched Douglas screaming and wondered why I was not doing the same thing. I was not thinking about my missing scream while I was creating collages, especially the later ones. I saw my images edging me closer to fulfilling my desire to scream and integrate a missing piece. I consciously and unconsciously allowed its energy to come into form.

I also saw those images as prophetic, in the sense that an inordinate number of images appeared in my collage work in April, right before Minuit died. I felt that the multiple and repeated references were not a coincidence. At the time I did not make the connections between my art work and my scream; that happened years later. Writing about my collages took me there as I entered a process of reflection and synthesis.

The presence of scream images right before Minuit's fall was mysterious, and I wondered how it happened. I had no rational answer to this mystery, other than the answers that came from the spiritual side of me, from the side of beliefs and faith in an order and purpose to things. I sensed God's presence, because my images pointed the way toward what I never saw coming. I felt that I was prepared and readied for what would happen. I felt supported. I was not alone in this life and was blessed with healing.

The sense I had of my journey was not some elusive notion. I held it in my hand, a tangible reflection of what had transpired over time. I indeed released unwanted waste, my lungs emptied, my throat opened, and I let go. I screamed and there was healing.

In May 2006, collage #40: "Clenched Heart," I was given a visual record of my hearts condition. It offered me a snapshot of myself so that I could make a comparison a few short weeks later when Minuit fell from my hands. Fragments of Kristin's death and missing pieces became integrated, and I felt a measure of wholeness. This newfound sense of myself gave me strength. I had a better understanding of closure and completion and replaced those words with growth and evolution. I was even more aware of my process, in the very substance of my body. Kristin died, and I shattered and floated like dust. We returned to the earth, Kristin's body and mine, mine mixing with tears, clay-like and ready for grief's hand to begin its work.

In June 2006, collage #42: "Gift Boxes," I observed myself and noticed my physical transformation over time from clay to rock, to black-and-white marble, to flesh and blood. I held my head up high with an open heart. I remembered my 2001 walled garden dream, when I saw little blue boxes within the heart of an alligator resting in mud. All these years later I interpreted the boxes as grief gifts and understood their promise of personal growth and transformation. I sensed how I was moved through the prayer wheel of my life, as past and present connected. The grief gifts cascaded along my body, my journey highlighted by the words "All about the Fall."

July 4, 2008:
Presence

It was the Fourth of July, and we invited our friends over. We had not entertained very much over the years, not like we used to. I had not had the desire or the ability to endure the stresses of planning, hosting, and cleaning up. Today I felt happy setting up the large square table in the studio space for the eight of us to celebrate. I covered it with old newspapers and added red, white, and blue napkins and some flowers. I opened the doors and windows and put on beautiful soulful music. I placed candles in the garden outside. I felt strong and capable.

In this refuge Kristin was everywhere, and when they came in, they went right over to her photograph and picked her up. They turned and we looked at each other; there was nothing that needed to be said. We sat and picked at crabs all night. I talked and laughed. Perhaps only I realized the changes and knew the difference. I listened with presence and really cared about what was being shared. This empathetic and engaged part of myself disappeared when Kristin died. I had no strength for anyone but myself and my survival. It had taken a long time for this part of me to return to the ways with which I was familiar. I had cherished deep and intimate relationships with family and friends and had missed those kinds of interactions over the years, mostly because I sensed my own diminished capacity and inability to connect. The breeze wafted through this celebration and the music played and I had the wherewithal to feel and listen.

In the past, when I heard mothers talk about the never-ending details of their children's lives, it was traumatizing. I could hardly stomach those who complained about their children and the petty difficulties of their lives. However, it was worse listening to those who boasted of their children's and grandchildren's success; the gushing would drive me to a frozen place. I remembered sitting across from someone as she went on and on, feeling myself falling apart and wanting to reach across the table and shake her as I yelled, "Do you have any sense about you? Do you have any idea what you are doing?" I sat and said nothing, though I was tortured.

It hurt, even when family and friends were conscious that their stories might be difficult for me, a mother of a child who ended her own life, along with surviving children whose lives were broken and tenuous at best. Most often I disappeared, watching myself recede to some distant place and hoping that my eyes would not give me away as I died inside. Sometimes I would suddenly change the subject—or better yet, simply walk away, saying I needed a drink, to go to the ladies room; I'd pick from a host of other self-protections in my arsenal. These were normal conversations that happened naturally between women. It was part of the aftermath with which I was forced to contend. It was part of loss.

My sisters and very close friends were compassionate, and they silenced themselves in order to protect me. I was eternally grateful for their tender caring. I knew their silence came at a cost to them because they not only lost Kristin, they lost their sister and friend with whom they naturally would have wanted to share the fullness of their own mother journeys and pride in their children's accomplishments.

It took strength and compassion and commitment to stand by me, unwavering day after day and week after week for years. We each did our best. I knew over time I had gotten stronger in my capacity to listen, to share, and to genuinely care. I could be with them because I could be with myself, all of myself. I sat today among my friends and noticed my capacity to be fully present, to listen with all of my heart and not fly away.

August 27, 2008:
Myself

My birthday was a time when I reflected on myself. The year was a poignant movement through, a seventh year marked by months of writing, by months of remembering as I wove back and forth between image and word. I loved what I was doing. I looked in the mirror and was please with my reflection.

The moment of Kristin's death marked a before and after. I thought I knew who I was before that moment. After the phone call, I broke into a million pieces and floated out into the universe. I had no concept of myself, no sense of my own body. My eyes were lifeless. I existed in that void for over a year until the creation of my first collage in December 2002.

I pasted my naked, flesh-colored self onto the page and found comfort, steadied by the fact I could see my nearly invisible self. As the weeks went by, I noticed how I identified myself with Kristin's suicide. I merged with Kristin and experienced her broken and bleeding body as my own. I wondered which one was which as I placed another falling figure into the frame work of my creation. I had become the horror that she inflicted on her own flesh.

In February 2003's collage #3: "Once Upon a Time," I marked myself with the stigma and shame of it all, and I pasted the word "suicide" on my forehead. I was in pieces. I dripped. I floated about. I was cut in half. I was disconnected. I loved sitting with this image of myself, strangely grounded in the truth of my everyday experience.

For the next six months I systematically made my way into Kristin's physical destruction before I returned to myself again. In November 2003's collage #10: "Rage: Code Red," I was an iconic figure of pulsating rage. I explored various aspects of my still fragmented self. I sat in a chair on fire and asked, "Why?" I was dark and brooding, barely visible. I was an inhuman artist's rendition with an exposed heart. I sensed progress when I placed collage #10 alongside collage #3.

In December 2003, collage #11: "The Wisdom," I was front and center, naked and exposed. I looked at myself in a mirror and saw my cruciform reflection. I was less fragmented; I was more whole.

In January 2004, collage #12: "The Goldfish," I wondered if I was the goldfish that had everything it needed. The goldfish appeared whole, in an environment that was in pieces and floated among stars. I saw movement and sensed healing.

In April 2004, collage #14: "Seen," I played with two distinct parts of myself. One was cloaked in light and ascended a set of stairs while the other one was stone-faced and inhabited the underworld. I was particularly drawn to a black-and–white, partially naked figure that arose in the submerged wasteland. She gave me hope.

In September 2004, collage #16: "Forgiveness," I was grounded in compassion and a single whole figure.

In March 2005, collage #18: "Letting Go," I explored my innocent, untouched self; at the same time I acknowledged my wounded part, the one in the yellow dress. I was intrigued by the one with the capacity to witness it all, to silently observe. I felt possibility in that field of colorful flowers.

In July 2005: Collage #19: "Transformation," I was covered in black and white butterflies. I sensed change.

In January 2006, collage #23: "Golden Creatrix," I was a powerful figure in command of her creative energies, and I was haloed in golden light. The creation of that collage was a defining moment, because all references to myself after that were whole rather than fragmented.

In March 2006, collage #33: "Ascension," I arose on a shaft of gold and moved toward a single diamond sparkling with light. I sensed movement.

In September 2006, collage #47: "Reborn," I imagined myself tattooed. I had become my own creation. My identity was reshaped by my process; I had recreated myself. I was pleased with myself as artist. I had imaged myself into my future.

In September 2007, collage #60: "The Book," I embraced myself as writer, and my book sprung like wings from my back. I continued to grow.

In February 2008, collage #71: "The Dance," I wrapped myself in multicolored jewels and danced. I was alive.

I sat quietly before myself with a cup of tea. My pieces had rearranged themselves not as they had been before Kristin's suicide, but in another way. I was reborn.

The Missing Chair

We went home from our vacation in Jackson Hole by way of Los Angeles, a small detour so that we could visit Kimberly. Kevin happened to be in LA, too, still traveling and exploring after being let go from his Wall Street job. It was the first time the four of us had been together since Thanksgiving.

It was early evening, and the breeze that kept the temperature bearable had ceased. We arrived at Kimberly's thirties style pink stucco apartment. We were tired after a long day followed by a long wait in line for carryout. There were hugs and kisses, yet underneath it was an air of detachment and formality. Red plates were set out and four chairs pulled up—four, not five. Years after Kristin's death, she filled the space just like the aroma of the various vegan dishes sitting at the center of the table. We began talking, and I looked over at Kevin and smiled. That moment dislodged something in Kimberly and once it began there was no stopping it. It gathered in intensity and uprooted more and more debris. Her body trembled in the midst of it as tears gave way to silence. Kristin's suicide mixed with our individual issues. Time and distance had not been kind to us but rather created the perfect conditions for an explosion. In truth we were a fragmented family made up of still fragmented individuals.

I was stunned and unable to predict or control an episode like this. The vigilant part of myself had receded into the background over the years; it only took an incident like that to alert me to our fragility. A pregnant silence created a pause and then a breadth. We stayed with it, we listened, we talked, we shared, we cried. We did not turn away. It would have been easy to get up and leave. We did not.

We sought each other out again the next night. We shared dinner at a restaurant with outdoor seating. In that garden setting we revisited our pain, our lives together as a family, our individual paths, our failures and successes. We continued to be present to what needed tending. I had the impression that the restaurant was glad when we left; it was obvious we were in the middle of intense interactions. My tears flowed freely, as well as everyone else's. I allowed them rather than holding them in. We moved into new territory over those few days, ultimately lighter, torn up by the fall, ready for new skin to form. Family healing was complicated by the individual journeys that intertwine, but it was not impossible.

September 23, 2008:
Monica's Massage

It was a remarkably better summer and fall, one I never imagined possible. At the same time I enjoyed this, I was aware of a very subtle pain in my back. My pain was along my spine where my right shoulder blade rested. I blamed it on too much tennis and on too much writing. Then I blamed it on my grief, because the body was always the last to heal. I went to Monica for a massage. I'd seen Monica consistently throughout the years, scheduling appointments as needed depending on the level of stress. I rested on the massage table and was confident she would massage the pain out of my back. I wanted it to be as simple as that, and so I was not prepared for what happened. I should have known by now that healing comes over a life time, in bits and pieces.

Our session was almost over, and she asked how I was feeling. I told Monica that my back still hurt, "Like I have been stabbed." As soon as I uttered those words, my heart began to ache as the word "betrayed" entered me. "Betrayed, betrayed, betrayed," echoed inside as tears fell along the contour of my face. I did not move to wipe them away and just lay there.

In seven years, that word had not made its way into my consciousness. Shame, guilt, fear, anger, and a hundred other words and feelings had entered my heart … but never betrayed. "You betrayed yourself. You betrayed me. You betrayed my trust. You said you would never do something like that. You said you loved me. You lied to me. You shocked me. You stabbed me in the back. You murdered yourself; you committed the ultimate betrayal."

Kristin's willful disregard for the life I had given left a permanent scar on my body and soul. I was surprised that the pain in my back ultimately revealed a healing opportunity. I was surprised by the intense feeling that seemingly appeared out of nowhere. Monica allowed me the time to be with what was moving through me.

In that space an image took form. Betrayed manifested as a woman impaled. The image was downloaded into my imagination. I could not wait to get home and create a collage from what I'd just experienced. I knew she was waiting for me with her back exposed, a lady in red.

This was the territory of my journey.

I noticed the pain in my back was gone as I drove home.

 October 10, 2008:
Sacred Seven

Tomorrow marks seven years, seven portals in my journey out of the abyss. In Hebrew, seven (Sheh'-Bah) comes from a root word that means to be complete or full. It's considered a sacred and holy number. It is a prime number that combines the spiritual three with the material four. There are seven acts of creation, seven stars in the Pleiades, seven sacraments, seven colors in the rainbow, seven days of the week, seven chakras, seven virtues and deadly sins, seven stages of alchemy, seven ages of man, seven candles on the Menorah, seven pillars of wisdom, and seven joys and sorrows, just to name a few.

I pulled two books from the middle shelf of my refuge. In *Anatomy of the Spirit*, Carolyn Myss says,

The chakra system is an archetypal depiction of individual maturation through seven distinct stages. The chakras are vertically aligned, running from the base of the spine to the crown of the head, suggesting that we ascend toward the Divine by gradually mastering the seductive pull of the physical world. ... The first chakra lessons are related to the material world; the second chakra to sexuality, work and physical desire; the third chakra to ego, personality and self esteem; the fourth chakra to love, forgiveness and compassion; the fifth chakra to will and self expression; the sixth to mind, intuition, insight, and wisdom; and the seventh chakra to lessons related to spirituality.

I had touched all those places over the years. I'd seen it in my work and knew I would continue to touch those places over and over again as I made my way along the spiral of my life.

In *Interior Castles,* Teresa of Ávila said that in the seventh mansion the soul reaches the "Spiritual Marriage where the two lighted candles join and become one: the falling rain becomes merged into the river. There is completion, transformation, ineffable and perfect peace."

I remembered Collage #24: "Blue Wisdom," created in January 2006. I was seated with my arms outstretched in an attitude of receptive surrender. I was raised up. I celebrated. A column of light, in the form of a waterfall, cascaded through the top of my head. Like falling rain, it merged into the river below. It captured the essence of my spiritual journey, a sacredness that was my foundation.

October 11, 2008: Seventh Anniversary of Kristin's Death

I woke this morning and thought of her. The memory of her passed through me without bringing me to tears. I would have loved a dream, but it did not happen. I wondered if she would come to me in some other special way today. I felt a sense of calm and peace and wondered if this was temporary. I smiled, for all was temporary. A part of me silently watched for grief's arrival as I moved through the hours of her anniversary. I wondered about it seeping in and overtaking my heart and bringing me to my knees, but it didn't, not today.

blessings

January 1, 2011:
A Decade

I was aware of my movement toward the tenth anniversary of Kristin's death, which technically began in October but seemed to officially begin with the new year. I had a sense of its place in the flow of my life a decade later. I woke up happy, anticipating all the year might offer.

Kevin; his girlfriend, Sierra; and I shared a coffee this morning. We had celebrated the new year together. They had surprised Douglas and I with a candlelight dinner, balloons, streamers, and all the necessary bells and whistles to bring in 2011. We opened a bottle of Dom Perignon.

Kevin had come home on September 26, 2008, after leaving Wall Street. He completed his post baccalaureate at Goucher College, picked up all his sciences, and was in the process of applying to medical school. Sierra was just months away from completing the same coursework. They were both headed in the same direction.

It was a blessed time having Kevin with us. There had been healing in the three years that he was home. We had the opportunity to get to know each other as adults transformed by life and death, adults making space for each other and all that entailed. We had the opportunity to witness Kevin's and Sierra's love in the fullness of blooming. The alchemy of love was healing.

March 2, 2011: Trauma

It might have been the shocking phone call that woke me up in the middle of the night. It might have been the stress of the weekend workshop I had organized. It might have been the class I facilitated under the watchful eye of my mentor. Separately, I would have handled them; together, they were a trigger to my nervous system. Up until that point, I was successfully handling life's normal stresses.

As the days proceeded, I experienced a range of symptoms that I recognized from the early days of my grief journey. I had read several books about complicated grief, trauma, and posttraumatic stress disorder (PTSD). It all sounded so clinical compared to my direct experience. I wondered how my journey fit into that framework, and in what way I would have been labeled. How I faced the trauma was what mattered to me, because in the end it was the only thing in my control.

These three convergent stresses had activated something in my nervous system, already imprinted with the shock of Kristin's suicide. I was suffering again—not in the same way I had in the past, but a soft and subtle version. It caught me by surprise and reminded me that Kristin's suicide had permanently altered the composition of my being. Life would continue to happen, and when it did, I would face it head on as I had in the past. I was not afraid; I was more annoyed than anything else. It clearly invited me into Kristin's tenth anniversary year.

I took stock of my symptoms and considered my healing options. I did not have the time I once had. I was busy with my workshops and presentation. I was busy with my monthly collage circles and my weekly meditation circles. I was busy with tennis, playing several times a week. I was busy with Kevin and Sierra. I was busy with getting *Artful Grief* published. I was busy with my life in ways I had not been from 2001 to 2004. It was a good busy.

Because of my current symptoms, I made an effort to spend more time in my studio, creating. I added another massage to my regular monthly appointment with Monica, and I added acupuncture. I never considered acupuncture before. I do not know where the idea came from, other than a little voice that said, "Forget that you're terrified of needles and just do it. It will be great."

I made an appointment with Elizabeth, and it *was* great. It worked. Within six weeks I felt better than I had in a long time. A "better" that I did not even know was possible until I felt that way. I likened it to a tune-up: everything was humming perfectly. The disturbing energy that had crawled over the surface of my skin had disappeared. I was grounded in my body and slept better. I was clearer and more focused. I played better tennis. I was peaceful. I was very grateful.

I wished I had taken advantage of this ancient form of healing from the beginning. I wondered in what way my physical suffering may have been eased. I wondered how these past years may have been different. I will never have the answer to that. I have recommended it wholeheartedly to survivors, as another tool for their grief toolbox.

May 20, 2011:
Kimberly's Graduation

Kimberly had been in California for several years, getting her MFA in film and video from the California Institute of the Arts. I had envisioned Kristin getting an MFA, but ironically it was Kimberly who found her way there. Her healing path was forged by her own creative processes as well as her stewardship of Rita Project. All of it had evolved into her work with others.

Ten years later, Kimberly had moved from in front of the camera to behind the camera. She was happy and loved her life in California. She loved the promise her future held. On May 20, 2011, we yelled and screamed for her as she crossed the stage. We took pictures. She held a large bouquet of pink roses, and we were proud.

Kimberly's relationship with Joseph did not survive. He graduated from Columbia University with an MFA in photography. We thought of him on his graduation day and wished him much success.

June 13, 2011: Tenth Anniversary Yellow Dress Golf Classic

We celebrated our Tenth Anniversary Yellow Dress Golf Classic and brought in Active Mind's "Send Silence Packing" exhibition of 1,100 backpacks, representing the number of suicides on college campuses each year. Many of the backpacks were decorated by surviving families in memory of their loved ones, complete with personal pictures and memorabilia. I created one for Kristin using the North Face backpack she carried her senior year. I attached her pink hairbrush, two large paintbrushes, pictures, Pink J Crew flip-flops, a black-and-white camisole, and the green running shoes that did not fit but that she insisted on buying a few weeks before she died. I added Kristin's backpack to the bunch on the grassy knoll. It was a powerful visual statement of loss that brought most of the golfers to tears. We have raised almost $750,000 in ten years, still devoted to mental health awareness, education, and suicide prevention.

I remembered how difficult it was as I stood before a packed room of family and friends on October 7, 2002, our first Yellow Dress Golf Classic. I had no idea what I was doing. I seemed in the flow of something that gathered me up and moved me forward. I remembered how helplessness rested beside purpose, and how the senselessness of Kristin's suicide rested beside my passion to make a difference. I remembered and was overcome with gratitude for this part of my journey, so supported by a community that stood with me for years.

Kristin lived through the Kristin Rita Strouse Foundation. This was her legacy.

July 4, 2011: Jess

Today was a special day. Today we remembered Sierra's seventeen-year-old brother Jess, who was killed in a car accident in 1995. Last year Sierra and Kevin ran up the hill in our yard with sparklers. They celebrated life as the night sky filled with the light of neighborhood fireworks. It seemed strange that Sierra and Kevin would share the loss of a sibling, and yet it seemed somehow perfect. It bound them together in places that I cannot know as a parent. It and other life experiences had molded them into the adults they had become. Life was precious; they meant to make a difference.

I smiled as I imagined Jess and Kristin together.

July 13, 2011:
Medical School

Douglas and I stood on the sidewalk and waved to Sierra and Kevin as they boarded a bus that took them to New York for a flight to Paris. Their final destination was Tel Aviv University, Sackler School of Medicine. We stood with smiles and tears, wishing them the best as they moved into their dreams.

As the bus turned the corner and was out of our sight, I thought of all that had happened in the past ten years. I thought of the experience of loss that wove through my children's lives, and the impact it had on their life decisions. Kimberly and Kevin came to terms with Kristin's death in unique and individual ways. Kristin's suicide had extracted a terrible price. It took a good ten years to see the fruits of their labors, to see them moving on, to feel a sense of hope, to have a sense of future. I had worried, I had wondered, and I had watched.

Today I celebrated.

July 14, 2011:
My Work

Life moved me forward, and I headed to Minneapolis, Minnesota, for The Compassionate Friends (TCF) national conference. It was a time to connect with old friends like Carla and Mitch, as well as to continue on with my collage and meditation workshops, "The Art of Healing: Loss, Grief and Grace" and "Wisdom Bowls: The Inner Journey of Healing." I loved seeing survivors from years past. I loved hearing how my workshops had positively impacted their healing journeys. Some had started collage circles in their home towns; a few had entered graduate school, working toward degrees in art therapy. I came home enriched and encouraged by the process of survivors reaching out and helping other survivors.

I also came home feeling humbled and inspired by what moved through my workshops. There were always compelling moments, more like blessings than anything else. Over the past ten years, one experience stood out, and I always shared it during my workshops and presentations. Over the years I had forgotten in what city it happened; it was early in my journey with TCF.

In that workshop, a young mother drew my attention. Perhaps it was her tears, because she cried from the moment she began her collage. I was surprised when she raised her hand to share. She stood before a packed room of sixty and clutched her collage to her heart. She said, "I lost my eighteen-month-old daughter just two months ago. We had her cremated and released her ashes at sunset in a park in Hawaii, where we played when she was alive. I have prayed to feel a connection to my daughter. I have prayed for a sign. I have prayed, but to no avail." Amidst her tears, she turned over her collage and said, "This is a picture of the exact park in Hawaii, where we released my daughter's ashes. The picture was taken at sunset. I feel my daughter's presence. I feel as if my prayers were answered." Everyone was crying. We stood and clapped. It was an extraordinary experience, a blessing.

She had her pick of any seat in the room. She had her pick of any number of magazines on the table in front of her. She chose a *National Geographic* and opened it to a random page. What are the odds of her finding a sunset picture of the park in Hawaii, where she released her daughter's ashes? I still got goose bumps when I remembered, it was a healing that touched every person in the room.

Over the years my work had grown. In March I was in Frankfort, Kentucky, for The Compassionate Friends (TCF) regional conference. It was a smaller gathering than the national conferences, and I loved that. April was filled with a special Rita Project Workshop for Grassroots Crisis Intervention Center in Maryland. May ended, as it had for the past few years, facilitating Rita Project Open Studio for the Tragedy Assistance Program for Survivors. (TAPS) Over that Memorial Day weekend, Julia, Rita Project's senior art therapist, along with a team of art therapy graduate students, provided a creative environment for those in the military who had lost someone in service to this country.

I had one more national conference after the TCF conference in Minneapolis, The Bereaved Parents of the USA, in Reston, Virginia. I had come full circle again, because BPUSA had been my very first national experience as a workshop presenter in July 2004.

I was recently asked to write articles for The Compassionate Friends magazine (*We Need Not Walk Alone*), The Tragedy Assistance Program for Survivors magazine, and the SoulCollage Neter Letter. I enjoyed this aspect of my healing journey; I loved writing and sharing.

I loved my work and giving back. I was very fortunate. This aspect of my life was different from my work on The Kristin Rita Strouse Foundation and from my involvement with Johns Hopkins Medicine, Department of Psychiatry and Behavioral Sciences. This was personal and intimate. I got down in the trenches with survivors. I shared myself personally and professionally. Kristin lived through my work. She lived on inside of me, in my heart.

August 27, 2011:
Invited

Jill called a few weeks ago. I met her at TAPS in October 2009, where she worked while finishing her PhD at the University of Pennsylvania. She subsequently moved on to the Center for the Study of Traumatic Stress as a senior field research clinician. She invited me to co-author a chapter in Robert Neimeyer's upcoming book, *Techniques of Grief Therapy: Creative Practices for Counseling the Bereaved*, due out April 2012. I said yes, excited by the thought of being a published author in a prestigious grief and bereavement publication. The short chapter, titled, "The Art Studio Process," needed to be completed before Jill left for vacation. We worked hard to finish it on time. I ordered two of Robert Neimeyer's books, *Meaning Reconstruction and the Experience of Loss* (2001) and *Grief and Bereavement in Contemporary Society: Bridging Research and Practice* (2011).

Jill's invitation gave me the opportunity to delve into an academic field of which I had no formal knowledge. Once the two books arrived, I was consumed in the writings of prominent authors in the field of grief and bereavement. I was overcome by the theories, research, and structures that seemed to support the body of my creative journey. It gave credence to the past ten years of my life.

Dr. Neimeyer included a Friedrich Nietzsche quote at the beginning of a chapter: "To live is to suffer; to survive is to find meaning in the suffering." It caught my attention. This professional arena was quite different from the survivors arena that I was a part of as a workshop facilitator and presenter. It felt like a door opened. I entered new territory and noted how this coincided with my birthday.

September 11, 2011:
In Remembrance, Waterfalls

I got up early and curled up with a cup of coffee on the sofa in our family room and watched the 9/11 ceremonies. I cried as I am sure millions cried, watching and remembering. I was not undone as I was in the past but filled by the stories of healing and resilience. I loved the garden and waterfall created in memory of so many who died that day. I planned on making my way to New York City so that I could sit in that sacred space that held such special meaning for me.

I spent the remainder of the day reflecting on my own journey. I spent some time in my studio. I collaged into an old children's book I found in a Cockeysville antique store on York Road. I loved this newfound form. I loved creating into the pages. I loved rewriting my story, reimaging myself and all around me. The actual title of the book was *Every Child's Story*.

October 11, 2011:
Tenth Anniversary of Kristin's Death

Douglas and I visited Kristin's grave on our way home from our getaway in the Poconos. We stood looking at her name, Kristin Rita Strouse. Dad shook his head and whispered, "Ten years," as I brushed the grass clippings away from her marker. We watched the ducks on the water near us. We were sad but did not cry this year as we had other years. There was peace.

It was late in the afternoon when we arrived home. I pulled the lounge chair from its place on the patio and dragged it through the garden bed, out beyond the border of the boxwoods. I had repositioned my chair many times over the years, a seasonal ritual that coincided with Kristin's fall. I sat there and watched the sun move behind the trees that marked the boundary of our property. The sun in its descent casts long shadows by late afternoon. I imagined Kristin swinging on the swing over by the tennis court. I imagined her running and playing with our yellow lab, Kakee, and sitting with Sienna in the leaves, under our two great maple trees. Black crows flew overhead and moved about the trees, calling to each other. I felt them calling me and reminding me of my journey.

We all have journeys as beings in human bodies, and we are capable of losing ourselves in many ways. We break apart through abandonment, abuse, addiction, betrayal, divorce, financial ruin, illness, neglect, and violence, just to name a few. No one forgets. We learn to integrate what is difficult into the fabric of our life. We learn. We grow. We make meaning. We heal.

I shared my joys and my sorrows. My greatest sorrow was Kristin's death. I compared my feelings now with those of the past ten years and noticed this moment's difference. I was humbled by all that had come my way through the agony of Kristin's death.

In *Comfort*, Ann Hood talked about the experience of the loss of her beloved five-year-old daughter, Grace. She said,

Time passes and I am still not through it. Grief isn't something that you get over. You live with it. You go on with it lodged in you. Lodged deep inside ... At first grief made me insane. It's true, I have been there. That is me making that sound which is both inhuman and guttural and the most human sound a person can make: the sound of grief. My hair is coming out, not in fistfuls, but in painful tangles, ripped from the roots, from my scalp. That is me running zigzagging, trying to escape what is inescapable.

I knew that insane, grief-ravaged part of myself. She was indeed inescapable. She found me, and when she did I had a choice: I could allow her in, or I could shut the door. I let her in when the moment presented itself. I stood and screamed and went insane, an insanity known only by those who lose their children. I made room for her, and she took her rightful place beside the other ravaged parts.

When I considered my own insanity as a result of Kristin's death, I realized that on my very worst days, my insanity paled to her experience of madness, for I never lost hope—not completely. I could not do what she did, not even in my darkest hours. That realization separated our experiences of madness. As I fell into the abyss with her, some part of me understood her a little better. As I sat with her on the ledge, some part of me never completely understood. I accepted the paradoxes that made up her life and death. I accepted the unanswerable questions. I accepted Kristin and I accepted myself. I came to this place because I found a way to retrieve the million pieces of myself, the ones that floated out into the universe when I found out she died. I was filled with gratitude for the one who whispered into my ear, "Why don't you make a collage?"

The bits and pieces of paper I endlessly touched allowed me to come to terms with the past, the present, and the future. I discovered myself in the process. I glued myself down and did not blow away. There was forgiveness. I collaged and wrote my way through it all. I breathed my way through and got very, very still. I listened. I learned to live in the moment. Living in the present allowed me to surrender my future; it will be what it is. I have embraced life and found purpose. I found meaning. It was an artful grief.

Before I went to bed, I opened Kristin's closet and touched the gray pleated skirt she wore one Christmas. I opened her sketchbooks and thumbed through her dreams that will never be. I opened her jewelry box and slipped on the silver ring from Ireland that we gave her. I adjusted the witch's hat on her favorite Madame Alexander doll. I opened her armoire and ran my hand over the shirts in which she painted. I sat at her desk and opened the little drawer that still held her pen and pencil collection. I looked into her brown eyes that gazed upon me from her portrait hanging above her desk.

I felt the deepest love and compassion for the seventeen years we shared. Knowing what I know, I would not trade them in. I felt into Kristin's life, and I felt into Kristin's death. I felt into all of it. I wanted her to know how very much I loved her.

In the end questions remained. I did not have all the answers. There was an element of mystery. I was opened to it all and at peace, for a majority of the time.

The work is always there; it will rise and fall into the river of my life. I accept my failures and embrace myself as a mother. I love my children completely. I don't know what else there is but returning to my center, remembering who I am, and being present to what is.

Kristin Rita Strouse

October 27, 1983–October 11, 2001

a c k n o w l e d g m e n t s

I am indebted to my family, who walked with me for years and whose hearts broke with mine. Devona Toher, Donna and Michael Naslund, Jim, Brian and Alana, Elizabeth and Keith Burton, Dan and Erin, Nancy Leiderman, Darla and Jim Strouse, David and Mimi, Cecily and Jay, Rosalie and Russell Hunt, Cynthia and Tim, Donna and Tom, Michael and Tamra, Laura and Jeff, Andrew and Megan, Rosemarie and Charles Strouse, Charlie and Stacy, Eric, Matt and Angie, Gale and Fred Rhodes, Zack and Abby. Our lives are intertwined, changed forever and bound by love.

Thank you my dear sisters, Donna and Elizabeth, who listened endlessly to me with compassion. Your love sustained me.

I am grateful to my teachers and mentors who created sacred spaces for healing and guided me through grief's labyrinth: Sheila Foster, Janet Cyford, Meredith Young-Sowers, and Martyn Young. Thank–you to Monica Staub, Gena Tampio and Elizabeth Kramer, who ministered to my body and soul.

Thank you to the Temenos community, whose presence was a life-affirming container of compassion.

Thank you to those who came to my refuge: you joined me in the unknown and simply said yes. A special thank-you to Chris, Christopher, Patrick, and Daniel, whose spirits permeate my Soul Gathering circle.

A special thank-you to our friends and neighbors who tenderly cared for our family not only on the day we buried Kristin, but in the weeks after. You fed us with your love: Darlene Jones, Nadia Farace, Marie Mullaney, Joy Andersen, Anne Scornavacca, Donna Nazelrod, Sloane Brown, Patty White, Freda Jasper, Trudy Wexler, Debi Rothstein, Carol Martorana, Sharon Mech, Ursula Lifson, and Gail Butler.

I will never forget those who, in the aftermath of Kristin's death, invited us to dinner. You reached out and gave us the opportunity to talk about our feelings. Joe and Meadowlark Washington, Lynne and Victor Brick, Freda and Tom Jasper, Sharon and Larry Sheets, Patty and Stan White, Heide and David Hungerford, Joan and Jon Schochor, Jan and John Kenny.

To Laura Jones, Kelly Kidd, Meadowlark Washington, Gail Butler, Darlene Jones, and all those who wrote notes and sent cards on holidays, anniversaries, and special occasions: your thoughtfulness comforted me in ways you will never know.

Thank you to those who spoke Kristin's name, remembering her, remembering her life, and daring to ask how we were doing.

I value my tennis friends, who urged me back on the court. During those initial years, you put up with me when I couldn't hit a ball. You were kind and gentle. Sharon Sheets, Debi Rothstein, Bonnie Glick, Phyllis Schuster, Nadia Farace, Jodi Fader, Kathy Piven, Muffy Rollins, Linda Stough, Caddy Shank, Betsy Cole, Michele Pearlman, Kathy Zarzecki, Esther Sharp, Nancy Cunningham, Michele Donehower, and Patti Faby.

Thank you to those who have supported the Kristin Rita Strouse Foundation for Mental Health Awareness, Education and Suicide Prevention (www.krsf.com), and The Yellow Dress Golf Classic. We have been a success because of your personal financial support and guidance. You have made a difference in the lives of survivors who attend Rita Project Studio New York, Baltimore. and Los Angeles. and Rita Project workshops and exhibitions locally and nationally (www.ritaproject.org). You have helped to educated countless adolescents through your support of the Johns Hopkins Medicine: Department of Psychiatry and Behavioral Sciences: Adolescent Depression Awareness Program (ADAP). Thank you, Christine and Andrew Burke, Gail and Larry Butler, Kevin Daye,

Michelle and Craig Kahl, Susan and Jon Levinson, Tom Rosato, and Joan and Jon Schochor.

Thank you, Gerry Sandusky, Stan White, Meadowlark and Joe Washington, Gail and Fred Rhodes, Rosalie and Russell Hunt, Sharon Wieciech, Muffy Rollins, Donna Naslund, Elizabeth Burton, Alana Naslund, Adhikari, Mary Tessman, Joan Schochor, Betsy Weinstein, and Jan Kenny, whose service to the Yellow Dress Golf Classic made each evening very special. Thank you to the golfers, dinner guests, and volunteers.

Thank you to the Johns Hopkins Medicine: Department of Psychiatry and Behavioral Sciences. Your support, as we continued to find our way through was an essential part of our healing. J. Raymond DePaulo, MD; Kay Redfield Jamison, PhD; Karen Swartz, MD; Elizabeth Kastelic, MD; Adam Kaplin, MD; Barbara Schweizer, RN; Sallie Mink, RN; Kathy Pollock, Jessica Lunken, and Barbara Verrier.

I am in gratitude for the healing experiences I have shared with the bereaved, locally and nationally. Thank you for your willingness to share from the deepest part of yourself, from the broken places. Thank you to all those who attended my workshops: I am richer in spirit because of you. Thank you, Mitch Carmody, Carla Blowey, Marie Levine, and Gloria and Heidi Horsley. Thank you Kelly, Kevin, Peter and Scott.

A thank-you to the Bereaved Parents of the USA, (BPUSA) who opened the door and invited me into my work with others. Thank you, Pat Loder and The Compassionate Friends (TCF), who minister to grieving parents around the world. A thank you to Bonnie Carroll, founder of the Tragedy Assistance Program for Survivors (TAPS), and to Kim Ruocco, whose work with military families is extraordinary. You placed the creative process in the foundation of programs offered to survivors. Thank you, Jill Harrington-LaMorie, DSW, LCSW; your invitation opened a door, and I am forever grateful.

Thank you, Joseph Michael Lopez, for the images of Kristin. Thank you for seeing us through the lens of your heart. You captured moments that are forever emblazoned on our soul.

Thank you to the photographers, graphic artists, editors, publishers, and all those involved with the magazines whose images became my soul's medicine. I returned to life through them.

Thank you to those who, after reading *Artful Grief,* will subscribe to magazines of every variety in search of images that will stimulate and support their own healing.

Max Regan, thank you for acknowledging me as a writer. You envisioned the story before it took form and invited me there. Thank you for holding my words with reverence and encouraging me every step of the way. I am forever indebted to you. Thank you, Brian Naslund: you offered me your youthful eye. You remembered your cousin and honored her life. Thank you, Donna Naslund, for your willingness to step into the final editing and shaping of *Artful Grief.* You guided me through the nuances in the text and challenged me to take it one step further than I imagined.

Thank you to my readers, who cried through my pages and offered me their guidance through many revisions: Douglas Strouse, Kimberly Strouse, Kevin Strouse, Devona Toher, Donna Naslund, Elizabeth Burton, Joan Schochor, Jane McCarthy, Sandra Magsamen, Carl Blowey, Rosalie Hunt, Gale Rhodes, Sierra Ferguson, Rebecca Matias, Kathy Piven, Martyn Young, Everett Siegel, and Jon Schochor.

Thank you, Douglas, for allowing me the space I needed to find my way with the paper, scissors, and glue. Thank you for supporting me all those years when I spent most of my time in the basement creating—and then hours at my computer, writing. Thank you for respecting my need to do it on my own. Thank you for walking with me every day of our married life. My love today, forever, and always.

Thank you, Kimberly and Kevin, for sharing yourselves with me and opening your hearts. Thank you for witnessing my images, listening to my musings, and reading the drafts of my manuscript. Your support and feedback were invaluable. I am proud of who you have become and honor each of you. It takes courage to walk this journey.

Thank you, Kristin, for seventeen precious years and the journey we continue to share.

references

Ardagh. A. *The Translucent Revolution: How People Just Like You Are Waking Up and Changing the World.* California: New World Library, 2005.

Brach, T. *Radical Acceptance: Embracing Your Life with the Heart of a Buddha.* New York: Bantam Books, 2003.

Chopra, D. *Life After Death: The Burden of Proof.* New York: Harmony Books, 2006.

Estés, C. P. *Women Who Run With the Wolves: Myths and Stories of the Wild Woman Archetype.* New York: Ballantine Books, 1997.

Goldberg, N. *Writing Down the Bones: Freeing the Writer Within.* Boston: Shambhala Press, 1986.

Hood, A. *Comfort: A Journey through Grief.* New York: W. W. Norton & Company, 2008.

Jung, C. G. *Man and His Symbols*. M. L. von Franz, (Ed.) Henderson, J. L., Jacobi, J. & Jaffé, A. New York: Doubleday & Company Inc., 1964.

Levine, M. *First You Die: Learn to Live After the Death of Your Child*. California: Silver Thread Publishers, 2004.

Martin, M., Crichlow, H., *Show Me the Meaning of Being Lonely*. Cheiron Productions: Martin, M. & Lundin, K. (Producers) 1998. In *Backstreet Boys: The Hits—Chapter One*, Zomba Recording Corporation, New York, 2001.

Myers, B., Bazilian, E., Child, D. *Kiss the Rain*. EMI Blackwood Music, BMI: Desmophobia Polygram International Publishing, Inc., Human Boy WB Music Corp., 1997. In Billie Myers: *Growing Pains*, Universal Records, Inc., New York, 1997.

Myss, C. *Anatomy of the Spirit: The Seven Stages of Power and Healing*. New York: Harmony Books, 1996.

Teresa of Ávila. *Interior Castles*. E. Allison Peers (Trans. & Ed.) New York: Doubleday, 2004, p. xvi.

American Psychological Association. (1994). *Diagnostic and Statistical Manual of Mental Disorders (4th ed.)*, Washington DC.

Perera, S. B. *Descent to the Goddess: A Way of Initiation for Women*. Toronto: Inner City Books, 1981.

Rumi, Jalal Al-Din. "Out beyond Ideas of Wrong-doing and Right-doing," from *The Illuminated Rumi*, Coleman Barks (Trans.) & Michael Green. New York: Broadway Books, 1997.

ShantiMayi. *In Our Hearts We Know*. N Season Books, 2007, p. 191.

selected bibliography

Allen, P. B. *Art Is a Way of Knowing: A Guide to Self-knowledge and Spiritual Fulfillment through Creativity.* Boston: Shambhala, 1995.

Blowey, C. *Dreaming Kevin: The Path to Healing.* Pennsylvania: Infinity Publishing Company, 2002.

Carmody, M. *Letters to My Son: A Journey through Grief.* Edina, Minnesota: Beaver Pond Press, Inc., 2002.

Chance, S. *Stronger Than Death: When Suicide Touches Your Life.* New York: W. W. Norton Company, Inc., 1980.

Chödrön, P. *When Things Fall Apart: Heart Advice for Difficult Times.* Boston: Shambhala, 1997.

Cori, J. *Healing from Trauma: A Survivors Guide to Understanding Your Symptoms and Reclaiming Your Life.* Philadelphia: Da Capo Lifelong Press, 2008.

Cyford, J. *Ring of Chairs*. Thirteen-O-Seven Press, 2000.

Didion, J. *The Year of Magical Thinking*. New York: Alfred A. Knopf, 2005.

Epstein, M. *Going to Pieces without Falling Apart: A Buddhist Perspective of Wholeness*. New York: Broadway Books, 1998.

Frost, S. B. *SoulCollage: An Intuitive Collage Process for Individuals and Groups*. Santa Cruz: Hanford Mead Publishers, Inc., 2001.

Guggenheim, B. & Guggenheim, J. *Hello from Heaven*. New York: Bantam Books, 1995.

Housden, M. *Hannah's Gift: Lessons from a Life Fully Lived*. New York: Bantam Books, 2002.

Jamison, K. R. *Touched with Fire: Manic-depressive Illness and the Artistic Temperament*. New York: Free Press Paperback, 1993.

Jamison, K. R. *An Unquiet Mind: A Memoir of Moods and Madness*. New York: Vintage Books, 1995.

Jamison, K. R. *Night Falls Fast: Understanding Suicide*. New York: Knopf, 1999.

Jamison, K. R. *Nothing Was the Same: A Memoir*. New York: Knopf, 2009.

Jordan J. R., McIntosh, J. L., (Eds.). *Grief After Suicide: Understanding the Consequences and Caring for the Survivors*. New York: Routledge, 2011.

Kornfield, J. *The Wise Heart: A Guide to the Universal Teachings of Buddhist Psychology*. New York: Bantam Books, 2008.

Kübler Ross, E. *On Death and Dying: What the Dying Have to Teach Doctors, Nurses, Clergy and Their Own Families.* New York: Macmillan Publishing Co., Inc., 1969.

Lesser, E. *Broken Open: How Difficult Times Can Help Us Grow.* New York: Villard Books, 2005.

Livington, G. *Too Soon Old, Too Late Smart: Thirty True Things You Need to Know Now.* Philadelphia: Da Capo Lifelong Books, 2004.

McCracken, E. *An Exact Replica of a Figment of My Imagination.* New York: Little Brown & Company, 2008.

McNiff, S. *Art Heals: How Creativity Cures the Soul.* Boston: Shambhala, 2004.

Neimeyer, R. A., (Ed.). *Meaning Reconstruction and the Experience of Loss.* Washington DC: American Psychological Association, 2001.

Neimeyer, R. A., Harris, D. L., Winokuer, H. R., Thornton, G. F., (Eds.) *Grief and Bereavement in Contemporary Society: Bridging Research and Practice.* New York: Routledge, 2011.

Neimeyer, R. A., (Ed.). *Techniques of Grief Therapy: Creative Practices for Counseling the Bereaved.* New York: Routledge, 2012.

Rynearson, E. K. *Retelling Violent Death.* New York: Brunner-Routledge, 2001.

Styron, W. *Darkness Visible: A Memoir of Madness.* New York: Vintage Books, 1990.

Tolle, E. *A New Earth: Awakening to Your Life's Purpose.* New York: Plume, 2005.

Weiss, B. *Many Lives Many Masters*. New York: A Fireside Book: Simon & Schuster Inc., 1988.

Young-Sowers, M. *Wisdom Bowls: Overcoming Fear and Coming Home to Your Authentic Self*. California: New World Library, 2006.

c o n t a c t   i n f o r m a t i o n

Sharon Strouse, MA, ATR is an Art Therapist who found meaning and healing after the suicide of her seventeen-year-old daughter Kristin, through collage making and meditation. She is a grief and bereavement specialist and acclaimed workshop presenter for The Compassionate Friends (TCF), The Tragedy Assistance Program for Survivors (TAPS), The American Association of Suicidology (AAS), and The Association for Death Education and Counseling (ADEC). She lives with her husband in Maryland, where she enjoys her art studio and private practice.

Sharon Redmond, Photographer

Artful Grief: A Diary of Healing
www.artfulgrief.com

The Kristin Rita Strouse Foundation
www.krsf.com